Teaching Critical Reading and Writing in the Era of Fake News

STUDIES IN COMPOSITION AND RHETORIC

Alice S. Horning
General Editor

Vol. 13

The Studies in Composition and Rhetoric series is part of the Humanities list.
Every volume is peer reviewed and meets
the highest quality standards for content and production.

PETER LANG
New York • Bern • Berlin
Brussels • Vienna • Oxford • Warsaw

Teaching Critical Reading and Writing in the Era of Fake News

Edited by Ellen C. Carillo and
Alice S. Horning

PETER LANG
New York • Bern • Berlin
Brussels • Vienna • Oxford • Warsaw

Library of Congress Cataloging-in-Publication Control Number: 2020018796

Bibliographic information published by **Die Deutsche Nationalbibliothek**.
Die Deutsche Nationalbibliothek lists this publication in the "Deutsche Nationalbibliografie"; detailed bibliographic data are available on the Internet at http://dnb.d-nb.de/.

ISSN 1080-5397
ISBN 978-1-4331-8819-0 (Paperback)
ISBN 978-1-4331-7507-7 (ebook pdf)
ISBN 978-1-4331-7508-4 (epub)
ISBN 978-1-4331-7509-1 (mobi)
DOI 10.3726/b16269

© 2021 Peter Lang Publishing, Inc., New York
80 Broad Street, 5th floor, New York, NY 10004
www.peterlang.com

All rights reserved.
Reprint or reproduction, even partially, in all forms such as microfilm, xerography, microfiche, microcard, and offset strictly prohibited.

We dedicate this book to all faculty members working hard to meet the challenges associated with teaching reading and writing in the era of fake news and to librarians, the true pioneers in the teaching of information literacy.

Table of Contents

List of Figures and Tables — ix

Acknowledgments — xi

1. Introduction — 1
   ALICE S. HORNING AND ELLEN C. CARILLO

PART I. Disciplinary Responses to the Era of Fake News — 17

2. The Reading Moves of Writing Teachers Debating Online — 19
   PAUL T. CORRIGAN

3. The Fox and the OWL: Pedagogical Lessons from a Real-World Fake News Controversy — 33
   JOSEPH FORTE

4. Search(able) Warrants: Fostering Critical Empathy in the Writing (and Reading) Classroom — 49
   WILLIAM FITZGERALD

5. What Is 'Fake News'? Walls, Fences, and Immigration: How Community-Based Learning Can Prompt Students to Employ Critical Reading and Research Practices — 63
   LARA SMITH-SITTON AND COURTNEY BRADFORD

PART II. Composition Classroom Practices in the Era of Fake News — 79

6. Factual Dispute: Teaching Rhetoric and Complicating Fact-Checking with *The Lifespan of a Fact* — 81
   DANIELLE KOUPF

7. Fighting Fake News with Critical Reading of Digital-Media Texts   95
   LILIAN MINA, DAKOTA MILLS, AND SHIFAT NIHA

8. Critical Science Literacy in the Writing Classroom: A Pedagogy for Post-truth Times   113
   ELLERY SILLS AND DANIEL KENZIE

9. The Resurgence of the Pacific Northwest Tree Octopus: How Instructors Can Use New Media to Increase Students' Awareness of Fake News   129
   JESSICA SLENTZ REYNOLDS AND STEPHANIE JARRETT

10. Teach from Our Feet and Not Our Knees: Ethics and Critical Pedagogy   145
    JEANEEN CANFIELD

11. News as Text: A Pedagogy for Connecting News Reading and Newswriting   161
    KRISTINA REARDON

PART III. Teaching Visual and Digital Media Literacy in the Era of Fake News   177

12. How Information Finds Us: Hyper-Targeting and Digital Advertising in the Writing Classroom   179
    DAN LAWRENCE

13. Preparing Students to Read and Compose Data Stories in the Fake News Era   193
    ANGELA LAFLEN

14. Sleuthing for the Truth: A Reading and Writing Pedagogy for the New Age of Lies   211
    CHRIS M. ANSON AND KENDRA L. ANDREWS

15. Hacking Fake News: Tools and Technologies for Ethical Praxis   229
    STEPHANIE WEST-PUCKETT, GENOA SHEPLEY, AND JESSICA GRAY

Notes on Contributors   247

Index   253

Figures and Tables

Figure 7.1:	Course Major Assignments: Source-Author	97
Figure 7.2:	Activity Prompt on Bias Detection in News Sources. Source: Author	102
Figure 7.3:	An Activity Prompt to Authenticate Visual Content Using Citizen Evidence Lab Source: Author	103
Figure 13.1:	A and B: Two Data Stories Based on the Same Data Set. Source: Author	199
Figure 13.2:	A and B: Comparison of Two Bar Charts. Source: Author	203
Figure 13.3:	Sample Data Story. Source: Author	207
Figure 14.1:	Wolf Pack Source: Nature Picture Library	212
Figure 15.1:	Evaluation Heuristic Source: Author	234
Table 9.1:	Expository Unit. Source: Author	135
Table 9.2:	Argumentative Unit. Source: Author	136

Acknowledgments

We are grateful to the Research Office (Dr. David Stone, Director) and the College of Arts and Sciences (Dr. Kevin Corcoran, Dean) at Oakland University for their support of this project.

1. Introduction

ALICE S. HORNING AND ELLEN C. CARILLO

The central goal of this collection is twofold: it will help faculty understand where students are with respect to reading and understanding the information they encounter on a daily basis (whether that information comes in the form of nonfiction prose they are reading in their courses or the news stories that pop up on their social media accounts), and it will help faculty improve students' critical reading, writing, and thinking abilities. In the current environment where it is difficult to evaluate claims of "fake news," "alternative facts," misinformation and disinformation, expert skills are needed more than ever. In this Introduction, we offer an overview of recent research that shows the current situation in college classrooms across the country, followed by an explanation of the basic psycholinguistic features of the reading process. We know from our own research and that of others that many teachers of college-level writing (and other subjects) have little or no background in the psycholinguistics of reading, so our goal here is to provide a solid backdrop for the chapters. Part of the context we provide in this Introduction also involves bringing to light research we have done separately that documents the absence of attention to reading in the field of composition and rhetoric. Finally, we demonstrate that there are sound reading pedagogies emerging from the field that, when taken alongside those discussed throughout this collection, will give faculty the tools they need to support students' development of the critical reading, writing, and thinking abilities they will need in this era of fake news.

Students' Reading Habits

If you get average college faculty from a variety of disciplines together in a room and ask them what the single biggest problem they face in the classroom today is, in less than five minutes, the discussion will be about reading. The focus will be on what Alice calls the "don't, won't, can't" problem. That is, students don't read as part of their regular range of activities, won't read assigned material unless it is tied to a grade, and really can't read in the ways most instructors expect or require. Their ability to comprehend, analyze, synthesize and make ethical use of extended nonfiction prose material is quite limited.

There is much evidence beyond faculty complaints to support the view that current college students have significant trouble with reading. The available evidence arises from an ever-growing stack of reports of studies on student reading from a variety of vantage points, quantitative, qualitative, online and off. Virtually all the studies suggest that half or more of students lack the critical reading skills to be successful in college. And while correlation is not causation, when the findings of reading studies are juxtaposed with data showing that roughly half of those who start any form of post-secondary education never complete a degree (Musu-Gillette et al. 2017), it seems at least possible that there might be a relationship between reading problems and crossing the finish line. Thus, there are many reasons to be concerned about students' reading situation; readers of this book need to be aware of students' ability levels as they consider strategies and approaches for the classroom.

The quantitative data come from large-scale tests of various kinds. The ACT organization has been tracking students' performance in a reading test for a number of years. The ACT test section devoted to reading comprehension consists of a 35-minute timed test. Students read four passages, answering ten multiple choice questions on each passage. Although there are many flaws in such an approach, ACT claims that it is measuring students' comprehension, vocabulary, ability to draw inferences and other features of critical reading. The most recent results from the ACT Reading test show an ongoing decline in the number of students scoring at or above the cut-off score that ACT has set. The latest results available as this book is being written are from 2019 when 1.78 million students or 52% of the US high school graduating class took the test. Of these students, only 45% met the ACT College Readiness Benchmark for reading, down from 46% in 2018 and 47% in 2017.

Related large-scale results come from the National Assessment of Educational Progress (NAEP), sometimes referred to as the "Nation's Report Card" because it tests a US Department of Education sample of students meant to reflect the student population as a whole. NAEP is not administered to high school students every year, so the latest results are from 2015, when some 37% of students in Grade 12 tested proficient in reading (NAEP, 2016). Thinking about the classroom implications of these findings, in a typical class of about 25 first-year college students, half or more of them are likely to lack the critical reading skills needed to do the reading instructors assign. And that's not even considering the time demands, the distractions, and the other dis-incentives to thoughtful, thorough critical reading expected in college. Again, the results from the ACT and NAEP are based on timed, multiple choice, paper and pencil kinds of tests. However, other measures, untimed, online and so forth, produce very similar findings.

For example, while a 2016 report of a sampling of college students' ability to evaluate news sources (Head et al. 2016) shows a weak ability to apply critical reading to news in both traditional and digital forms, more persuasive evidence comes from an earlier study done by this same team of librarians from the University of Washington (Head et al., 2013). The older study looked at more than 1900 first-year college students' responses to an online survey, along with follow-up interviews with 35 respondents conducted at six colleges and universities around the country. It found that students have difficulty finding, reading, understanding, evaluating and using research materials for their own purposes. In this case, the study relies on students' self-reported difficulties with college-level reading and research, and yet, it finds that a majority of students report that critical reading is difficult. Similar findings on international direct tests of reading ability with 15-year-old students in about 30 mostly Northern Hemisphere countries show again that half or more of students do not read as well as they could and should (Programme, 2012).

For those who have well-justified reservations about large-scale tests and surveys of this kind, there are other carefully done qualitative studies that offer similar findings. In a nutshell, no matter how critical reading skills are measured, half or more of the students currently in college classrooms lack the ability to analyze, synthesize, evaluate and make ethical use of what they read. Two of the many qualitative studies done to support this claim are the on-going work of The Citation Project and that of the Stanford History Education Group. The Citation Project has taken a national sample of students' use of sources in actual writing assignments from colleges and universities across the country (Jamieson & Howard, 2016). Researchers examined each source used in the sample of 2000 citations to see exactly what the writer did in each case. Here are the findings: only 6% use real summary; 46% cite from the first page of a source; 70% from the first 2 pages of the source, and a majority of the sources were cited only once. The implications of these findings will be clear to most readers: students do not read sources critically and in full to present the substance of an argument, relying instead on what these researchers refer to as "quote mining" to patch together sources for their own papers.

While the Citation Project results draw on students' use of sources they may have found in traditional print or online forms, the Stanford History

Education Group study relied entirely on online materials (Stanford, 2016). The researchers examined more than 7000 student responses to a series of age-appropriate tasks for middle school, high school and college students. Here are the tasks college students were asked to do in an untimed exercise: (1) Article Evaluation: In an open web search, students decide if a website can be trusted; (2) Research a Claim: Students search online to verify a claim about a controversial topic; (3) Website Reliability: Students determine whether a partisan site is trustworthy; (4) Social Media Video: Students watch an online video and identify its strengths and weaknesses; (5) Claims on Social Media: Students read a tweet and explain why it might or might not be a useful source of information. The results showed that somewhere between 50% and 80% of the students could not perform these tasks, a finding the researchers described as "appalling." A second study in 2019 showed that even PhD-holding historians and presumably well-prepared Stanford undergraduates were not as capable as professional fact-checkers at sorting trustworthy online material from fake and otherwise untrustworthy sources (Wineberg & McGrew, 2019).

The most recent study conducted by the Stanford History Education group (with support from Gibson Consulting) took place between June 2018 and May 2019 and involved 3,446 high school students from across the country. The goal of the study was to "explore whether the intense concern about information literacy since 2016 has had an effect on students' digital abilities." With their earlier study in mind, researchers wondered "Are young people today, over three years after our original study, prepared to make choices based on the digital information they consume?" (5). The short answer given by researchers in "Students' Civic Online Reasoning: A National Portrait" is no. The report explains that "overall, students struggled on all of the tasks," (14) tasks that "measured their ability to evaluate digital sources" (4). More specifically, "at least two-thirds of student responses were assessed to be at the "Beginning" level [the lowest level] for each of the six tasks." Moreover, "in four of the six tasks, over 90% of students received no credit at all" and "out of all of the student responses to the six tasks, fewer than 3% [of students] earned full credit" (14).

Given the findings of these studies and many others that will be discussed in the following chapters, it should be clear that secondary and postsecondary students are not the effective, efficient, critical readers instructors expect them to be. And now, more than ever, such skills are essential not only to success in college but also to careers and in the personal lives of students beyond college. Moreover, if we want these students to participate fully in our democratic society, they are going to need careful reading skills to evaluate traditional and digital sources of all kinds. The goal of this book is to support faculty as they help students develop these essential abilities.

Psycholinguistic Features of Reading

Reading is a complex activity that involves the interaction of the reader and the writer as they meet in and through the text. College-level academic reading can be defined as a complex, recursive process in which readers actively and critically understand and create meaning through connections to texts, broadly defined (i.e., not just alphabetic texts). The psycholinguistic process of creating meaning via print and/or sound, images, or on a page or screen is then often called upon to inform other processes, including analysis, synthesis, evaluation and application; these processes develop through formal schooling and beyond it, at home and at work, in childhood and across the lifespan and are essential to human functioning in a democratic society (Horning, 2012, p. 41). This process entails the interaction of what readers know (the psycho part) and the language on the page or screen (the linguistic part). But if no meaning is constructed, then the material has not really been read. The students who have run their eyes over lines of print but cannot report on or summarize the content have not read the material. For a different example, those who read mysteries will be focused on motive, method and opportunity of the suspects presented in a case, and may need, once the perpetrator is revealed, to return to the beginning of the book to see missed clues planted by the author. And readers can and will go back because of the focus on meaning in reading.

But those clues may have been missed because readers do not look at or see or need to see every word of a text in order to construct meaning. An exercise Alice does with groups of faculty involves having readers look at a text on the screen that is a simple story with some misprints (double words, spelling errors, and so forth). Most are focused on reading the story and miss the errors, though some do see them. When she puts the passage on the screen for a second look, many readers are surprised at what they did not see. When she puts a second similar passage on the screen, readers are so focused on seeing the errors that they have no idea what happened in the story. These insights are captured in the title of a somewhat dated article that makes this point most clearly, "Reading is Only Incidentally Visual" (Kolers, 1968). Kolers, a distinguished psychologist at the University of Toronto, shows that the brain fills in what readers do not see in the course of normal reading. Again, common sense experience shows that when writers think they have proofread a text carefully, and it is returned (by, perhaps, a vigilant English instructor) with assorted typos and other errors marked, this common experience is a by-product of readers' normal, speedy focus on meaning and on the ability of the brain to fill in what is not looked at or processed by the reader.

These basic features of reading are part of good readers' everyday experiences with texts of all kinds. But knowing about how reading works can help faculty demonstrate what happens in good reading so they can improve students' abilities. In fact, teachers in every discipline can reach their own course objectives more effectively by helping students with reading on every assignment. Focusing students' attention on meaning, even if that means spending some time on the specific vocabulary of the field, can improve students' comprehension of assigned texts, which is what most instructors want. Setting up a class in small groups to take apart a writer's argument to examine the evidence and reasoning used will show students the processes instructors expect them to use on their own reading, regardless of topic. Thus, it should be clear that even these few features of good critical reading can help students do the work and learn the material teachers present. The chapters in this book offer a variety of approaches with specific focus on the problems of the materials in the current information landscape.

Because a fundamental understanding of the psycholinguistics of reading is a first step for faculty who want to help students by supporting the development of critical reading skills, we recommend Wolf's *Reader Come Home* (2018) or Seidenberg's *Language at the Speed of Sight* (2017), which offer engaging and insightful explorations of reading. An older book with useful exercises that can be helpful in showing students how reading works is called *On Reading* by Kenneth Goodman (1996) that might be found easily in university libraries or through interlibrary loan.

Reading Compliance

Students' reading abilities are not the only issue we face as instructors. We know from studies that reading *compliance* is an issue for students at both community colleges and four-year institutions. If we cannot get students to complete the assigned reading and practice various reading strategies then we cannot help them become the engaged and informed citizens they must be in a so-called post-truth culture replete with fake news.

Studies show that students' lack of reading compliance often has much to do with the lack of attention given to reading by instructors. In many cases, instructors assign reading, but then don't follow up on it in any significant or sustained way. Students come to understand that the reading assignments are not particularly important as compared to other aspects of the course. In their study of community college students, Annie Del Principe and Rachel Ihara (2017) found that students realized that "often reading isn't truly 'required' in their classes and that it's possible for a student to get by, even succeed, in coursework without doing any/much assigned reading" (200–201). Taking their cues from instructors who are not consistently connecting the reading to the writing for the course, first-year writing students at the University of Michigan indicated that they "were more or less motivated to read assigned texts depending upon whether they viewed that reading as relevant to the writing assignment" (Bunn, 2013). In other words, if the reading was clearly connected to the writing or other major assignments in the course then students completed it. If the purpose of the reading was unclear then students did not feel motivated to read. Finally, in their study at the University of Arkansas, Jolliffe and Harl (2008) found that first-year writing students "were extremely engaged with their reading, but not with the reading their classes" (600). Based on their findings, these scholars make compelling cases for more clearly connecting reading assignments to the writing and other key aspects of courses. While these recommendations inflect this collection, we are proud that the chapters herein also present new research about students' reading habits that will expand our understanding about how students read, what motivates them to read, and how we can further support their reading.

Teaching in the Era of Fake News

Teaching in this particular climate, marked by the circulation of fake news and alternative facts, is especially challenging and has raised the stakes even higher for literacy instructors at all levels who are responsible for teaching students how to make meaning—through the practices of reading and writing—from the world that surrounds them. No matter where we position ourselves on the left-right political divide, this challenge is presumably something upon which we can agree.

Still being heavily debated, though, is whether the term "fake news," which appears in the title of this collection, is even useful. Some have pointed out that the increased circulation of the term "fake news" suggests that it is a new phenomenon. We certainly concede that fake news is not new. Satire, parody, propaganda, and false and misleading "news" stories have been around since the beginning of civilization. What is new, however, is the speed at which these stories spread because of social media and related technologies, as well as the ease with which they can be created because of our advanced digital technology.

The term "fake news" has also been criticized for how it has been taken up in certain political contexts and by specific people. In other words, what counts as fake news depends on who you ask. Some people believe that the term has been weaponized and politicized to pit one political group against another, both calling "fake news" on the opposing camp. As such, journalists and others have instead been using terms like "false news" or "disinformation" in attempts to de-weaponize and depoliticize the concept.

Still, we have chosen to use the term "fake news" in this collection's title for the very reasons that many have turned away from it, namely because it encapsulates the sort of complexity that faces us—the politically-charged manipulation of information that we and our students face daily. This does not mean, however, that we are not committed to incorporating other related, key terms into this collection's discussion. For example, the term "disinformation" is a crucial one for instructors to understand and to share with their students. While the terms "misinformation" and "disinformation" sound as if they might mean the same thing and are often used interchangeably, the difference between the two is noteworthy. While both terms describe factually incorrect information, the difference between the two is one of intent. Disinformation involves maliciously spreading wrong information while misinformation is incorrect information, but it is not spread with malicious intent. For example, you may have been misinformed about the daily hours at the local post office, but it is doubtful that the customer service representative spread incorrect information on purpose. That person was likely misinformed and so, now, are you. While misinformation can be problematic, it's usually not as dangerous as disinformation, particularly for a democracy. In fact, the Stanford History Education Group's "Evaluating Information: The Cornerstone of Civic Online Reasoning Study," mentioned above, noted that the consistent difficulties these students had evaluating the credibility of online sources led them to conclude that "democracy is threatened by the ease at which disinformation about civic issues is allowed to spread and flourish" (5). As this collection underscores, in an information-saturated culture and particularly one where disinformation abounds, students need to be taught how to understand, assess, analyze, and synthesize—how to read—the information that bombards them on a daily basis.

Unfortunately, though, instructors are not necessarily prepared to help students undertake this work. Data collected by Ellen in "Reading in the First-Year Writing Classroom: A National Survey of Classroom Practices and Students' Experiences," a qualitative study funded by a CCCC's Research Initiative Grant and conducted in the winter and spring of 2012, suggest that even instructors committed to attending to reading in their composition courses feel woefully unprepared to do so. More than half of the instructors interviewed as part of that study were not secure in their abilities to teach reading. This point has been underscored by Linda Adler-Kassner and Heidi Estrem (2007): "At the same time as instructors ask for more explicit guidance with reading pedagogy, that pedagogy is rarely included in composition research, graduate composition courses, or first-year writing programs' developmental materials" (36).

Whether composition instructors are simply not attending to reading or are committed to teaching reading alongside writing but must piece together their own reading pedagogies because of the lack of research, scholarship, professional development and graduate courses on the subject, the same problem remains—instructors generally do not have access to enough and consistent resources that would allow them to draw on best practices for teaching reading alongside writing at the postsecondary level. This collection can serve as one of those resources.

The landscape is beginning to change, however, as reading pedagogies are starting to emerge from the field. Daniel Keller's *Chasing Literacy* charts the challenges that instructors are facing in our current age of "acceleration." While the book does not directly outline new reading pedagogies, one can recognize the kinds of pedagogies that need to be developed as a result of the challenges Keller describes. Tanya Rodrigue has made some recommendations that seem to align with Keller's findings, as well as her own findings related to students' digital reading practices. Rodrigue recommends—among other things—helping students develop a vocabulary of digital reading practices, strategies and habits as well as ways of engaging multimodal texts (17). One of the more comprehensive approaches to incorporating reading alongside writing at the postsecondary level has emerged in the form of Ellen's mindful reading framework, which can be used in first-year writing courses, as well as across the disciplines.

The goal of this approach is to help students cultivate a repertoire of reading strategies and position them to transfer what they learn about reading to future courses and contexts. Mindful reading is not another type of reading that might appear on a list alongside rhetorical reading, for example, but a framework that contains the range of reading strategies that each instructor thinks is important in that particular course and/or discipline. The term "mindful" underscores the metacognitive basis of this frame wherein students become knowledgeable, deliberate, and reflective about how they read. Reading mindfully helps student-readers construct knowledge about reading; the reading strategies they are practicing and testing out on a range of texts; and themselves as readers, all of which is represented in reading journals and similar reflective assignments. When taught within a metacognitive framework like mindful reading in ways that directly connect reading to writing, students are not only more likely to complete the reading, but as they do so, they develop knowledge about the practice of reading and about themselves as readers, which they can take to future courses and contexts.

In response to our complex information literacy landscape, we are also seeing the emergence of a range of educational initiatives at all levels of the curriculum. Less than a year after the 2016 presidential election, Michael Rosenwald reported that there had "been a burst of interest in secondary education ... with legislators in at least 15 states introducing or recently passing laws mandating digitally focused media literacy instruction in public schools" (par. 8). The News Literacy Project and Common Sense, for example, both introduced curricula along these lines. The News Literacy Project designed a curriculum geared toward American middle school and high school students, describing itself as "a nonpartisan national education nonprofit" that "empowers educators to teach students the skills they need to become smart, active consumers of news and other information and engaged, informed participants in our democracy" (par. 1). Common Sense Education, an arm of the nonprofit organization Common Sense, introduced a newly revised K-12 Digital Citizenship Curriculum in late 2019. Free to all schools, the curriculum, which is described on the organization's site as "guided by the research of Project Zero at the Harvard Graduate School of Education" is committed to "prepar[ing] this generation of young learners to critically develop the skills and habits of mind as they face dilemmas in the digital world." Specifically, the curriculum "addresses current issues students face, including cyberbullying, online privacy, hate speech, news literacy, and more" (par. 1).

At the postsecondary level, these kinds of curricular interventions vary, particularly in terms of scope. Some institutions are making courses or competencies in digital literacy (also called information literacy, media literacy or 21st-century literacies) a graduation requirement while other institutions are introducing individual courses that focus on these literacies. Other institutions, still, are spending time building up their faculty members' expertise in this area with the expectation that they will incorporate attention to these emerging literacies in their courses across the disciplines.

Keeping in mind the need for more attention to these kinds of literacies, all of which include reading, this volume ultimately contributes to discussions about what instructors can do in and beyond first-year writing courses to attend more consistently, deliberately, and effectively to reading in their classes. The chapters herein bring fresh perspectives on a range of issues, including ways to teach critical digital reading, ecological models that help

Introduction

students understand fake news, and the ethical questions that inform reading and research. With each chapter offering practical, research-based advice this collection underscores not just the importance of attending to reading, particularly in the era of fake news, but precisely how to do so.

Overview of Chapters

In the opening chapter of this volume, "Disciplinary Responses to the Era of Fake News," Corrigan returns to the heated debate about "mansplaining" that took place in October 2018 on the Writing Program Administrators Listserv (WPA-L). He demonstrates how this debate showcases a rich chronicle of readings, misreadings, rereadings, and commentary on reading, and argues that by studying how scholars and teachers of English navigate this controversial subject we can delineate their rhetorical moves and share these with students who often find themselves having to negotiate similarly complex and controversial digital landscapes.

While Corrigan culls resources for teaching reading from a controversial thread on the WPA-L, in the following chapter, Forte looks to rhetorical ecology as a resource for teaching and, specifically, as a means to teaching students how to recognize, understand, and respond to fake news. Like Corrigan, Forte introduces a contemporary example to enrich his discussion, namely the real-world fake news controversy that followed an inaccurate Fox News segment claiming that the Purdue Online Writing Lab (OWL) had discouraged students from using the word "man." Through this example, Forte shows how rhetorical ecology, which posits complex audience/rhetor interactions, distributed networks of causation, and the overriding influence of affect within rhetorical contexts, illuminates the ways that fake news propagates as a self-reinforcing rhetorical phenomenon. Forte develops recommendations for teachers aiming to create curricula that encourage students to work with fake news critically and responsibly.

The next two chapters in the first section address how instructors can help students develop dispositions particularly useful in a climate marked by the circulation of fake news. In his chapter, FitzGerald describes his composition program's signature assignments that help foster the rhetorical virtues of critical empathy and civic responsibility by inviting students to keep open the possibility of dialogue and understanding as they explore their own rhetorical agency. Smith-Sitton and Bradford's chapter closes out the first section by exploring how students were especially motivated by community engagement projects, which allowed them to gain firsthand experience working with groups of individuals directly affected by fake news and public policy changes made since the 2016 US presidential election. In addition to helping upper-level composition students meet the course goals, these projects specifically motivated students to find new ways to understand the complexities of the immigration debates that followed the 2016 US presidential election. The authors also include recommendations for structuring community engagement projects in an apolitical manner to help students gain research and rhetorical skills without becoming distracted by the politics of the topic.

The second section of this volume, "First-Year Writing Classroom Practices in the Era of Fake News," opens with Koupf's discussion of D'Agata and Fingal's 2012 book *The Lifespan of a Fact*, which she situates in her classes as a hybrid work of literature and rhetorical criticism. In the book, Fingal fact-checks D'Agata's essay draft on a teenager's suicide in Las Vegas, identifies numerous inaccuracies in it, and engages in a complex dialogue with D'Agata about the essay draft's genre, audience, subject matter, and use of rhetorical appeals. Koupf describes how this hybrid work generates productive ambiguity concerning both the physical act of reading and the intellectual processing of what has been read, which allows students to reject binary thinking, engage in healthy skepticism, and experience what it feels like to dwell in uncertainty.

Mina's chapter, a portion of which is co-written by two of her students, also explores how she has transformed her classroom to help prepare students for engaging with the complexities that characterize the circulation of misinformation and disinformation. In the chapter, Mina draws on Richard Miller's idea that the professor must be the "master of resourcefulness" who prepares college students to be informed citizens in a digital world, and she outlines how instructors can take on this new role. The chapter also explores a course that she designed to help students become "quality-control checkers" and "digital-content evaluators" as they engage in accelerated rhetorical practices and read digital texts.

Unlike the first two chapters in this section, which take a broader approach to literacy instruction, Sills and Kenzie's chapter focuses specifically on science literacy. They argue for incorporating critical science literacy into writing classrooms because science literacy allows students to build a richer vocabulary for problematic information, attend to questions of circulation, and negotiate scientific (un)certainty claims.

While Sills and Kenzie argue for incorporating science literacy into the first-year writing classroom, a kind of literacy that will likely be new to many students, in their chapter, Reynolds and Jarrett describe the importance of drawing on what students already know and what they bring to the classroom with them. The authors describe two units from an integrated reading and writing course that draw on their students' preexisting digital identities, experiences, and abilities in order to help students develop academic literacies that can ultimately also be applied beyond academia.

In the following chapter, Canfield expands these earlier discussions of literacy by considering the role of ethics in literacy pedagogies. She argues that incorporating attention to ethics is an essential component of critical literacy pedagogies. Drawing on a study of student work she conducted, as well as a more in-depth case study of a single student's response to one of the advanced composition course's assignments, she offers a pedagogical framework that foregrounds ethics in reading and writing instruction.

Reardon's chapter closes this section by introducing a different kind of pedagogical framework, namely a news-as-text pedagogy. Reardon describes this pedagogy as a means of engaging with news writing to help students develop critical media literacy skills. She presents four critical reading strategies that involve writing, including writing a news report, analyzing news photography, assessing news for bias, and recommending sources of information to peers. The goal of this pedagogy, as Reardon explores, is to prepare students to do more than sift through information. Instead, this pedagogy encourages students to think like reporters as they read the news and, through Facebook, Snapchat, and other networks, share news with their peers.

The third section of the collection opens with Lawrence's chapter that takes a unique approach to teaching digital literacy. While most of the chapters in this collection describe ways to help students find and identify credible information online, Lawrence outlines the importance of helping students understand how information finds them. Through introducing the concept of procedural rhetoric and offering a sandbox approach for bringing the Facebook Advertising Manager technology directly into the classroom, he argues that instructors can better assist students in understanding the complex channels of distribution that digital content goes through to match with and find consumers. To support this work, the chapter includes recommendations for in-class activities and assignments about digital content distribution and digital content analysis.

Laflen's chapter builds upon Lawrence's chapter in its call for instructors to encourage students to uncover how data stories work. Powerfully persuasive texts, data stories combine words, iconography, and data displays to make numeric data comprehensible for the public, decision makers, and other audiences. Laflen argues that writing instructors are well-equipped to help students understand how data stories are composed to appeal to specific audiences and achieve particular persuasive goals. In the chapter, Laflen details a unit-long data storytelling assignment she uses with students at different levels to help them critically read the arguments presented in quantitative visuals and to produce their own data stories about issues relevant to their campus and local communities.

Like Laflen, Anson and Andrews recognize how persuasive digital information can be. As such, the authors have developed an approach to teaching first-year writing that foregrounds inquiry-driven research that consciously and deliberately focuses on the subject of truth and falsehood, as well as methods for distinguishing between the two. The goal of the course is to help students not only recognize the extent to which they are regularly being deceived, but to encourage students to take on the mindset of skepticism and to acquire a robust set of tools for ferreting out the truth about any piece of information. While the authors concede that a classroom framed by a curriculum of curiosity or inquiry-based pedagogy necessarily resists uniformity in design and implementation, Anson and Andrews offer a plethora of suggestions and recommendations for instructors interested in adopting this approach.

The collection closes with a chapter that, like Anson and Andrews', seeks to empower students by helping them develop agency as they navigate the complicated digital landscape. In their chapter, West-Puckett, Gray, and Shepley describe how their first-year writing program is committed to engaging students in the participatory practice of writing fair, accurate, and verifiable news. The authors describe how students learn about the very real impacts of fake news, use heuristics adapted from the News Literacy Project to identify fake news and work in an open-source application to hack existing fake news web texts. This work not only helps students develop the literacy skills they need to both produce and consume digital information, but also honors the professionalism of journalism and its commitment to ethical codes in a time when journalism has been cast as the enemy.

References

ACT. (2019). *The condition of college and career readiness 2019 national ACT.* Retrieved from https://www.act.org/content/dam/act/secured/documents/cccr-2019/National-CCCR-2019.pdf

Bunn, M. (2013). Motivation and connection: Teaching reading (and writing) in the composition classroom. *College Composition and Communication, 64*(3), 496–516.

Carillo, E. C. (2015). *Securing a place for reading in composition: The importance of teaching for transfer.* Utah State University Press.

Commonsense Education. (2019). *All new digital citizenship curriculum.* Retrieved from https://www.commonsense.org/education/webinars/all-new-digital-citizenship-curriculum.

Del Principe, A. & Ihara, R. (2017). A long look at reading in the community college: A longitudinal analysis of student reading experiences. *Teaching English in the Two-Year College, 45*(2), 183–206.

Goodman, K. S. (1996). *On reading.* Heinemann.

Head, A. J. (2013). *Learning the ropes: How freshmen conduct course research once they enter college.* (Project Information Literacy Passage Studies research report). University of Washington. Retrieved from https://www.projectinfolit.org/uploads/2/7/5/4/27541717/pil_2013_freshmenstudy_fullreportv2.pdf

Head, A. J., Wihbey, J., Metaxas, P. T., MacMillan, M. & Cohen, D. (2016). *How students engage with news: Five takeaways for educators, journalists, and librarians.* Project Information Literacy Research Institute. Retrieved from https://www.projectinfolit.org/uploads/2/7/5/4/27541717/newsreport.pdf

Jamieson, S. & Howard, R. M. (2016). *The citation project.* Retrieved from http://www.citationproject.net/

Jolliffe, D. A. & Harl, A. (2008). Texts of our institutional lives: Studying the "reading transition" from high school to college—what are our students reading and why? *College English, 70*(6), 599–617.

Kassner, L. A. & Estrem, H. (2007). Reading practices in the writing classroom. *WPA: Writing Program Administration, 31*(1–2), 35–47.

Keller, D. (2014). *Chasing literacy: Reading and writing in an age of acceleration.* Utah State University Press.

Kolers, P. A. (1968). Reading is only incidentally visual. In K. S. Goodman & J. T. Fleming (Eds.), *Psycholinguistics and the teaching of reading* (pp. 8–16). International Reading Association.

Musu-Gillette, L., de Brey, C., McFarland, J., Hussar, W., Sonnenberg, W., & Wilkinson-Flicker, S. (2017). *Status and trends in the education of racial and ethnic groups 2017* (NCES 2017-051). U.S. Department of Education, National Centerfor Education Statistics. Retrieved from http://nces.ed.gov/pubsearch.

National Assessment of Educational Progress. (2016). *Mathematics and reading at grade 12.* Retrieved from https://www.nationsreportcard.gov/reading_math_g12_2015/#reading

News Literacy Project. (2019). *Giving facts a fighting chance.* Retrieved from: https://newslit.org/wp-content/uploads/2019/10/NLP-Brochure-10-10-19-DIGITAL.pdf

Programme for International Student Assessment. (2012). *2012 Results.* Retrieved from http://www.oecd.org/pisa/keyfindings/pisa-2012-results.htm

Rodrigue, T. K. (2017). The digital reader, the alphabetic writer, and the space between: A study in digital reading and source-based writing. *Computers and Composition, 46,* 4–20.

Rosenwald, M. (2017). Making media literacy great again. *Columbia Journalism Review*. Retrieved from https://www.cjr.org/special_report/media-literacy-trump-fake-news.php

Seidenberg, M. (2017). *Language at the speed of sight: How we read, why so many can't, and what can be done about it*. New York: Basic Books.

Stanford History Education Group. (2016). *Evaluating information: The cornerstone of civic online reasoning*. Retrieved from https://sheg.stanford.edu/upload/V3LessonPlans/Executive%20Summary%2011.21.16.pdf

Stanford History Education Group and Gibson Consulting. (2019). *Students' civic online reasoning: A national portrait*. Retrieved from https://stacks.stanford.edu/file/gf151tb4868/Civic%20Online%20Reasoning%20National%20Portrait.pdf

Wineburg, S. & McGrew, S. (2019). Lateral reading and the nature of expertise: Reading less and learning more when evaluating digital information. *Teachers College Record, 121*, 1–40.

Wolf, M. (2018). *Reader, come home: The reading brain in a digital world*. HarperCollins.

Part I. Disciplinary Responses to the Era of Fake News

2. The Reading Moves of Writing Teachers Debating Online

Paul T. Corrigan

"Look fellas .... I'm feeling just a little 'mansplained' here," Michelle LaFrance wrote on October 22, 2018, in an email to the Writing Program Administrators Listserv (WPA-L), the most prominent online forum in writing studies. The day before, LaFrance had asked scholars and teachers on the list for examples of "Rubrics to Assess Writing Assignments." While a few folks responded to share examples, a few others responded to comment more broadly, and skeptically, on the use of rubrics. Those folks, senior scholars in the field, were men. LaFrance's reply reading their comments as "mansplaining" lit a heated debate about that term that blazed through the end of the month, sparking over five hundred posts from more than two hundred readers, with an unknown number of folks, including me, reading along silently.

This fractious discussion reproduced some negative features of the larger political discourse in the United States, including polarization, willful ignorance, sexist and racist comments, personal attacks, and drastic misreadings. "Frankly, I blame Trump for all of this," wrote Steve Krause six days in. "We are all constantly bombarded with a political climate that is so crass, unhinged, combative, mean, stupid, and balkanized ... This toxicity is leaking into our daily lives" (Oct 27). But while Krause saw toxicity reproduced, Janet Zepernick saw it also repudiated. "This has been by far the most transformative instance of discourse in any community of practice I have ever witnessed," she wrote a few days later (Oct 29). It was "something truly worthwhile and beautiful at a time that has seemed to be a wasteland for public discourse." Indeed, the debate did also include skilled, genuine, extended efforts by folks to understand and communicate across significant differences of experience and perspective.

In the age of fake news, patent lies are but one symptom of a larger jettisoning of thoughtful discussion, deliberation, and debate. In their chapter in this volume, Lara Smith-Sitton and Courtney Bradford describe countering fake news with real people—through service learning projects, students encounter firsthand in the local community the stories of folks affected by misinformation, the lives behind the lies. Such a pedagogy exemplifies a larger principle: to equip students to navigate the toxicity Krause condemned and cultivate the transformation Zepernick celebrated, we need to teach students not only how to assess the credibility and accuracy of information but also how to engage with others with intelligence and integrity. We need not just credibility but meaning, not just accuracy but understanding.

If service learning is one way to accomplish such ends, deep reading is another. In her chapter in this volume, Kristina Reardon advocates teaching students to read news stories not unlike one reads poetry or novels, not merely evaluating veracity but also sitting with, interpreting, and making meaning out of such texts. In *Teaching Readers in Post-Truth America*, Ellen C. Carillo (2018) similarly notes that "readers generally, and our students specifically, are under unprecedented pressure within this post-truth culture to navigate the range of texts (broadly defined) that vie for attention and acceptance" and makes the case "that foregrounding and teaching the interpretive practice of reading . . . is one way of responding to this contemporary moment and is absolutely crucial to preparing our students to participate in an information-rich democratic society" (p. 7). Moreover, as Joseph Forte and Lilian W. Mina make clear in their chapters in this volume, we specifically need to teach students to read well under the treacherous conditions of online discussion and debate where so much public discourse now takes place. Doing so, observes Mina, requires developing new ways of "conceptualizing and teaching reading."

The archive of the WPA-L mansplaining debate presents a rich resource for teaching students to read well while deliberating online in the era of fake news. In *Arguing about Texts: The Rhetoric of Interpretation*, Martin Camper (2017) posits that every reading is rhetorical, that every attempt to make sense of a text is also an attempt to persuade an audience of that sense, even if the audience is only the reader's own self (p. 10). By the same token, I posit that every act of rhetoric also entails reading, even if only an implicit reading of the rhetorical situation. In practical terms, every email in the WPA-L debate includes or implies a reading of other emails. The archive comprises a chronicle of readings and misreadings. In addition to examples of how not to read, we can find instances of exceptionally skilled scholars and teachers of English reading under difficult circumstances.

In this chapter, unpacking five key "moments of reading" in and of the debate, I am "making reading visible," as Carillo (2009) encourages (p. 37).

Mariolina Rizzi Salvatori (1996) similarly advocates teaching students to reflect on their own ways of reading: "to become conscious of their mental moves, to see what such moves produce, and to learn to revise or to complicate those moves as they return to them in light of their newly constructed awareness of what those moves did or did not make possible" (p. 447). But while both Carillo and Salvatori have student reading in mind, my present analysis extends their insight to expert reading. When students look not only at their own practices but also at how other and stronger readers read, they can expand their "repertoire" of reading moves (Blau, 2019). Showing students how experts read under the conditions of online debate in the era of fake news, we can help students adopt or adapt such ways of reading for themselves.

Moment of Reading 1: "Expert Readers Are Meta-Readers"

The first moment of reading to unpack is my own reading of the WPA-L debate. In this chapter, I make several moves that also appear in the debate emails—first and foremost analyzing how readers read. For instance, when Kristin Milligan reflected on the effort she put into reading others' emails (Oct 25), when Suzanne Sink compared reading emails to reading poems (Oct 26), and when Melissa Elston exhorted another reader to "Please read more carefully before you #notallmen me" (Oct 26), they each added a "meta" layer to their reading. According to Alice Horning (2011), such a layer is a defining characteristic of expert reading: "expert readers are meta-readers" (pp. 4–5). In this analysis, I follow suit, reading the reading that took place in the debate.

The second move I make is to build on the readings of others. One benefit of online deliberation is that collaborative reading—readers going back and forth, extending, contesting, and borrowing from each other—can unfold faster and more fluidly than in print. During the debate, Angela Crow, Eileen E. Schell, and others called for analyses of the WPA-L archives (Oct 25, 30). "Please get to work dear scholars and friends," Janet Zepernick wrote. "I can't wait to read the theoretical accounts of this moment in composition history" (Oct 29). In addition to responding to and thus building on these broad calls, my analysis also cites specific insights about reading from scholars in and outside of the debate. Instead of starting from scratch, I add the next turn in a larger reading.

My third reading move is to acknowledge that my analysis is partial. The complexity of "the text" of the WPA-L debate renders impossible any definitive reading. While deconstructionists theorize the fragmentation and instability of all texts, readers online experience those as immediate, practical challenges. Though some folks wanted to compile the entire discussion into a single document (William Thelin, Oct 25, Caitlyn H. Laughner, Oct 26), that project proves implausible, as the conversation forked into threads, with hundreds of participants reading, writing, and posting simultaneously, "replying" to different prior emails, and creating new subject headings altogether. As Dawn Shepherd noted, "the back channeling, subtweeting, and hashtagging have been epic" (Oct 27). In addition to emails officially posted to the list, the conversation spilled over into private emails (Lynn Lewis, Oct 26), social media (Thomas Wright, Oct 26), and talks with colleagues not on the list (Kristin Milligan, Oct 25). While readers who tried to read every single email couldn't be sure they didn't overlook some (Kristin Milligan, Oct 25), others jumped into the conversation knowing they skimmed or missed some or most of what came before (T. J. Geiger, Oct 27; M. W. Jones, Oct 27; Chet Pryor, Oct 24). Apparently, technological hiccups delayed some messages (Vyshali Manivannan, Oct 28) and delivered others "out of order" and possibly not at all (Sonja Andrus, Oct 26). With so many complications in mind, the best I can offer is a partial reading of a partial text. So I leave my interpretation open to revision, complement, and critique by other readers.

These readings moves that I make in this analysis begin a list to which each of the remaining moments of reading will add: *analyzing how readers read, building on the readings of others,* and *appreciating the partial nature of every reading*.

Moment of Reading 2: "Mansplaining"

The next moment of reading I want to look at is an early exchange in the WPA-L debate about the meaning of the central term "mansplaining." A day into the discussion, William Thelin confessed, "I am genuinely confused here" (Oct 23). Specifically, he elaborated, "I haven't seen 'mansplaining' explained. I would really like to hear a definition that describes the features and patterns of this rhetoric." He requested an example to distinguish between mansplaining and "mere explaining." He went on to describe what folks using this term might mean, that mansplaining indicated factors in addition to gender, such as "experience" and "age," and that avoiding mansplaining on the listserv involved following certain "rules," such as attending carefully to what folks ask for before responding. Thelin presented his summary as an exploration of what he did not understand, pitched as a set of implied questions, as if to ask, "Is this what you are saying?"

While novice readers often get stumped by not understanding, expert readers get working to construct an understanding out of not-understanding. In *Teaching Literature as Reflective Practice*, Kathleen Blake Yancey (2004) describes just what Thelin did in his email: "Not-understanding is not an absence, but rather an acquired art. As students learn, articulating what they don't understand is a critical first move toward a fuller, more complex understanding" (p. 45). Although Thelin could have bypassed this particular not understanding if he were already more familiar with the term "mansplaining"—drawing on background knowledge is itself a mark of expert reading (Willingham, 2009)—anyone deliberating with folks with starkly different perspectives and experiences will encounter texts and terms they do not already know. Knowing how to proceed is a vital reading skill.

The next move Thelin could have made would have been to look up the information he was missing, as Melissa Nicolas recommended: "Bill, if you don't know what mansplaining is, there are *plenty* of articles on-line that explain it quite lucidly" (Oct 23). But online deliberation allows reading to unfold collaboratively and over time, so readers can perform meaningful reading moves without having to present an already fully formed reading. Making a few initial moves, particularly questions like Thelin's, invites others to contribute additional moves, as Em Ramser did next. "Hi Bill!" she wrote. "You mentioned that there was not an explanation of mansplaining on this thread, so I wanted to pop one in." She then quoted *Merriam-Webster*: "what occurs when a man talks condescendingly to someone (especially a woman) about something he has incomplete knowledge of, with the mistaken assumption that he knows more about it than the person he's talking to does" (Oct 23).

After looking up this information, Ramser proceeded to make use of it, articulating overtly how it shaped her reading. "It applies in this thread," she wrote, "because several male listserv participants gave Michelle [LaFrance] advice on if she should use outside rubrics when she simply asked for example rubrics." The definition of the term matched several aspects of this situation, including that these men had "incomplete knowledge" of why LaFrance requested the rubrics, that LaFrance's academic credentials in writing studies ought to have led them to assume that "she knows a lot about rubrics," that the men instead "assumed she was going to use them," and that they "proceeded to give her unasked for advice" on the basis of that assumption. In short, Ramser concluded, "They automatically assumed they knew more than her and that is where the problem" is. Spelling out a detailed application of a theoretical concept in this way is a productive reading move. Others have described this move as applying a "paradigm" (Fahnestock and Secor, 1991) or a "theoretical lens" (Wolfe and Wilder, 2016).

This moment of reading, then, demonstrates several productive reading moves: *taking not-understanding as a chance to understand, asking clarifying and probing questions, describing tentative current understandings, looking up missing information*, and *applying concepts to texts*.

Moment of Reading 3: "Exactly the Same Thing"

In a third moment of reading, two readers offer competing interpretations of several prior emails taken to represent the debate as a whole. A few days into the debate, Rich Haswell wrote, "this three-day thread on 'mansplaining' . . . has been scapegoating, singling out and piling on, plain and simple" (Oct 26). He grounded his broader interpretation in a detailed reading of a couple emails by Elizabeth Wardle, one of the women critiquing mansplaining (Oct 26). Yes, Haswell pointed out, several men had responded to a request for example rubrics by expressing skepticism about the use of rubrics, but so had Wardle. Haswell quoted specific sentences to document this point: "I get a lot of requests for help with rubrics," wrote Wardle, "that I tend to resist because of the many complications and because it is easy for faculty to use them to try to solve problems that should be otherwise solved. I thus don't have any sample rubrics to share." "So in effect," Haswell wrote about this quotation, "she agrees with" the men "on the problems with rubrics." By responding to LaFrance's initial request for rubrics with such comments, Wardle did "exactly the same thing" as the male scholars, but only the men were critiqued for it. Therefore, Haswell concluded, the critiques were not honest criticisms of that behavior but rather personal attacks.

One productive reading move Haswell made here was paying careful attention to textual details. In *Literary Learning*, Sherry Linkon's (2011) description of "expert reading" beings with careful attention "to the text itself" (p. 16). This same move came up elsewhere during the conversation as well, such as when Elizabeth Hutton requested, "Let's read and respond more carefully" (Oct 26). Haswell's reading also relied on comparing and contrasting texts—which Robert Scholes (1989) calls "a proper move in any critical reading" (p. 80)—and noticing both patterns and exceptions, also moves discussed in the conversation, with Angela Crow urging readers to "find out the patterns of discourse" on the list (Oct 25) and Melissa Elston acknowledging, "Yup. There are exceptions to every general pattern" (Oct 26). Additionally, when Haswell presented his reading as a direct alternative to, and indeed contradiction of, a prior reading made by a number of others, he made the move Joseph Harris (2006) in *Rewriting* calls "countering," building meaning by way of disagreement (p. 56). Setting opposing readings side by side, even if a reader only accepts one of them, results in a greater, more multilayered understanding.

Responding directly to Haswell, Jennifer Maher performed two additional moves to arrive at an opposite interpretation. She, too, paid careful attention to details of the emails, but she also weighed those details, showing how some had more import than others to the reading at hand. "[I]n your comparison," she wrote, "you failed to include the important framing elements that differentiate" Wardle's emails from the emails by the men (Oct 27). Maher then presented several long quotations, putting key phrases in bold, to show those key difference. Haswell had quoted the parts of Wardle's emails similar to the male scholars' emails. But he did not quote what set her emails apart: "I'm curious now, Michelle," Wardle had also written, "as to what you are doing with these rubrics you are collecting, as I suspect it is not what your interlocutors are imagining.... [I] would love to know more about your project." In other words, while the details Haswell quoted highlighted *what* Wardle was saying (that she, like the male scholars, was skeptical about rubrics), the details he did not quote highlighted *how* Wardle said it (she asked questions instead of making assumptions).

About this selection of details, Mahar commented: "Instead of recognizing the really significant difference that these two sentences make—a difference that constitutes an invitation to conversation rather than subjection by schooling—you erase it in order to illustrate a supposed hypocrisy, deflection, double standard, whatever." Since the mansplaining conversation revolved not around what was said but how it was said—"It's more behavior than content," as Patricia Donahue put it (Oct 26)—differentiating between the greater and lesser salience of different textual details on that basis is an important reading move. Maher used this move to conclude that Wardle did not do the same thing as the male scholars. By way of implication, the conversation as a whole similarly did not amount to personal attacks.

In this exchange, these two scholars add the following moves to our list: *comparing and contrasting texts, presenting an opposing interpretation, noticing patterns and exceptions, attending to textual details,* and *weighing the relative import of different textual details.*

Moment of Reading 4: "Digital Lynching"

Next we will consider the most heated moment in the debate, an extended exchange to which many readers contributed about the language of violence. In a later email than the one we just looked at, Haswell described the collective critique of the male scholars' initial emails in still stronger language.

It was an "attack" on the way they had written. It was an "attack" on their "intentions and morals." It was "a digital lynching" (Oct 26). Not surprisingly, this last phrase became the focus of intense scrutiny. The most common reading found it "inappropriate" (Adam Hubrig, Bernice Olivas, Greer Murphy, Oct 26, among others, used this exact word) because comparing the discussion to lynching exaggerates the discussion and, worse, minimizes lynching. While readers forwarded this reading through a range of moves—including describing experiences of shock and disgust at reading the word (Mandy Olejnik, Caitlin Martin, Oct 26), interrogating the qualifier "digital" (Ryan McCarty, James Eubanks, Oct 26), distinguishing between what Haswell probably intended and what his language conveyed (Ryan Skinnell, Oct 26), and applying Aristotle's theory of metaphor (Jennifer Maher, Oct 27)—the most common move was to draw on historical context.

Specifically, readers drew on the history of white supremacist lynchings in the United States, particularly in the South during the Jim Crow era (Megan McIntyre, Ruth D. Osorio, Brandy Brown, Kimberly Merenda, Estee Beck, Cara Messina, Patricia Donahue, Oct 26). To make that context all the more vivid, Jennifer Maher shared as an email attachment a "newspaper account of the lynching of Matthew Williams in Salisbury, MD in 1932" (Oct 27), while Roxane Gay linked to websites for the National Association for the Advancement of Colored People's history of lynching and the Equal Justice Initiative's lynching memorial (Oct 26). The move of drawing on historical context to inform a reading of a text is part of what Robert Scholes (2001) means when in *The Crafty Reader* he exhorts readers to "Situate, situate" (p. 67). Contexts shed light on texts. Accordingly, Gay continued, "lynching does not apply. It is audacious to think it does. Lynching is the hanging of black people for white entertainment. Lynching was the ad-hoc justice and terrorism enacted throughout the South and other parts of the United States . . . . You do not get to co-opt that word and that horrific rather recent history because some men's feelings are hurt on an e-mail list" (Oct 26). Gay explained both the historical context most closely associated with the word "lynching" and how that context informed her reading of Haswell's use of that word.

Challenging these readings with his own, Haswell drew on a different set of historical contexts, listing examples from around the world to establish that "lynching" is "larger than just the USA South" (Oct 26). From that broader use, he posited that the term "can refer to a universal group psychology—as evil as evil can be—where an individual, accused (often falsely) of some minor offense, is persecuted by a mob of people who take justice into their own hands. Psychologically it is connected with victimizing, blaming, bullying.

That group psychology was what I meant." Bringing in additional contexts, beyond the most obvious ones, can be a productive reading move, resulting in a more complex understanding of a text. In this case, Haswell failed to weigh the relative import of the different contexts. Yes, other historical contexts exist for the word "lynching." No, they are not sufficient to dislodge the American South as the central context for how that word will be understood by the vast majority of college-educated readers in the United States in the 21st century, including most of the participants in the discussion. This is a case where additional contexts could complicate but would not override the meaning drawn from the most obvious context given that that context is so powerfully and painfully evocative in the minds of readers.

Another reader did draw on additional contexts, both historical and personal, more productively. Vyshali Manivannan first acknowledged the same central context that others had pointed to: "In the South, I grew up around people with family in the KKK, who took pride in the history of lynching" (Oct 26). To this context, she added another: "In a Sri Lankan home, I grew up with stories of journalists disappeared or assassinated for speaking truth to power." By pointing to political violence in Sri Lanka, Manivannan, like Haswell, pulled in an additional, alternative context for understanding the word. But instead of overriding or diffusing the word's overwhelming association with violence in the American South, the additional context sharpened the significance that the primary context already gave the term. "I'm incredibly troubled," she wrote, "by the flippant deployment of analogies and metaphors whose cross-cultural meanings contain lived, felt, material consequences of the utmost gravity." Rather than rendering violent language merely psychological, these additional contexts, both historical and personal, made the term's sense of literal violence all the more immediate and pressing.

When considering additional contexts, Manivannan also weighed their import. The additional contexts may complicate but do not "erase" the meaning already so vividly established by the most obvious context. In this case, the complication was intensification. "We should know these metaphors come with pain, torture, death," she wrote. "With historical and cultural context that can't be neatly parsed out. No figure of speech or additional word [i.e. 'digital'] will give them connotations that erase their old meaning." Recognizing that her personal context contributed to her experience of the language of violence and "wondering how many other readers have histories similar to mine," she still concluded that having or lacking such personal contexts would not weigh enough to override the clear significance of the terms: "the words alone signify, regardless of our experiences." In this way, by both considering and weighing multiple historical and personal contexts, she constructed a layered and compelling reading of the language of violence.

From this extended exchange about the language of violence, we gather several more reading moves: *drawing on social and historical context, drawing on personal context,* and *weighing the relative import of different contexts.*

Moment of Reading 5: "It Has Made Me Look Inward"

One last moment of reading for us to consider, among the most striking of the entire debate, comes in a single email near the end of the conversation. In this email, Jeffrey Galin changed his mind. Not long before, he had clashed with other readers over gender generalizations and expressions of anger. He had read the conversation as necessary but insufficiently nuanced. He had seen his own comments as simply "point[ing] out complexities" others were overlooking (Oct 28). But, in this final email, he offered outright an "apology to the list" for this earlier reading and presented how his understanding of the conversation and of his contributions to it had changed. In *Literary Learning*, Sherry Linkon (2011) writes that expert reading "involves changing one's view of a text over time as one gains additional information, engages in conversations with others (whether in actual conversation or by reading critical analyses from other readers), and rethinks one's own response" (p. 21). In the WPA-L debate, a few other readers made the same move, such as when Susan Schorn expressed "regret" over using a particular word (Oct 26) and Thomas Wright told another reader, "your post is making me reconsider my last one" (Oct 27). But the move was rare in this conversation, as it likely is in most conversations, and no one made it more profoundly and productively than Galin.

Several other moves appear to have paved the way. First, after becoming "overwhelmed," Galin stepped away from the conversation for a day. Previously, Susan Schorn, recognizing many readers' emotions were running high, had written, "I'd like to suggest that we all consider taking a breath and a step back from the current conversations" (Oct 26). As far as reading goes, it was sound advice. In *Teaching Readers in Post-Truth America*, Ellen Carillo (2018), upon explaining "how truly entangled reason and emotion are," argues that we must attend to our and our students' affective states as integral aspects of critical reading—all the more so in situations of conflict (p. 47). Although Galin stepped away to quit altogether, not simply take a few deep breaths, that pause appears to have given him space and time to navigate his emotions. It was the day after quitting, as he sat down to write a different email, that he "realized" he needed to write this one.

Next, Galin made the move of taking readers' responses into account. On one hand, he considered his own experience of the conversation as "tough," "painful," and "downright hurtful" to see men, including friends of his, "get pummeled." On the other hand, he also considered other readers' very different experience of the conversation as "a defining moment of solidarity" and of his own comments as "an interference." While acknowledging his own experience appears to have helped Galin understand where his earlier reading had come from, acknowledging others' experience appears to have helped him shift his understanding. He was helped by hearing from other readers. Earlier, for instance, Mandy Olejnik had described how she and other women, particularly graduate students, experienced certain comments: "This makes us think, 'oh, gosh; we shouldn't have posted .... We do not belong here .... Shame on us. Let's retreat'" (Oct 23). In *Literature as Exploration*, Louise Rosenblatt (1995) urges readers to put their own responses to texts in conversation with others' experiences, to see how the responses differ, and to consider whether they might not need upon further reflection to change their own view of the text (p. 104). From Galin's email, this appears to be precisely what he did.

A superficial reading of a text considers only the intentions of the writer, while a deeper reading also considers implications of the text that might not be exactly what the writer meant. Aside from intention, the implications of a text can stem from patterns that the text fits into, effects the text has on readers, and so forth. As Susan Schorn wrote, "I can, and often do, cause harm without intending to" (Oct 26). In the debate, critiques of particular emails often focused on implication, while defenses of particular writers often focused on intention. Where that difference was not recognized, readers talked past each other, often arguing legitimate points about separate things. William Lalicker described these layers this way: "It may be that the earlier commenters (or mansplainers) had no ill intent. But when it comes to rhetoric, we are fortunate to operate in a very interesting and complex field where we can all keep learning, where every exchange merits analysis; misunderstanding between rhetor and audience is the disciplinary ocean in which we swim daily; and our discourse can easily fall into tropes of which we are previously unaware" (Oct 23).

In his revised reading, Galin distinguished between these aspects of meaning and shifted his focus from intentions to implications. He realized that, in light of the "emotional importance" of the collective critique, his "pointing out of contradictions or limitations" in the term mansplaining was no "use." In light of the larger implications of the moment, his comments pursing that line of reasoning were not so much correct or incorrect as "irrelevant." That is why "my attempts to participate in the conversation, to point out complexities, were perceived as an interference and an intentional changing of the subject. While that was in no way my intent, I can see how it was perceived that way." Although he does not discard his intentions as an aspect of meaning (he asserts positive intentions multiple times), he no longer sees intentions as the sole or even most important aspect of meaning, which leads him to a far fuller and deeper understanding of the text of the conversation.

Finally, reading the conversation in this new light led Galin to make one more move. In *Protocols of Reading*, Robert Scholes (1989) writes, "reading, though it may be a kind of action, is not the whole action but a part of it, remaining incomplete unless and until it is absorbed and transformed in the thoughts and deeds of readers" (p. x). Elsewhere in the conversation Timothy P. Oleksiak offered, "part of hearing is demonstrating how the hearing has transformed our behavior into something new that allows us to resist old patterns of hurt" (Oct 27). So it was with Galin's revised reading. In this email, he described realizing that he, too, in his own daily conversations, tended to act in some of the ways that folks in the conversation had been critiquing. "This conversation has done something that I did not realize as I was responding," he wrote. "It has made me look inward and to acknowledge that I am complicit and need to be more careful how I respond and engage." His revised reading of the conversation led him to reread and revise his own life as well.

This email, the last of the moments of reading we will look at, rounds out our list with multiple powerful reading moves: *revising a reading over time, pausing and breathing to navigate emotions, taking readers' responses into account, differentiating between intention and implication,* and *applying texts to life.*

Conclusion

In this analysis of the WPA-L mansplaining debate, I have sought to make visible expert reading. Unpacking key moments in the emails exchanged by teachers and scholars of English debating with each other, I've identified reading moves made by experts reading online under the chaotic conditions of the fake news era. These reading moves ranged from attending to textual details, to drawing on historical and personal context, to revising a reading over time. In this way, the archives of WPA-L mansplaining debate offers a rich resource for teaching students how to read critically and empathetically online.

In closing, I offer a few brief ideas of what such a pedagogy could look like. To begin with, we could encourage students to pay more attention to the role of reading in deliberating and debating online. Just as students often do not consider the writing they do on, say, social media as "real writing," so they may also not consider the reading they do in online spaces as real reading either. By helping students see it is, we can help them navigate it more skillfully. Next, we could directly share with students the list of expert reading moves that I have developed through this analysis, presenting both descriptions and examples of ways experts make meaning of texts online. We could follow instruction with practice, asking students to apply the moves in their own reading, either by sending them out to try the moves in whatever real-life online discussions they already participate in or by simulating online discussions in our classes so students can experiment in a safer environment and so we can purposely design sticky reading situations to consider together. Most importantly, we could invite students to practice meta-reading—analyzing how readers read. We could bring to class texts from online discussions (perhaps including the WPA-L mansplaining debate) to unpack with our students. We could ask students to gather and consider instances of reading online on their own. We could ask students to write out intentions and strategies for how they would like to read and grow as readers online in the future.

By making reading visible, we can equip students to find and make meaning with intelligence and integrity of the texts they encounter online in the era of fake news. Critical and empathetic reading can help students navigate and perhaps even restore what Janet Zepernick called the wasteland of public discourse.

Acknowledgments

I am grateful to the participants in the WPA-L debate for modeling critical and empathetic reading under challenging conditions, to editors Ellen Carillo and Alice Horning for putting together this valuable collection and improving my manuscript along the way, and to my colleague Scott Morgan for diving into the debate archives with me and offering valuable input and feedback as I worked on this project.

References

All emails cited in this essay were accessed in the WPA-L archives hosted by Arizona State University (lists.asu.edu).

Blau, S. (2019, May 30). Becoming the kind of person who does these things: A conversation with Sheridan Blau. *Teaching & Learning in Higher Ed.* https://teachingandlearninginhighered.org/2019/05/30/becoming-the-kind-of-person-who-does-these-things-a-conversation-with-sheridan-blau/

Camper, M. (2017). *Arguing about texts: The rhetoric of interpretation.* Oxford University Press.

Carillo, E. C. (2009). Making reading visible in the classroom. *Currents in Teaching and Learning, 1*(2), 37–41.

Carillo, E. C. (2018). *Teaching readers in post-truth America.* Utah State University Press.

Fahnestock, J., & Secor, M. (1991). The rhetoric of literary criticism. In C. Bazerman & J. Paradis (Eds.), *Textual dynamics of the professions: Historical and contemporary studies of writing in professional communities* (pp. 77–96). University of Wisconsin Press.

Harris, J. (2006). *Rewriting: How to do things with texts.* Utah State University Press.

Horning, Alice S. (2011). Where to put the manicules: A theory of expert reading. *Across the Disciplines 8*(2). https://wac.colostate.edu/docs/atd/articles/horning2011.pdf

Linkon, S. L. (2011). *Literary learning: Teaching the English major.* Indiana University Press.

Rosenblatt, L. (1995). *Literature as exploration.* MLA.

Salvatori, M. R. (1996). Conversations with texts: Reading in the teaching of composition. *College English, 58*(4), 440–54.

Scholes, R. E. (1989). *Protocols of reading.* Yale University Press.

Scholes, R. E. (2001). *The crafty reader.* Yale University Press.

Willingham, D. (2009). *Why don't students like school?: A cognitive scientist answers questions about how the mind works and what it means for the classroom.* Jossey-Bass.

Wolfe, J., & Wilder, L. (2016). *Digging into literature: Strategies for reading, analysis, and writing.* Bedford/St. Martins.

Yancey, K. B. (2004). *Teaching literature as reflective practice.* National Council of Teachers of English.

3. The Fox and the OWL: Pedagogical Lessons from a Real-World Fake News Controversy

JOSEPH FORTE

The recent focus on "fake news" in popular discourses suggests widespread anxiety about the ways that digital technology can be used to spread harmful falsehoods. A Pew Research Center study carried out in the wake of the 2016 presidential election found that 64% of American adults believed that made-up news stories have caused "a great deal of confusion" about current events (2016). A more recent survey suggested that a plurality of Americans (47%) find it "somewhat" or "very" difficult to determine the veracity of information they regularly encounter (Associated Press-NORC & USA Facts, 2019). Moreover, despite broad academic agreement on the importance of critical thinking, relevant research suggests current educational approaches may not adequately address the problem. For example, a recent large-scale study of middle school, high school, and college students documented astonishing failures in each age group to evaluate whether digital sources of information were reputable (Stanford History Education Group, 2016). In one exercise, fewer than 10% of high school and college participants could determine that a lobbying industry website represented a biased source of information (p. 5)

Fake news poses serious problems for educators at all levels. If students graduate university unable to make reliable judgments about the accuracy of the information they encounter every day, their lives' horizons will meaningfully shrink. They will be easier to swindle, easier to deceive, and easier to mislead. Moreover, university courses that purport to teach critical thinking skills risk losing credibility, and administrators may question whether these courses are worth their expense.

Thus, this chapter argues that, to prepare students for lives as intelligent, responsible citizens (and to assert the discipline's relevance), English educators should use rhetorical ecology to conceptualize the phenomenon of fake news. Ecological models illuminate how the disparate, distributed audiences for fake news tend to form networks of shared affect. They account for the ineffectiveness of fighting fake news with "true news" (i.e., objective facts) by showing how the affective qualities of these networks pre-interpret factual information. Most importantly, the ecological model points to pedagogical practices that can help students reject fake news. In sum, ecological models represent an opportunity for educators to update curricula to deal with an increasingly pressing civic challenge.

To illustrate how rhetorical ecology can be used to understand fake news, this chapter uses an account of a real-world controversy sparked by fake news. This controversy briefly embroiled Purdue University's Online Writing Lab (OWL) in early 2018 following an inaccurate segment that ran on *Tucker Carlson Tonight*, a political commentary program on Fox News. Following this account, the chapter uses the ecological lens to analyze the controversy, demonstrating how it was the product of a rhetorical ecology. Finally, the chapter concludes by elaborating on the pedagogical implications of the ecological metaphor for college English educators.

The Ecological Metaphor: A Primer

In rhetoric and composition, the metaphor of "ecology" is frequently used to describe texts, actors, practices, and relationships that comprise systems of communication. Early work offered ecology as a response to process-centered paradigms in writing instruction. Marilyn Cooper, for example, noted that "the ideal writer the cognitive process model projects is isolated from the social world [. . .] The solitary author works alone, within the privacy of his own mind" (1986, p. 365). In response, she posited an ecological model for writing "whose fundamental tenet is that writing is an activity through which a person is continually engaged with a variety of socially constituted systems" (p. 367). Later theorists investigated how ecological models for communication might be applied in composition classrooms, finding support in disciplines like cognitive and systems science (Syverson, 1999). Others applied the ecological metaphor to professional realms. For instance, Spinuzzi extended the metaphor to textual genres to posit a "genre ecology" model for the flow of information within workplaces (2003).

These extensions of the ecological metaphor helped scholars model the ways that everyday communicative situations defy traditional models of rhetoric and communication. Moreover, each extension involved at least a cursory engagement with political or social concerns. Syverson, for instance, noted that ecology allows for the "distribution of cognition (or text-composing)" social dimensions (as well as other dimensions) (1999, p. 23). Similarly, Spinuzzi acknowledges that given genres can embody "a galaxy of assumptions, strategies, and ideological orientations" (2003, p. 43). Even Cooper's foundational work contains explicit acknowledgment of ecology's political ramifications. One advantage of the model, Cooper writes, is that it "encourages us to direct our corrective energies [...] toward imbalances in social systems that prevent good writing" (1986, p. 373).

Subsequent work by Jenny Edbauer expanded the notion of ecology to directly engage with political rhetoric. Drawing on Syverson as well as contemporary cultural theorists Shaviro (2003) and Reynolds (2004), Edbauer formulated a theory of rhetorical ecology that complicated the discrete borders between sender, receiver, and text traditional notions of rhetorical situation assumed. These, Edbauer argues, do not accurately model public, political enactments of rhetoric, which involve complex interactions between rhetor, audience, text, and affective contexts. Edbauer writes, "A given rhetoric is not contained by the elements that comprise its rhetorical situation (exigence, rhetor, audience, constraints). Rather, [it] emerges already infected by the viral intensities that are circulating in the social field" (2005, p. 14). Edbauer posits that the rhetorical situation itself operates as "a framework of affective ecologies" (p. 9) occurring "within a network of lived practical consciousness or structures of feeling" (p. 5). This ecological model, Edbauer argues, "allows us to more fully theorize rhetoric as a public(s) creation" (p. 9).

Rhetorical ecology has found use as a theoretical lens for understanding complex public phenomena. For example, researchers have used rhetorical ecology to explain how public stakeholders engage with science (Lerner & Gehrke, 2018). Similarly, an analysis of US university presidents' responses to the 2016 American election cites Edbauer to establish how the composition of university audiences influenced the responses (McNaughtan et al., 2018). Topinka (2016) invokes rhetorical ecology to examine how an anonymous racist blog influenced local news coverage of a contest to design Chicago's official vehicle registration sticker. Buchanan (2016) likewise examines the discourses surrounding the integration of female personnel into American submarine crews in 2010 using ecological models. In each of these contexts, a few particular qualities of Edbauer's ecological model enable analysis of sociopolitical exigences:

- Rhetorical ecology posits that rhetoric is not formulated by an independent rhetor and transmitted to a tacit audience, but instead comes from complex interactions of rhetor and audience.
- Rhetorical ecology accounts for the crucial importance of affect in determining how communication is formulated and perceived.

- Rhetorical ecology posits distributed networks of causation. In other words, they conceptualize rhetoric as something that emerges due to seemingly uncoordinated actions of disparate rhetors, audiences, and texts.

The next section provides an account of a controversy that embroiled the Purdue OWL in 2018 after a Fox News segment suggested that the OWL was advocating for a ban of the word "man."

The OWL "Man Ban"

In the interest of full disclosure, the author of this piece wishes it to be known that he has been employed as Content Coordinator for the Purdue OWL since May 2018.

The Purdue OWL is a website operated by the Purdue College of Liberal Arts that offers a wide variety of free writing resources. During the 2017–18 school year, the site received over 515,000,000 visits, making it one of the most popular educational sites in the world (Purdue Writing Lab, 2018).

The "man ban" controversy began on February 9, 2018 when OWL staffers made a minor edit to a page on the Purdue OWL entitled "Stereotypes and Biased Language." At that time, the page cited 2002 NCTE guidelines on sexist language to describe how writers might make terminological changes to avoid bias (e.g., by using "firefighter" rather than "fireman"). One particular passage on the page reads as follows: "Although MAN in its original sense carried the dual meaning of adult human and adult male, its meaning has come to be so closely identified with adult male that the generic use of MAN and other words with masculine markers should be avoided" (Driscoll & Brizee, 2017).

OWL staffers interviewed for this chapter believe that the February 9 edit to the "Stereotypes" page was what led *Campus Reform* to publish a story with the headline "Purdue writing guide: Words with 'MAN' 'should be avoided'" on February 20 (Sabes, 2018). *Campus Reform* is a digital publication whose mission statement asserts that "... *Campus Reform* exposes liberal bias and abuse on the nation's college campuses" (Campus Reform, n.d.-a). OWL staffers speculated that a *Campus Reform* reader may have mistakenly thought the edit to the "Stereotypes" page constituted the publication of a brand-new resource and notified *Campus Reform* via the outlet's anonymous tip page, which invites readers to report campus "abuse" (Campus Reform, n.d.-b).

The *Campus Reform* piece describes the "Stereotypes" OWL resource in exhaustive detail, noting, for instance, its suggestions to use "humanity" rather than "mankind" and "mail carrier" instead of "mailman." Though the article presents the OWL resource as an example of left-wing bias in higher education, and though it is interrupted with ads soliciting donations with messages like "The radical left will stop at nothing to intimidate conservative students on college campuses" (Sabes, 2018), the piece itself is essentially accurate. It quotes the OWL resource faithfully, and its writer does not editorialize.

Several days later, Tucker Carlson, a Fox News pundit, aired a segment titled "Campus Craziness" on his show "Tucker Carlson Tonight." The segment claimed that Purdue University had launched a "new writing guide" that called for writers to avoid words that include "man," as well as instances of masculine language more generally, on the grounds that they are sexist. The section was structured as a dialog between Carlson and Cathy Areu, a liberal contributor charged with defending the OWL resource. While Carlson occasionally posed serious questions (asking at one point, for instance, whether "a small group of super-unhappy people get to control what the rest of us say and think"), much of the segment takes a sardonic tone. In addition to levying several humorous jabs at Purdue University (referring to it, for instance, as an institution that grants "fake degrees"), Carlson spent much of the segment's five-and-a-half-minute runtime lampooning how the OWL page's alleged recommendations might function in everyday usage. He joked, for instance, that investment firm Goldman Sachs should be referred to as "Gold-person Sachs." At several points, Areu appears on the verge of laughter, seemingly unconvinced by her own pro-censorship arguments.

Despite its humorous tone, the segment made several factual errors. The largest of these was implying that the OWL page argued for a ban on any usage of "man," including terms merely containing M, A, and N in sequence. This, of course, was untrue. Some of the page's examples, like the recommendation to use "manufactured" in place of "man-made," even contradicted this. Also, contra Carlson's claims, the OWL page was not new: it was more than a decade old. The "man" suggestions were also not recommendations of Purdue University itself. Instead, the page presented 1975 instructions from the National Council of Teachers of English (NCTE) (revised in 2002) with commentary.

A few days after the Carlson segment, the "Stereotypes" page was quietly modified to present alternative terminologies as mere suggestions and urge student writers to defer to the conventions of their academic discipline. Nevertheless, as the Carlson story attracted attention on social media, Writing Lab staff were soon inundated with irate messages from around the world. Nearly all of these cited an attempt to ban the word "man" from everyday usage. Some took the form of fairly banal complaints. One user who identified himself as a Purdue alumnus wrote, "I cannot believe you have decided that any words with the letters M-A-N in them can be biased or sexist. [...] I can't truly express my disappointment." However, some messages contained vulgar or bigoted remarks. For example, one user wrote, "All that ever falls within your realm of observation is so-called 'female oppression' Do all of your neurons still fire? Cunt?!??!" [*sic*]. A small minority of messages even contained violent threats. One user, in a message with a subject line reading "Females are super special n' stuff," wrote "Do you understand your bias and unilateral approach or do I need to lobomitize [*sic*] you?". Writing Lab social media accounts and even unaffiliated grad students received similar abuse. In addition, at least one parent lodged a formal complaint with the College of Liberal Arts under the mistaken assumption that the OWL page was course material for one of his child's classes. While it is unfortunately impossible to determine exactly how many messages Writing Lab staff and affiliates received, the volume and nature of these messages led at least one Writing Lab staffer who feared for her safety to contact the Purdue Police Department for assistance.

The "Man Ban" controversy was intense, but it was also fairly brief. A small number of messages trickled in for the rest of the year (one user, for instance, sent an irate message in November 2018, roughly nine months after the *Campus Reform* piece), but the worst was over by April. Curiously, neither the university's administration nor its president, former Republican governor of Indiana Mitch Daniels, initially issued any official statement in support of the OWL, despite several media inquiries (Bangert, 2018). On March 19, nearly a month after the *Campus Reform* piece was published, Provost Jay Akridge acknowledged the controversy during a session of the University Senate, noting that the "assertion that there was this 'ban on man' obviously was a gross misstatement," but that it was not worth "going tit for tat" with Fox. Daniels eventually made an official written acknowledgment of the controversy in a March letter to alumni and friends of the university. Wrote Daniels, "You may have seen a couple of news reports that Purdue was attempting to ban the word "man" [...] These accounts were inaccurate; it [...] Purdue has [never] advocated for a ban on the word "man" in any fashion." However, Daniels also noted that coverage of the controversy "... helped [the administration] realize that the website [...] has not had the level of supervision something this prominent should have." Indeed, in the aftermath of the controversy, Purdue's administration mandated a new advisory board through which the College of Liberal Arts could exercise direct oversight of the OWL, which had previously operated semi-autonomously.

The Man Ban Controversy as Ecology

The Purdue OWL "man ban" controversy demonstrates how fake news can function as a rhetorical ecology. This section reflects on three notable aspects of the "man ban" controversy, demonstrating how an ecological model can account for each.

The first is that empirical truth exerted virtually no influence. Despite most users' complaints, the OWL page did not call for a ban on the word "man," nor did it represent official Purdue policy, nor was the page a new resource, nor were the NCTE guidelines featured on the page new. These facts would have been obvious to anyone who visited the page, including the Carlson segment's producers. They might even have been apparent to careful, attentive readers of the original *Campus Reform* piece, which quoted the OWL page accurately. The fact that so many individual actors—including Carlson—expressed grievances that were contradicted by observable fact suggests Carlson et al. either interpreted the content of the OWL page in ways at odds with objective truth, or they made no attempt to verify the content of the page at all.

Rhetorical ecology can account for the improbability of so many individual actors making concurrent errors by illustrating how affect pre-interprets facts in fake news ecologies. Rhetorical ecology does not assume neutral, objective audiences—instead, it acknowledges that every audience is made up of distributed individuals, and that these individuals form a coherent audience by way of sharing implicit features that affect how they interpret rhetoric. Citing Amin and Thrift (2002), Edbauer posits audiences as collections of individuals inhabiting metaphorical "spaces" characterized by experiences, affects, beliefs and processes. Thus, rather than facilitating persuasion via traditional criteria (e.g., some combination of ethos, logos, and pathos) rhetorical ecologies instead coordinate actors based on "shared structures of feeling" (2005, p. 20). Instead of assuming neutral audiences who must be persuaded, ecologies model non-neutral collections of individuals who must be *mobilized* on the basis of shared feelings. Thus, the ecological model suggests Carlson did not deceive his audience into thinking something false, per se. More accurately, Carlson directed the attention of a particular group of people toward a particular set of circumstances, and this group's shared affect essentially pre-determined its interpretation of them.

A second aspect of the OWL controversy is that both *Campus Reform* and Tucker Carlson tended to shift or blur traditional ideological reference points. In the *Campus Reform* piece, this was mostly implicit. For example, the piece presented quotes from the OWL page adjacent to ads warning readers that "the radical left will stop at nothing to intimidate conservative students on college campuses." The unstated message, of course, is that the OWL page is an example of liberal intimidation. Similarly, in Carlson's segment, left-wing stances were portrayed as vengeful and radical. As mentioned above, Carlson questions whether "a small group of super-unhappy people get to control what we say and think." At another point in the broadcast, the chyron read "Left's new target: 'mankind.'" In the case of both the *Campus Reform* piece and the Carlson segment, the overarching implication is that left-wing stances represent wild ideological aberrations, while, right-wing stances are common-sense, clear-headed, and non-ideological. Of course, in reality, both stances are the products of ideology.

Again, rhetorical ecology offers explanations. By positing that rhetoric is created not by an independent author, but instead by the affective interactions of author and audience, the model demonstrates that fake news ecologies function as morally and ideologically relativistic communities. The affective connection between Carlson and the audience acts as a center point for moral and ideological judgments. While Carlson makes the argument that colleges are home to ideological conspiracies, Carlson cannot himself be perceived as an ideologue because this would undermine his supposed raison d'etre: fighting ideological bias. Thus, Carlson couches his rhetoric in the trappings of neutrality, presenting his arguments as common sense, rather than partisan. Carlson's audience accepts this framing to avoid the cognitive dissonance that might come with the realization that they, too, are ideological beings, as this dissonance would disrupt the affective relationship that binds them to the rest of the rhetorical ecology. In short, innocuous texts like the OWL "Stereotypes" page can be perceived as profoundly ideological when Carlson's ideology and morality are first perceived as neutral.

A final important feature of the controversy is that many of the users who sent angry or harassing messages to the OWL interpreted ideas originally presented as jokes instead as facts. As previously mentioned, the Carlson segment dedicated a significant amount of time to absurd, sarcastic examples clearly intended to ridicule. For instance, Carlson chided Areu for recording her portion of the segment in "Man"-hattan. In response, Areu gamely replied that renaming New York City "The Big Apple" would make it "less offensive" (a suggestion made more preposterous by the fact that "Manhattan" derives from an Algonquian term, not the English "man"). However, viewers like the alumnus who expressed anger at the OWL's deciding "that any words with the letters M-A-N in them can be biased or sexist," appeared to have taken these sorts of jokes seriously (or at least internalized the inaccurate portrayal of the OWL they provided). Carlson's apparent ability to generate such passionate responses via jokes and derision rather than straightforward calls to action suggests a disquieting thought: that purveyors of fake news might evade scrutiny by claiming to be satirists or entertainers, even if their audiences do not interpret them as such.

Here, again, the behavior of fake news audiences is illustrated via rhetorical ecology, which allows for meaning to shift as rhetoric circulates through distributed social fields. Edbauer illustrates this in an account of how political rhetoric in Austin, Texas evolved as diverse groups adopted it. She documents how the phrase "Keep Austin weird," originally an anti-corporate slogan, accumulated a variety of new contextual meanings as local rhetors adapted it for various purposes. "The original rhetoric has been expanded in the course of new [uses], which adopt the phrase and transform it to fit other purposes," writes Edbauer (p. 17). However, when large corporations like Cingular adopted the phrase in advertisements, they imbued the phrase with the opposite meaning it originally carried: that Austin residents should support out-of-town corporate interests, rather than resist them.

Similarly, the perceived meaning of Carlson's rhetoric shifted and evolved as it circulated through distributed audiences. The nature of that circulation may have played an important role accelerating this process, as social media users can present clips of Carlson's segment to followers alongside their own commentary. There is evidence that this sort of accompanying social media commentary can color perceptions of the shared content itself. One study, for instance, found that subjects who were made to read social media posts from "elite" sources about fake news were subsequently unable to distinguish fake news from real news when presented with both (Van Duyn & Collier, 2019). However, this sort of deliberate priming may not even be necessary in online social groups that are already ideologically homogenous. Huckfeldt et al. (2004) find, for instance, that "insular social networks can be especially ripe for misinformation, in that homogeny can make acceptance of a falsehood appear socially 'normal' by decreasing the visibility and familiarity of contradictory information" (as cited in Scheufele & Krause, 2019, p. 7665). In sum, the distribution of Carlson's segment via social media may have enabled the segment to be interpreted in a manner incongruous with its tone and content.

Implications for Educators

Conceptualizing the OWL "Man Ban" controversy as a rhetorical ecology illuminates how, via distributed circulation and multiple interactions between rhetor, audience, and affect, partisan reporting by a relatively niche outlet transformed into something much more rhetorically potent. It also underscores the importance of helping students gain the skills necessary to avoid being swept up in similar controversies. Most importantly, it provides a starting point for corrective action in the form of a theoretical framework English educators can use to arrive at pedagogies that convey these skills. Considered alongside current empirical research, this framework suggests several productive paths for teachers concerned about fake news.

First, teachers should design interventions that reflect the ecologies in which students come into contact with fake news. Research suggests that these differ from the corresponding ecologies for adult professionals. Leeder (2019) finds that a strong majority of college students use social media as a primary source of news, which aligns with Pew data showing that younger age cohorts not only use social media for news more than older cohorts, but also view social media more positively in terms of its potential to inform (Pew Research Center, 2018). Research suggests that this trust is misplaced. Fake news spreads farther and quicker on social media than real news (Vosoughi, Roy, & Aral, 2018), and social media users tend to prioritize affective qualities like self-expression over accuracy when sharing social media news content (Chen et al., 2015). Moreover, one study suggests young peoples' news consumption habits are characterized by an "incidental" quality: that is, they tend to encounter news items passively during social media usage and spend little time reading or watching stories themselves. Instead, they tend to absorb the information in the headline and skim-read the rest of the piece (if they read it at all) unless it is especially attention-grabbing (Boczkowski et al. 2017).

This set of circumstances suggests the value of interventions that meet students where they stand with regards to news consumption, rather than assuming habits and values that might be more familiar to older generations. Assignments that have students engage with the sorts of genres that are more common in print and broadcast media, like op-ed pieces or cable news segments, risk wasting class time on skills that students will never use. Instead, teachers should try to mirror the rhetorical ecologies most likely to provide fake news in students' lives—in other words, the fake news ecologies found on social media. This does not necessarily mean teachers must work complicated new technologies or pedagogical techniques into their courses. To the contrary: relatively straightforward lesson sequences that include lectures, discussions, instructor modeling, and in-class activities can produce significant gains in terms of students' ability to differentiate true and false information encountered on social media (McGrew, 2020).

The ecological model also highlights the potential of interventions that change the way students interact with the rhetorical ecologies that tend to convey fake news to them. Though it is unlikely that educators will be able to rewire students' media habits in a single class, even relatively modest progress on this front could disrupt the set of circumstances that make young social media users so susceptible to fake news in the first place.

One initial goal might be to challenge the "incidental" behavior that broadly defines young students' interactions with news (real and fake). This means teaching students to be more skeptical, discerning navigators of social media ecologies. In particular, teachers should develop interventions that have students assess not only the trustworthiness of the sources they might encounter on social media, but also the trustworthiness of those sources' creators. Students are unlikely to consider the origin of a given source's information when evaluating its quality (Barzilai & Zohar, 2012; List, Grossnickle, & Alexander, 2016). One study found that, rather than attempting to determine whether a source's author was reputable, "... students made judgments about trustworthiness [of online news] based on factors like the content of a post and surface features of the page on which it appeared" (McGrew et al., 2018, p. 183). This can make students susceptible to misinformation that mimics the appearance and "feel" of reliable sources. The same study found, for example, that a majority of student participants were deceived by content on a lobbying group website presenting misleading information about a proposed minimum wage increase because of the site's professional appearance and the fact that the post linked to credible sources. Because fake news can similarly achieve "surface" trustworthiness, teachers should not fall back on the rote, tired conventions of source evaluation: privileging .org sources, sources with perfect spelling and grammar, sources with professional, authoritative aesthetics, and so on. None of these formal features signify truth.

Fortunately, pedagogical practices like lateral reading represent potentially powerful correctives. Lateral reading is the practice of seeking out additional sources to evaluate the trustworthiness of an original source, rather than evaluating a source using the content and features only of the source itself (i.e., vertical reading). Note that, insofar as lateral reading requires students to venture beyond individual texts and authors, it overlaps with critical science literacy, the ability to interpret scientific scholarship as a social endeavor. Pedagogical practices for imparting critical science literacy are described in detail in Sills and Kenzie's chapter within this collection.

A recent study of students, historians, and professional fact-checkers found that experienced lateral readers reached true conclusions relatively quickly when presented with sources of ambiguous trustworthiness (Wineberg & McGrew, 2019). By comparison, vertical readers struggled to differentiate reliable information from unreliable (and took longer to do so). Crucially, lateral readers appeared to be abler navigators of informational structures. Write Wineberg & McGrew, "[lateral readers] knew that the first result was not necessarily the most authoritative . . . they understood how search engine optimizers use sophisticated keywords and other techniques to game results." By contrast, vertical readers "often clicked on the first few search results, rarely articulating a rationale for why they selected a particular link."

Skills like lateral reading that change students' relationships with the digital rhetorical ecologies that deliver fake news may not necessarily be terribly difficult for teachers to work into existing curricula. Despite Wineberg & McGrew associating the technique with professional fact-checkers, lateral reading does not require any advanced technical proficiency or special equipment: it can be performed with any modern computer and web browser. This is also true for two complementary skills Wineberg & McGrew describe. Both "click restraint," the tendency to examine search results rather than immediately clicking on a prominent link, and "taking bearings," the strategy of plotting a path forward before delving into unfamiliar content, involve behaviors and thought patterns that can ostensibly be conveyed and assessed straightforwardly. There is no readily apparent evidence that traditional teaching practices like instructor modeling, discussion, reflection, and practice would not suffice for these skills. That said, two chapters within this collection offer additional guidance. Anson and Andrews' chapter explores how instructors might approach these everyday pedagogical interventions in ways that promote analysis, inquiry, and synthesis (rather than incidentalism). Similarly, Mina, Mills, and Niha's chapter describes the process of creating a course designed to impart the skills of good digital citizenship.

The ecological model also helps instructors identify which pedagogical strategies are unproductive. For example, while a well-meaning educator might train students to immediately debunk any piece of online misinformation with counter-information from neutral, reputable sources, the ecological model hints at the futility of such an approach. The powerful role that affect plays within rhetorical ecologies dictates that political opinions can rarely be reshaped solely by appeals to logic. Moreover, direct attempts at refutation can be particularly counterproductive in the context of fake news, as the affective characteristics of fake news audiences can cause corrective information to function merely as a "reminder" of the falsehood. For example, a recent study of untrue beliefs surrounding healthcare policy found that "merely repeating a rumor increases its strength [. . .] even when rumors are repeated in the context of debunking that misinformation" (Berinsky, 2015, p. 242). The same study found that partisan affiliation determined how subjects interpreted the neutrality of sources used to debunk false beliefs, making ostensibly "reputable" sources less useful than they might initially appear. However, the study also found that corrective information originating from an ideologically affiliated source (i.e., a source on the same "side" as the reader) appeared to have the most persuasive potential. Thus, teachers would do well to teach students to choose their battles carefully by first considering how other members of fake news ecologies will perceive them and their preferred sources before starting debates.

If there is one final lesson the ecological model and the OWL "man ban" controversy can teach educators, it is that fake news thrives not merely due to naivety on the part of ordinary citizens, but also due to the deliberate actions of powerful bad-faith actors. It was not some radical screed on a fringe message board that motivated people to send violent threats to OWL staffers. It was a professionally-produced segment that ran for five minutes on a well-known political commentary show. Whether influential rhetors like Carlson fully understand the consequences of their misleading words, they exert a continuous negative influence on the grand rhetorical ecology that constitutes global political discourse every day. Absent any sort of political effort to curb this influence, ordinary educators may represent the most important social bulwark against misinformation insofar as they, too, exert rhetorical influence over billions of human beings every day.

Fortunately, the evidence is clear: when classrooms engage explicitly with fake news in the forms and contexts in which students encounter it, students learn. Of course, even the most expertly-crafted curricula cannot serve as panaceas for misinformation. It should also go without saying that educational efforts to combat misinformation must involve the contributions of stakeholders of diverse ideological backgrounds to maintain legitimacy in the eyes of administrators, parents, and students. Despite these qualifications, it is not easy to imagine an issue of greater import for writing teachers in the early 21st century than the global fight against fake news. Nor is it easy to imagine a contest with a greater prize—that is, the enduring happiness and security of our students—should we teachers win.

References

Amin, A., & Thrift, N. (2002). *Cities: Reimagining the urban*. Polity.

Associated Press-NORC Center for Public Affairs Research & USAFacts. (2019). State of the facts 2019 [PDF document]. http://www.apnorc.org/PDFs/USA%20Facts%202019/State%20of%20the%20Facts.pdf

Bangert, Dave. (2018, March 19). Purdue breaks silence on fake 'man' ban. *Journal & Courier*. https://www.jconline.com/story/opinion/columnists/

dave-bangert/2018/03/19/bangert-purdue-finally-breaks-silence-after-fox-news-mocks-fake-campus-ban-man/438596002/

Barzilai, S., & Zohar, A. (2012). Epistemic thinking in action: Evaluating and integrating online sources. *Cognition and Instruction, 30,* 39–85. https://doi.org/10.1080/07370008.2011.636495

Berinsky, A. (2015). Rumors and health care reform: Experiments in political misinformation. *British Journal of Political Science, 47*(2), 241–262. https://doi.org/10.1017/S0007123415000186

Boczkowski, P., Mitchelstein, E., & Matassi, M. (2017, January). Incidental news: How young people consume news on social media. In *Proceedings of the 50th Hawaii international conference on system sciences.* https://doi.org/10.24251/HICSS.2017.217

Buchanan, L. (2016). A few good (wo)men: Integrating the US submarine force. *Rhetoric Review, 35*(1), 35–48. https://doi.org/10.1080/07350198.2016.1107826

Campus Reform. (n.d.-a). *About.* https://www.campusreform.org/about/

Campus Reform. (n.d.-b). *Send us a tip.* https://www.campusreform.org/TIP/

Chen, X., Sin, S. C. J., Theng, Y. L., & Lee, C. S. (2015). Why students share misinformation on social media: Motivation, gender, and study-level differences. *The Journal of Academic Librarianship, 41,* 583–592. https://doi.org/10.1016/j.acalib.2015.07.003

Cooper, M. (1986). The ecology of writing. *College English, 48*(4), 364–375.

Driscoll, D. L., & Brizee, A. (2017). Stereotypes and biased language. https://web.archive.org/web/20180221163237/https://owl.english.purdue.edu/owl/resource/608/05/

Edbauer, J. (2005). Unframing models of public distribution: From rhetorical situation to rhetorical ecologies. *Rhetoric Society Quarterly, 35*(4), 5–24.

Huckfeldt, R., Mendez, J., & Osborn, T. (2004). Disagreement, ambivalence, and engagement: The political consequences of heterogeneous networks. *Political Psychology, 25*(1), 65–95. https://www.jstor.org/stable/3792524

Lerner, A., & Gehrke, P. (2018). *Organic public engagement: How ecological thinking transforms public engagement with science.* Springer.

List, A., Grossnickle, E. M., & Alexander, P. A. (2016). Undergraduate students' justifications for source selection in a digital academic context. *Journal of Educational Computing Research, 54,* 22–61. https://doi.org/10.1177/0735633115606659

McGrew, S. (2020). Learning to evaluate: An intervention in civic online reasoning. *Computers & Education, 145,* Computers & Education. https://doi.org/10.1016/j.compedu.2019.103711

McGrew, S., Breakstone, J., Ortega, T., Smith, M., & Wineburg, S. (2018). Can students evaluate online sources? Learning from assessments of civic online reasoning. *Theory and Research in Social Education, 46*(2), 165–193. https://doi.org/10.1080/00933104.2017.1416320

McNaughtan, J., Garcia, H., Lértora, I., Louis, S., Li, X., Croffie, A. L., & McNaughtan, E. D. (2018). Contentious dialogue: University presidential response and the 2016

US presidential election. *Journal of Higher Education Policy and Management, 40*(6), 533–549. https://doi.org/10.1080/1360080X.2018.1462437

Pew Research Center. (2016). Many Americans believe fake news is sowing confusion. *Journalism & Media.* https://www.journalism.org/2016/12/15/many-americans-believe-fake-news-is-sowing-confusion/

Pew Research Center. (2018). News use across social media platforms 2018. *Media & News.* https://www.journalism.org/2018/09/10/news-use-across-social-media-platforms-2018/

Purdue Writing Lab. (2018). Services offered. *Purdue University writing lab annual report: May 2017–May 2018.* https://blog.apastyle.org/apastyle/blog-guidelines.html

Reynolds, N. (2004). *Geographies of writing: Inhabiting places and encountering difference.* Southern Illinois University Press.

Sabes, A. (2018). Purdue writing guide: Words with 'MAN' 'should be avoided.' *Campus Reform.* https://www.campusreform.org/?ID=10539

Shaviro, S. (2003). *Connected, or what it means to live in the network society.* University of Minnesota Press.

Spinuzzi, C. (2003). *Tracing genres through organizations: A sociocultural approach to information design* (Vol. 1). MIT Press.

Stanford History Education Group. (2016). *Evaluating information: The cornerstone of civic online reasoning* [PDF file]. https://stacks.stanford.edu/file/druid:fv751yt5934/SHEG%20Evaluating%20Information%20Online.pdf

Syverson, M. (1999). *The wealth of reality: An ecology of composition.* Southern Illinois University Press.

Topinka, R. (2016). Race, circulation, and the city: The case of the Chicago city sticker controversy. *Western Journal of Communication, 80*(2), 163–184. https://doi.org/10.1080/10570314.2016.1139173

Van Duyn, E., & Collier, J. (2019). Priming and fake news: The effects of elite discourse on evaluations of news media. *Mass Communication and Society, 22*(1), 29–48. https://doi.org/10.1080/15205436.2018.1511807

Vosoughi, S., Roy, D., & Aral, S. (2018). The spread of true and false news online. *Science, 359*, 1146–1151. https://doi.org/10.1126/science.aap9559

Wineburg, S., & McGrew, S. (2019). Lateral reading and the nature of expertise: Reading less and learning more when evaluating digital information. *Teachers College Record, 121*(11), 1–40. https://purl.stanford.edu/yk133ht8603

4. Search(able) Warrants: Fostering Critical Empathy in the Writing (and Reading) Classroom

WILLIAM T. FITZGERALD
Rutgers University-Camden

A naive assumption informed the assignment sequence for Writing 101 when, in 2015, I took on the role of writing program director at Rutgers University-Camden. It was in many ways a quaintly conservative approach to composition that I would articulate, akin to models of rhetorical argumentation fashionable a generation or more ago (Fulkerson, 2005). My assumption was that students benefit from a curriculum in which civility and civic responsibility are paramount. What made it naive is that our culture pays lip service to norms of civility. Read comments online, watch cable news. The exchanges one finds are anything but civil or responsible. Public discourse grows ever more partisan. We are endlessly recapitulating battles between present-day Cavaliers and Roundheads. I suspect many of us routinely wonder of those we meet: one of *us* or one of *them*?

Today, 2015 seems so long ago. If anything, we have grown even further apart as a polity, our norms of civility not even given lip service. Yet the model adopted then no longer strikes me as quaint. In fact, I believe it is just the opposite. The election, in 2016, of Donald J. Trump as the 45th president of the United States has reinforced for me the notion that developing capacities for listening and for reflecting on the nature of how beliefs are formed, held, and subject to change is something vital for our moment. These capacities are vital for the rhetorical education we need to meet the challenges we face in an era of "fake news and alternative facts" (Cooke, 2018).

In this chapter, I present the first-year composition course we teach at Rutgers-Camden, one that takes as its pedagogical mission to foster skills of critical empathy in reading and writing. It reflects a commitment to teach toward the rhetorical virtues of honesty, open-mindedness, and accountability and against the smash-and-grab model of argumentation now prevalent, in which we speak from hardened silos, yet rarely listen.

Of course, when I first conceived of a new curriculum for our Writing 101 course, few could have predicted that Donald Trump would become president of the United States, least of all many who feel at home in the academy. There, one pursues truth for its own sake, reasons ethically with like-minded others, and embraces the dialectic whereby our inevitably partial insights yield to shared beliefs based on discoverable knowledge. It may be that learning to navigate one's way through the groves of academe is poor preparation for a world where facts are met, in the now infamous words of White House advisor Kellyanne Conway, with "alternative facts" (Bradner, 2017).

Even so, before Trump or Conway, before this chilling culture of disinformation, we drifted for decades toward "truthiness" (Colbert, 2005). The gist of this term is the *semblance* of truth without the *substance*. Truthiness is what *feels* true, what we believe ought to be the case, whether facts exist to back up an assertion or not. I think, especially, of claims by the Bush administration concerning weapons of mass destruction that served as a pretext for the invasion of Iraq in 2003. On later inspection, evidence for such weapons proved to be much less than initially met the eye (Duelfer, 2004).

Yet even here we were in a domain where at least the *ring* of truth was honored. Truthi*ness* had yet to concede to *post*-truth (Keyes, 2004; Biesecker, 2018; Carillo, 2018). If truthiness is over-invested in *pathos*, it does not forswear *logos*. A residue of norms for civic argumentation remains as our inheritance from the Enlightenment, succinctly expressed in the Declaration of Independence: "To prove this, let facts be submitted to a candid world" (Jefferson, 1776). These words follow not long after more familiar words, "We hold these truths to be self evident ..." (1776). We mourn for a lost world of accountability, in particular for the principle that the more partisan our belief, the more we, like the Founders, must present our case "to a candid world."

Notwithstanding—or in order *to withstand*—the erosion of these long-established norms for reasoned discourse, I imagined a first-year writing (and reading) course for authors who stayed true to truth, *almost* as if we did not live in a post-truth world. I thus outline a course in Writing 101 that imagines a space for reasoned discourse with a sequence of assignments and a rationale for their individual and collective agency.

For the course I imagined, several key questions arose: How do we reason with others, and ourselves? How do we represent our beliefs and those of others? How do we stay open to the possibility of changed minds, including our own? I am hardly alone in posing such questions. How could I be in the field of rhetoric and composition, in good company with others (Booth, 1970, 1974; Crosswhite, 1996; Perelman and Olbrechts-Tyteca, 1969; Roberts-Miller, 2007) wrestling with these concerns and reminding us of *our* civic responsibility as teachers of rhetoric? I stand with scholars and teachers eloquent in articulating how the virtues of "honesty, accountability, fair-mindedness and intellectual courage" are *foundational* to both the academy and the civic sphere and who argue that "the first-year writing class offers a robust defense against the post-truth culture and provides a model for constructive, fact-based public discourse" (Duffy, 2019). When reasoned discourse itself is under siege and people retreat to their echo chambers of choice, the composition classroom offers a vital contrast to the culture of alternative facts.

From Common Read to Authorial Agency

From the start, I imagined first-year composition as a space for the discovery and practice of argument and the cultivation of civic virtues. In practical terms, I conceived of a productive arc from the salon of the classroom to the agonistic domain of the public square. Consequently, the units of Writing 101 proceed from the communicative arts of *reading* to those of *writing*, with the first two units (five to six weeks) centered on reading as an intellectual and civic act.

The program I inherited had a long tradition of reading, reflective of an older model of writing pedagogy centered in critical response to (literary) texts. After all, this is where most of our instructors—graduate students in English and Creative Writing—excel. Apart from local culture, I was sympathetic to arguments (Salvatori, 1996; Carillo, 2015) that the disappearance of reading from the composition classroom needed a literal as well as figurative course correction. I was eager to *deepen* a tradition of reading in Writing 101 even as I took new steps to composition as civic rhetoric. We kept the "summer read" as an gateway to college literacy, focusing on a common text in the first weeks of the course.

In 2015, we selected a work of science reporting in David Quammen's *Ebola: The Natural and Human History of a Deadly Virus* (2014), a text published at the height of the public health crisis that anticipated the Ebola virus becoming a global pandemic. This choice led efforts to select a book relevant to a broader cultural conversation, a move common to many colleges and writing programs in selecting a campus book (Strawser & Hume, 2019). Beginning with reading responds to a call to address the affordances and obstacles associated with college-level reading through explicit instruction

(Bunn, 2013; Carillo, 2015, 2017; Jolliffe & Harl, 2008; Horning, 2007, 2011; Keller, 2013).

In 2016, our first-year book was Ta-Nehisi Coates' (2015) *Between the World and Me*. This choice reflected a belief that encounters with literacy in composition should be consequential in expanding horizons and challenging students with voices and concerns that, for many, are fresh and provocative. As I explain to new instructors, reading in first-year composition serves multiple purposes. It is a gateway experience to college—a place where people read books and discuss ideas. It thus serves as a microcosm of academic culture. And it is an opportunity to experience reading at a deeper level to understand how texts work on readers and readers on texts.

These first few weeks are a mini-course on reading by *introducing* strategies for encountering, and also countering, texts. Such "mindful reading" (Carillo, 2017) practices include annotation, exploring the connotations of particular words, reading aloud to make reading visible, connecting passages to personal experience, responding to authors, and also quick takes on research stimulated by the book. Importantly in this first unit, students do not write a paper but assemble a portfolio of reading-based responses to the text. This early focus on exploring a repertoire of reading strategies resonates with approaches identified by Danielle Koupf in her chapter, "Factual Dispute," in this volume.

In 2017, our summer book became Rutgers Reads, with a substantial investment by the Office of the Chancellor. The book is now complementary to first-year students; and each September, as classes complete this unit, the author of the selected book comes to campus. In addition to a public lecture the author participates in a question and answer session just with first-year students. Three authors have visited: in 2017, Margot Lee Shetterly (2016); in 2018, Colson Whitehead (2016); in 2019, Matthew Desmond (2016).

Only after this immersive experience in reading—curiously, responsively, critically, and authentically—does the pedagogy of writing begin. A second unit in close reading called "Analyze This!" builds on reading skills previously introduced. This assignment asks students to perform rhetorical analysis by explaining how a text works and applying rhetorical terms and concepts to characterize an argument based on textual evidence. Their experiences with this unit parallel those of students analyzing news photography in Kristina Reardon's "News-as-Text" chapter in this volume.

To no surprise, students struggle with these tasks of academic writing, especially negotiating the binary between what a text "says" and what it "does" (Bean, 2011, pp. 170–71). Here, instructors might choose to remain with the common book of unit one. More often, they choose another text, for example Martin Luther King's *Letter from a Birmingham Jail* (1992) or Ta-Nehisi Coates' "The Case for Reparations" (2014), to profile strategies for text-based arguments. While students struggle, this unit helps to create a shared lexicon for future use and to further develop critical reading strategies.

Exploring the Nature of Belief

At this point, the course shifts to the nature of belief and the possibility of change. In particular, the third unit asks students to compose a variation on the popular radio genre "This I Believe," introduced in 1951 by journalist Edward R. Murrow and revived several times since ("This I Believe", 2019). In this genre, people voice individual philosophies of life by reading a short essay on the air. These essays were intended to be non-sectarian and non-political, focusing on values that contribute to a meaningful life. It is not surprising that the series "This I Believe" began at the height of the Red Scare era in American politics, under the sway of Senator Joseph McCarthy. To state one's beliefs in the public square, or its "on air" equivalent, is an act of civic courage.

For Writing 101, students write, then record, a three to four minute audio essay for a hypothetical podcast series, "This I (now) believe." As explained on assignment sheets, students reflect on a belief they have come to over time, one they are aware of not always holding, and explore how they came to that belief. Many instructors share advice from the latest revival of "This I Believe": "be positive"; "be personal"; "tell a story about you" ("This I Believe").

For many students this is a breakthrough assignment. It inspires, but also invokes fear. Consider what is involved. In the flux of thought students have to isolate something as localizable as a belief. They have to identify this belief, put a name to it. They have to share a story about themselves that crystalizes recognition of having a belief. They have to do this *in writing*, wrestling with words on the page, representing their thoughts and experience. For those who were told never to use *I* in a paper, composing this essay is no small hurdle. Finally, they must *read* and *record* their text, performing it in their own voice as a public genre.

The movement from disembodied text to spoken word is the element of "This I (Now) Believe" that looms largest for most students. Things happen in that passage as writers discover what they did and did not mean to say, as they try to give voice to their words and words to their thoughts and experiences. Supporting this assignment is our Writing and Design Lab, where consultants help students compose, revise, and record their essays. Students typically find that recording a three-minute essay is a complex undertaking, one involving many takes. The effort can spark unanticipated conversations on writing and revising because students feel compelled to tell their story well.

In implementing this assignment, my colleagues and I did not anticipate the extent to which students would see it as an invitation to write about highly personal matters, at times surfacing trauma. Consequently, some resist sharing their recordings with anyone but their teacher. However, most see the audio essay as an opportunity to experience the writing classroom as a "proto-public space" (Eberly, 2000, p. 170). By composing and sharing, they engage the nature and variability of belief, with opportunities to reflect on how beliefs are formed and to what extent they are malleable or even within our control.

This unit ends with a different notion of *reading*—performing one's *own* writing—than the one with which Writing 101 begins. It opens up a space for reflecting on common as well as idiosyncratic dimensions of how we come to and hold the positions we do and how we might change those positions. As such, it is a first step in fostering a spirit of empathy for the beliefs and experiences of others.

Interlude: A Pedagogical Pre-history

From the start, two concerns were central to my blueprint for Writing 101. First, I wanted students to experience themselves in performance on the page *and* in their own voice. Hence, the audio essay "This I (Now) Believe" as an exercise in *speaking* one's truth. Second, I wanted students to *own* a position and to consider the rhetorical choices involved in doing so while also acknowledging alternative views. Writing 101 concludes with three linked assignments that give an opportunity to stake a claim in "My Take: An Open Letter to X" but also construct a more nuanced statement of that position in "Take Two." Between these takes is "To Think That, One ...," an exercise in critical empathy.

Before expanding on these units, I offer a pre-history of Writing 101 to recognize several pedagogical forbears. They include a direct mentor in Jeanne Fahnestock at the University of Maryland, who, with Marie Secor, reintroduced stasis theory from classical rhetoric to contemporary audiences in their landmark textbook, A *Rhetoric of Argument* (Fahnestock & Secor, 1982). The stases of fact, definition, value, and policy form a coherent framework for discovering points of agreement and disagreement on any issue. Indeed, the stases identify what is *at issue* in a given debate. However, I was less interested in organizing a first-year writing course around the stases as heuristics for inventing arguments than in foregrounding argument as a rhetorical mode centered on identifying sites of disagreement.

I cite stasis theory here because it provides an anatomy of argument at once accessible and generative. The idea that arguments can be assembled or broken into parts is a breakthrough insight. So, too, is the notion that facts and definitions are starting points for arguments. The choice of facts (or "alternative facts") is motivated by and supports chains of reasoning that move from claims of fact and definitions of terms to arguments over cause, value, and policy. One person's *pro-choice* position is another's *anti-abortion* stance, each with its attendant facts that opponents would challenge. That is, claims of policy (e.g., what we allow under law) and value (e.g., whose rights should take precedence) rest on logically prior beliefs (e.g., when *life* begins or what constitutes personhood). Previous experience with the stases as a generative model for inventing and analyzing arguments showed me the value of examining generally unarticulated links between claims and beliefs.

A second source for a rhetorical approach to argument is Stephen Toulmin (2003). The so-called Toulmin model offers a structure for examining and elaborating on the informal reasoning common to all civic debate. According to Toulmin (2003), arguments can be broken down into at least three (and as many as six) parts: claim, data, warrants, (qualifiers, rebuttal, backing) (p. 97). A *claim* is an assertion: *it rained last night*. The *data* are various forms of evidence that support a claim: *the ground is wet*. The *warrant* is the connection, often unstated, linking a claim with its grounds: *rain makes things wet*. Again, I did not intend to *teach* the Toulmin model in first-year writing, for it rarely aids invention. But I did want Toulmin's terms, especially *warrant*. If we are to understand *dis*agreement, we must first understand how warrants connect claims and their data. How is *this* evidence for *that*? Why do we reject evidence others point to as the proverbial smoking gun? Indeed, the civility and accountability that I posited as core goals of a composition course were connected to the connections made by warrants.

Finally, I cite the influence of literary critic and rhetorician Wayne Booth. In ways both broad and specific, I was keen to enact a Boothian pedagogy (Baker, Dieter, & Dobbins, 2014). In *Modern Dogma and the Rhetoric of Assent* (1974), Booth ponders the inability of students and faculty and administrators to understand or even to listen to one another at the height of protest movements in the 1960s, much like today in "red" and "blue" America. Here and in later works (1979; 1988; 2009) Booth addresses the ethical obligations of rhetors *and* audiences. He considers on what basis we *should* change our minds and assumes a willingness to do so is essential for true communication. Against traditional notions of rhetoric as the art of persuasion,

Booth (1974) defines rhetoric as "the art of discovering warrantable beliefs and improving those beliefs in shared discourse" (p. xiii). This notion of "warrantable beliefs" is the key concept of Writing 101. A course in the rhetoric of argument, rooted in inquiry and open to the possibilities of "improving" (Booth, 1974, p. xiii) beliefs through dialogue should foster our abilities to *make* arguments as well *listen to* them. It should go along with Booth (2009) toward a vital listening rhetoric by "paying full attention to opposing views" (p. 10).

I present this backstory because I believe it useful to name our pedagogical beliefs and commitments when we design curricula and invite our students and fellow instructors into spaces of teaching and learning. A writing curriculum negotiates between prevailing practices and idiosyncratic choices. As I noted earlier in discussing the place of reading in our curriculum, the approach to teaching writing is shaped by contextual factors. It is informed by a program's institutional setting and thus what is possible in a local context in terms of students, staff, resources (including class size), and program leadership.

Writing 101 at Rutgers-Camden is part of a two-semester sequence required of all students. A second course, Writing 102, is focused on research. Our program is 'in-house' in its training and staffing, depending primarily on graduate teaching assistants and part-time lecturers (most of whom were TAs at one point). Notably, Rutgers-Camden does not offer a doctoral degree in English. Composition instructors are students in the master's program in English or the MFA in Creative Writing. On average, our instructors teach two years; most take a required Practicum in the Teaching of Writing concurrently with a first semester of teaching. These details explain the need for a top-down curriculum, one that provides an accessible on-ramp for relatively inexperienced writing instructors. Beyond the first units focused on reading, Writing 101 does not demand large amounts of reading or much writing in response to assigned texts. Students choose their own topics within the framework of the assignment sequence.

Teaching towards Critical Empathy

The focus in "This I (Now) Believe" on articulating an individual *credo* in an established public genre set the expectation, for some an unfamiliar one, that students will address an audience beyond the teacher. Rather than reinforce egocentric tendencies, or tribalistic ones, this assignment ideally invites students to construct for themselves a participatory role in the public square. Here they can recognize diverse perspectives and reflect on the many factors that shape *coming to believe*. The hope is that this effort in "discovering warrantable beliefs" (Booth, 1974, p. xiii), in this initial case their *own*, will contribute to an ethic of mutual understanding. As the course proceeds, students see that a personal *credo* is but one type of public statement when they next encounter the genre of the open letter in a sequence of linked assignments: "My Take: An Open Letter to X" (unit 4); "To Think That, One..." (unit 5); and "Take Two: Academic Revision of the Open Letter" (unit 6). This approach to linked writing assignments of increasing depth and complexity differs from that outlined in Anson and Andrews' "Sleuthing for the Truth" in this volume.

The open letter presents a natural complement to the personal credo. Each of these two genres is demonstratively civic—a form of personal witness in the public square. A *credo* is arguably an instance of *epideictic* rhetoric, one of three classic speech situations identified by Aristotle along with *forensic* and *deliberative* (Kennedy, 2006). Epideictic discourse articulates, even celebrates, the shared values of a community. A "This I (Now) Believe" essay contributes to a society that welcomes pluralism and civic participation. By contrast, the open letter participates in public *debate*. It falls under a heading of *deliberative* rhetoric in bringing attention to a problem and calling for a resolution.

Among many famous examples of the genre is Emile Zola's (2011) 1898 letter, "J'accuse," (known by its provocative opening) to the president of France accusing the government of anti-semitism in the Dreyfus affair. The open letter directly calls *on*, and often calls *out*, an addressee (person, group, or abstraction) whether or not the addressee is in a position to respond. At the same time, it appeals indirectly to a broader audience positioned as readers of the letter on its way to the addressee. The most famous instance of the genre in American culture is Martin Luther King's "Letter from a Birmingham Jail" (1963), in which the briefly jailed King addresses a group of prominent white clergymen in Birmingham who questioned King's tactics of civil disobedience.

Why ask students to write this particular genre? For one, the open letter affords an opportunity to imagine and inhabit a civic space through discourse, with a suitably rich rhetorical situation. There is a problem, and also disagreement. With two audiences, one explicit and one implicit, students explore matters of stance and rhetorical appeals. And, of course, a letter is not a paper. Students must depart from writing in an objective stance in the third person in favor of an "I" speaking to a "you." Finally, an open letter advances an argument, typically a motivated (one-sided) statement of a case without the rigor and nuance we associate with academic argument. For Writing 101, it is thus a *first* take.

This initial stance-taking is followed by "To think that, one ...," as an effort in articulating alternative views. Here, the goal is to *think with*, not *against*, alternate views as an exercise in *critical empathy* (DeStigter, 1999). The task is not to argue *for* the other side, however, but rather to understand how others might *reasonably* hold different beliefs as a form of "rhetorical listening" (Ratcliffe, 2005). For Booth, this "listening rhetoric" entails "the whole range of communicative arts for reducing misunderstanding by paying full attention to the opposing view" (2009, p.11). *Real* attention to opposing views is rare. And it is difficult work, intellectually and emotionally. We might change our mind in finding common ground with those whom we oppose.

The effort to listen to opposing views has echoes in Peter Elbow's (2008) "believing game." Yet it need not go as far as Elbow advises:

> be as welcoming or accepting as possible to every idea we encounter: not just listening to views different from our own and holding back from arguing with them; not just trying to restate them without bias; but actually trying to believe them (2008).

In "To think that, one ..." students try to *understand* counter arguments by seeking—and by spelling out, as fairly as possible—the warrantable beliefs that might support them, in effect, to go underneath those arguments. For example, *to think that* gun rights are sacrosanct, *one* might believe that an individual's right to self defense always outweighs collective rights in the form of government regulation. To listen with empathy to this perspective is to consider how it *feels* to hold to that view, not just recognize it intellectually. Of course, when we find ourselves arguing against positions that seem, to us, grounded in racism, sexism, or any form of injustice we do not *want* to see things from the other side or, especially, to *feel* those arguments working inside us.

Hence *critical empathy*, a term I use hesitantly. It's fair to say that in rhetoric and composition the concept of empathy has enjoyed a good run of late (Fleckenstein, 2007; Leake, 2016; Blankenship, 2019). Empathy is generally deemed something we could use more of. There are limits to empathy. We do not suspend our capacities for judgment when confronted with claims and reasoning that defy credulity. We thus find wisdom in how Todd Destigter defines critical empathy:

> the process of establishing informed and affective connections with other human beings, of thinking and feeling with them at some emotionally, intellectually, and socially significant level, while always remembering that such connections are complicated by sociohistorical forces that hinder the equitable, just relationships that we presumably seek. (1999, p. 240)

Critical empathy goes beyond framing arguments along dialogic lines of "they say, I say" (Birkenstein & Graff, 2018). It extends to efforts to understand *why* "they" say it. It is a variation on Booth's "critical understanding," in contrasted with "overstanding" (1979, p. 236). Where *over*standing privileges the view of the interpreter, *under*standing searches for the bedrock of "warrantable beliefs" (Booth, 1974, p. xiii). For Booth (1979), this understanding is "the goal, process, and result whenever one mind succeeds in entering another mind or, what is the same thing, whenever one mind succeeds in incorporating any part of another mind" (p. 262). Again, this is dangerous, work. Why *under*stand when *over*standing will do?

Practice in listening rhetoric counters notions that we can win over others to our side simply by making clear and forceful arguments. *Thinking with* opposing views in "To think that, one ..." sets up the final writing assignment in "Take Two," in which students revise their open letter into an *academic* argument addressed to an audience of peers. This last unit recognizes the 'sidedness' of any perspective by acknowledging the existence, even the reasonableness, of other views. In this second effort, students can draw on insights generated from their exercise in critical empathy to consider which opposing arguments to address and to what extent their own arguments would benefit from articulating of warrants.

To be clear, this last unit is *not* a research paper, even as it requires students to being the process of research by locating opposing arguments and shoring up their own claims with relevant data. The course to follow, Writing 102 uses the same textbook (Lunsford et al., 2020) and extends the rhetoric of argument introduced here by teaching information literacy and other aspects of conducting and reporting on research. Writing 101 stays focused on rhetorical features of argument: staking a position, addressing an audience, taking bias and belief into account, and respecting the principle of a sincere effort to find common ground as a starting point for argumentation.

Conclusion: Democratic Life After Charlottesville

Way back in 2015, the goal of fostering critical empathy and civic responsibility seemed quaint, if consistent with a model of composition an as introduction to the rhetoric of argument (Fulkerson, 2005). A rising tide of "fake news" complicates assumptions about this goal, as it would seem to demand ever higher walls of *in*credulity to protect ourselves from those who have discovered the weaknesses in our defenses. Yet I am advocating in this post-truth era (Keyes, 2004) for a *more* vulnerable mode of "listening rhetoric" (Booth, 2009) in engaging the arguments of others. I am advocating that we attend to the affective dimensions of belief, including how we come to hold and to let go of beliefs.

The weaponizing of doubt as the rejection of any truth claim we find inconvenient or inconsistent with our worldview and the refusal to be open to the testimony and the experiences of others not in our camp in informing our beliefs—these trends do not augur well for our politics. We have to learn to become adept players of both the "doubting game" *and* the "believing game" (Elbow, 2008). Indeed, we have to confront the challenge in living not only in a post-truth era but in a post-Charlottesville America.

"Very fine people on both sides" is the summary judgment offered by President Trump on the protesters and counter-protesters at the "Unite the Right" rally in Charlottesville, Virginia in August of 2017, after the murder of counter-protester Heather Heyer (Jacobs, Zhang, and Jackson, 2019). For many, this characterization is outrageous on its face. And I agree. Notions of false equivalence are stock in trade for demagogic rhetoric. At the same time, the emphasis in this chapter on developing our capacities for a listening rhetoric and for critical empathy, even with those whose beliefs repel us, call for the possibility of constructive dialogue with *those* people on the *other* side, whether or not they are "very fine." As difficult as it may be, this is something we must prepare our students to be able to do if we, collectively, are to repair the ruptures and divisions in our civil society in the era of "fake news."

References

Baker, M. L., Dieter, E., & Dobbins, Z. (2014). The art of being persuaded: Wayne Booth's mutual inquiry and the trust to listen. *Composition Studies, 42*(1).

Bean, J. C. (2011). *Engaging ideas: The professor's guide to integrating writing, critical thinking, and active learning in the classroom.* John Wiley & Sons.

Biesecker, B. A. (2018). Guest editor's introduction: Toward an archaeogenealogy of post-truth. *Philosophy & Rhetoric, 51*(4), 329–341.

Birkenstein, C., & Graff, G. (2018). *They say/I say: The moves that matter in academic writing.* WW Norton & Company.

Blankenship, L. (2019). *Changing the subject: A theory of rhetorical empathy.* University Press of Colorado.

Booth, W. C. (1970). *Now don't try to reason with me: Essays and ironies for a credulous age.* University of Chicago Press.

Booth, W.C. (1974). *Modern dogma and the rhetoric of assent.* The University of Chicago Press.

Booth, W. C. (1979). *Critical understanding: The powers and limits of pluralism.* University of Chicago Press.

Booth, W. C. (1988). *The company we keep: An ethics of fiction.* University of California Press.

Booth, W. C. (2009). *The rhetoric of rhetoric: The quest for effective communication*. John Wiley & Sons.

Bradner, E. (2017). Conway: Trump White House offered 'alternative facts' on crowd size. *CNN Politics*, 23.

Bunn, M. (2013). Motivation and connection: teaching reading (and writing) in the composition classroom. *College Composition and Communication*, *64*(3), 496–516.

Carillo, E. C. (2015). *Securing a place for reading in composition: The importance of teaching for transfer*. University Press of Colorado.

Carillo, E. C. (2017). *A writer's guide to mindful reading*. WAC Clearinghouse.

Carillo, E. C. (2018). *Teaching readers in post-truth America*. University Press of Colorado.

Coates, T. N. (2014). The case for reparations. *The Atlantic*, *313*(5), 54–71.

Coates, T. N. (2015). *Between the world and me*. Spiegel and Grau.

Colbert, S. (2005). Truthiness. *The Colbert Report*.

Cooke, N. (2018). *Fake news and alternative facts: Information literacy in a post-truth era*. ALA Editions.

Crosswhite, J. (1996). *The rhetoric of reason: Writing and the attractions of argument*. University of Wisconsin Press.

Desmond, M. (2016). *Evicted: Poverty and profit in the American city*. Broadway Books.

DeStigter, T. (1999). Public displays of affection: Political community through critical empathy. *Research in the Teaching of English*, *33*(3), 235–244.

Duelfer, C. (2004). *Comprehensive report of the special advisor to the DCI on Iraq's WMD: Regime strategy and WMD timeline events* (Vol. 1). Central Intelligence Agency.

Duffy, J. (2019). *Provocations of virtue: Rhetoric, ethics, and the teaching of writing*. University Press of Colorado.

Eberly, R. A. (2000). *Citizen critics: Literary public spheres*. University of Illinois Press.

Elbow, P. (2008). The believing game or methodological believing. *The Journal of the Assembly for Expanded Perspectives on Learning*, *14*(1), 3.

Fahnestock, J., & Secor, M. (1982). *A rhetoric of argument*. Random House.

Fleckenstein, K. S. (2007). Once again with feeling: Empathy in deliberative discourse. *JAC*, *27*, 701–716.

Fulkerson, R. (2005). Composition at the turn of the twenty-first century. *College Composition and Communication*, *56*(4), 654.

Horning, A. S. (2007). Reading across the curriculum as the key to student success. *Across the Disciplines*, *4*, 1–18.

Horning, A. S. (2011). Where to put the manicules: A theory of expert reading. *Across the Disciplines*, *8*(2), 8–33.

Jacobs, C. S., Zhang, X., & Jackson, S. A. (2019). *Transcript of journalists questioning of President Donald Trump about his response to white supremacist protest in Charlottesville*.

Jefferson, T. (1776). "The declaration of independence as adopted by Congress". *The Papers of Thomas Jefferson*, 429–432.

Jolliffe, D. A., & Harl, A. (2008). Studying the "reading transition" from high school to college: What are our students reading and why? *College English, 70*(6), 599–617.

Keller, D. (2013). *Chasing literacy: Reading and writing in an age of acceleration.* University Press of Colorado.

Kennedy, G. A. (2006). *On rhetoric: A theory of civic discourse.* Oxford University Press.

Keyes, R. (2004). *The post-truth era: Dishonesty and deception in contemporary life.* Macmillan.

King Jr., M. L. (1992). Letter from Birmingham jail. *UC Davis L. Rev., 26,* 835.

Leake, E. (2016). Writing pedagogies of empathy: As rhetoric and disposition. *Composition Forum, 34.* Association of Teachers of Advanced Composition.

Lunsford, A. A., Brody, M., Ede, L. S., Moss, B. J., Papper, C. C., & Walters, K. (2020). *Everyone's an author*, 3e. WW Norton.

Perelman, C., & Olbrechts-Tyteca, L. (1969). *The new rhetoric: A treatise on argumentation* (trans. John Wilkinson and Purcell Weaver). University of Notre Dame Press.

Quammen, D. (2014). *Ebola: The natural and human history of a deadly virus.* WW Norton & Company.

Ratcliffe, K. (2005). *Rhetorical listening: Identification, gender, whiteness.* Southern Illinois University Press.

Roberts-Miller, P. (2007). *Deliberate conflict: Argument, political theory, and composition classes.* Southern Illinois University Press.

Salvatori, M. (1996). Conversations with texts: Reading in the teaching of composition. *College English, 58*(4), 440–454.

Shetterly, M. L. (2016). *Hidden figures: The untold true story of four African-American women who helped launch our nation into space.* Harper.

Strawser, M. G., & Hume, J. (2019). A "common" campaign: Reinventing the book in common program on a liberal arts campus. *Journal of College Reading and Learning, 49*(3), 252–259.

This I Believe (2019). thisibelieve.org.

Toulmin, S. E. (2003). *The uses of argument.* Cambridge University Press.

Whitehead, C. (2016). *The underground railroad.* Doubleday.

Zola, É. (2011). *J'accuse.* Les Editions de Londres.

5. What Is "Fake News"? Walls, Fences, and Immigration: How Community-Based Learning Can Prompt Students to Employ Critical Reading and Research Practices

LARA SMITH-SITTON AND COURTNEY BRADFORD
Kennesaw State University

> "Before, I recognized that there were a lot of issues surrounding immigration in this country, in this world, but when you come into a class like this and you put yourself into that community and you see the faces, you can't help but be like, 'I don't care what is going in on in my life, I want to learn more about this right now.'"
> —Marie, Student Editor, *Green Card Youth Voices: Stories from an Atlanta High School*

> "Before this I always knew that a lot of decisions are made by government officials, but after this project, I realized that citizens play a role too. If we are informed, it is better for the community. I will now follow the narratives I hear in the media more closely and differently than before."
> —Melissa, Student Editor, *Immigration Integration Toolkit*

An October 2018 report entitled *How Students Engage with News: Five Takeaways for Educators, Journalists, and Librarians* reveals interesting details about college students' news consumption: while 82% surveyed advised they feel news is essential to democracy, 68% reported they were overwhelmed by the amount of news available each day, and 45% reported it difficult to discern "fake news" from "real news" (Head et al., p. 14). In addition, students reported they obtain their news from multiple sources, including social media sites and established national media outlets as well as through conversations with professors and peers (Head et al., p. 4). Although this may not be surprising to faculty teaching in English and writing programs, what is noteworthy is that our students are turning to dialogue with others for help discerning fact from fiction. This, however, can also be problematic given the overload of information available—facts are sometimes misrepresented or omitted, creating more confusion for today's students. Much like the contribution of Lilian W. Mina, Dakota Mills, and Shifat Niha to this collection, "Critical Digital Reading between the Role of the Professor and Students' Responses," this chapter explores how course design deliberately focused on developing critical reading and analysis skills can help students become more informed citizens outside of the classroom.

In fall 2018, *Journal of American Folklore* published a special issue entitled *Fake News: Definitions and Approaches* to examine not only the etymology of the term "fake news" but also its historical and contemporary usage. Recognizing that the term is more significant than simply the inclusion of inaccurate facts or false representations by media sources, Tom Mould (2018) specifically notes the harm that "fake news" can cause to vulnerable groups when used by those with political power: "Fake news that appears to originate with political actors rather than in response to them is more explicit about the fears and anxieties it evokes, and it is more consistently negative in doing so, targeting marginal or marginalized populations rather than elite or institutional ones" (p. 374). Helping students understand the impact of "fake news" on individuals, families, and communities seems a way to argue for the importance of engaging with research and evaluating the sources we rely upon for information. But how can faculty and students engage in these conversations without the politics of certain subjects distracting from the goals of developing stronger research and rhetorical analysis skills?

This question became an important consideration when seeking to implement service learning/community writing projects related to immigration in two upper-level writing courses—one in spring 2017 and another in spring 2018. The hope was that by including authentic projects where students could engage with the topic of immigration without political frameworks, they could direct the inquiry and knowledge acquisition. As Ashley J. Holmes (2015) explains, "Those of us who incorporate service and community-based learning into our courses often hope to expose students to diverse populations, prompt them to confront 'real world' problems in their community, and offer a reflective classroom space for students to work through the dissonance that may accompany these experiences" (p. 48).

The first project was small. Working with a local organization, students contributed research and editing for a resource guide, the *Immigrant Integration Toolkit: Strategies for Investing in Our Community* (Rodriguez & McDaniel, 2018), which was created for immigrants and their families resettling in

Georgia. The second project, *Green Card Youth Voices: Immigration Stories from an Atlanta High School* (Rozman Clark et al., 2018) was a significantly larger initiative. In this project, students worked with a national nonprofit to publish an edited collection of essays written by young immigrants living in Atlanta. These experiences called upon students to explore the topic of American immigration during a time when public and political discussions surrounding the topic could be misleading, inaccurate, and difficult. As John Dewey's (1938/1997) work in *Experience and Education* suggests: "every experience lives on in future experiences ... [and an] education based upon experience ... select[s] the kind of present experiences that live fruitfully and creatively in subsequent experiences" (p. 23).

The major goals of these projects were multi-faceted. The first goal allowed students to apply skills to authentic projects with objectives aligned with course learning outcomes: the assignments became tools for teaching and learning. Through the second goal, given that both projects included information about the issues and challenges faced by immigrants, students were presented with opportunities to understand more about the lives of immigrants who are their neighbors and fellow community members. Finally, because these projects were implemented from an apolitical stance, the third goal encouraged students to pursue more knowledge about US immigration policy and practices beyond what might be represented in short news articles or media clips. This goal sought to motivate students to research, read, listen, and learn independently of class requirements.

Upon completion of the project, two IRB-approved studies investigated what students found valuable and impactful about working on the immigration-related projects and how their ideas about immigration were shaped or changed as a result of the project. In addition, the concept of "fake news" and the students' new understanding of the immigration debates were important facets of the data collection. What these studies revealed was that by working on community-based projects surrounding this highly visible topic in culture, news, and social media outlets, students found themselves independently identifying misleading information represented in the public narratives. The students took control of their research, often choosing to consider more deeply the topics related to their assignments and course activities. The value of giving students the freedom to prioritize their individual research interests and sources also prompted them to discern what was "accurate" and what "misleading" within the media. Stephanie West-Puckett, Genoa Shepley, and Jessica Gray's research in this collection, "Hacking Fake News: Tools and Technologies for Ethical Praxis" also saw the value in letting students develop their own definition of "fake news." They found that creating opportunities for students "to develop more sophisticated tools to discriminate between reliable information and fabrication" occurred through understanding the differences between fake and reliable news. In the IRB-approved studies following the Toolkit and *GCV-Atlanta* projects, students confirmed that these projects were not only beneficial academically and professionally but also allowed them to gain new perspectives about the complexities of this topic and the lives of immigrants to the US. In addition, the projects prompted an interest in learning more about the term "fake news" and how this concept affects student learning and engagement in English studies and writing courses.

Exploring the Etymology and Impact of the Term "Fake News"

According to an article entitled "The Real Story of 'Fake News,'" published in the "Words We're Watching" section of *Merriam-Webster*, the term "fake news" finds its roots in the 19th century, beginning approximately 125 years ago. The article cites early uses of the term by example of an 1890 *Cincinnati Commercial Tribune* headline, "Secretary Brunell Declares Fake News About His People is Being Telegraphed Over the Country." Another example was found in an 1891 *Buffalo Commercial* article that describes fake news as "distortions of facts and enlargements of incidents" ("The Real Story," n.d.). These early uses of "fake news" provide important etymological considerations that contradict assertions that it is a new term. What is different in current usage is that it is largely used to undermine established media outlets and reshape public narratives through arguments that the facts disseminated to the American public are false.

Though first connected to the practice of "yellow journalism" where the press was "driven to sensationalize stories and fabricate facts, in a quest for eyeballs and dollars" (Samuel, 2016), this historical foundation of the term is often unknown individuals in the 21st century. Many, including our students, first heard the term "fake news" during the 2016 US presidential election when then Republican candidate Donald J. Trump frequently employed the term when endeavoring to debunk media coverage that he disliked or disagreed with, regardless of whether the news was actually truthful or accurate (Mould, 2018, p. 373). Since the election, President Trump continues to tout that he created the term, and while this claim is false, what is not in dispute is that the term is now more commonplace in American public discourse: in the year following the election, when *Merriam Webster* selected "fake news" as the "Word of the Year," its use had increased 365% according to *Google Trends* (Graves, 2018).

The impact of the pervasive use of this term changed its meaning from a literal understanding of misleading or incorrect news to a term that now has powerful, persuasive, and false intentions. As Lucia Graves (2018) explains, "Trump weaponized the term, turning its meaning on its head. Instead of using it to describe a specific corrupt phenomenon ... he used it to discredit the non-fake news sources that might keep his power in check." For some, the term "fake news" might have prompted eye-rolling or frustration during the presidential election and early days of a new presidency; the effect on our students and in our classrooms, however, has been significant. The 2018 Project Information Literacy Report noted the term's influence specifically on students: "More than anything, students mentioned the 'fake news' phenomenon in their comments and interviews, particularly its far-reaching impact on people's ability to distinguish truthful and accurate news coverage from misinformation and outright lies" (Head et al., 2018, p. 15). This term did not simply confuse a public trying to keep up with a 24-hour news cycle: it ultimately resulted in discouraging individual efforts to follow the news.

Evidence of declining engagement with the news is also affirmed in a 2019 Reuters Institute study where 41% of Americans report they "often or sometimes actively" avoid the news. The study contends key reasons include consistently negative coverage, powerlessness to affect change, and the likelihood of false information (Newman et al., 2019, p. 25). Another 2019 study by Pew Research Center revealed that over 60% of the adults surveyed believe "the news media intentionally ignores stories that are important to the public" (Rainie et al., 2019). Knowing that students in our classrooms are distrustful and possibly disengaged from news stories creates challenges for implementing projects. Motivating students to become interested in the context of contemporary topics and the need to evaluate credible and non-credible sources for academic and other research inquiries create hurdles that are difficult to overcome.

Building the Framework for Impactful Community-Based Projects in Writing Courses

The community-based projects that are the subject of this chapter were developed and completed while national media coverage focused on a range of fiercely debated initiatives impacting US immigration practices and policies. While at first it seemed to complicate the projects, the conflicting discourse actually presented rich opportunities for students to discern fact from fiction about the topic of immigration—testing their critical and close reading skills as well as their research abilities in a cacophony of narratives. For example, on

January 27, 2017, the first of three Muslim bans were initiated by Presidential Executive Order—this development occurred during the third week of the course and one week before the *Immigration Integration Toolkit* project was introduced to the class. While the Supreme Court did not confirm the lawfulness of the first two bans, the attempts to place significant restrictions on immigrants and refugees from seven Muslim-majority countries ("One Year After," 2019) and the heated rhetoric, accusations of discrimination, and assertions of "fake news" were covered extensively by media outlets throughout the project.

In contrast, a year later during the 2018 spring semester, just as work got underway on *Green Card Youth Voices: Immigration Stories from an Atlanta High School*, critical conversations were underway about "Dreamers" and the continuation of Deferred Action for Childhood Arrivals (DACA). As the developmental editing stage of was ongoing, DACA and immigration reform were not taken up by the US Congress, placing millions of immigrants in uncertain situations. Ironically, on April 6, 2018, the day the editing was completed on the book, Attorney General Jeff Sessions issued a memorandum of "Zero-Tolerance for Offenses Under USC § 1325(a)," which addressed undocumented entry into the US (Smith-Sitton et al., 2019). The implementation and completion of these projects occurred during a particularly turbulent and difficult chapter in America's immigration history.

The first project was a resource guide entitled the *Immigrant Integration Toolkit: Strategies for Investing in Our Communities* (Toolkit) that came about through a partnership between the Georgia Immigration Research Network (GIRN) and the English Department beginning in fall 2016. The aim was to create online and print materials that share "best practices strategies for working with and on behalf of newcomer or immigrant communities" (Georgia Immigration Integration Network, 2015). Covering a wide range of topics relevant to immigrants, refugees and their families, including civic engagement, public safety, health services, workforce and economic development, language access, education, and housing, the Toolkit also has a Community Resource Guide section providing additional support. GIRN, as an organization, seeks to provide "human, social, and/or service needs" to immigrants and refugees in Georgia and the US South as well as offer spaces for discussion about prioritizing issues that impact immigrants and refugees in Georgia (Georgia Immigrant Integration Network, 2015). The project was implemented in an upper-level professional writing course where one unit was dedicated to authentic, community-based projects that provided opportunities for students to work in teams as editors, researchers, and writers.

Each team working on this project had three team members. One of the teams served as copyeditors and proofreaders for the full draft of the Toolkit project. The second group of three students conducted research for the Community Resource Guide section to identify approximately 100 state and national organizations working with the Georgia immigrant community and to write summaries of their work and mission statements. At the start of the project, students met with the authors of the Toolkit, Dr. Darlene Xiomara Rodriguez and Dr. Paul D. McDaniel, and received an overview of the project. They were welcome to ask questions, but little information was provided about the topic of immigration directly to the students—their focus was working on the community—writing, editing, and research facets of the project. This approach also would allow the post-project IRB-approved research project to collect data about the students' perception of the value and impact of their work in order to draw some conclusions about student learning through community engagement activities. The research project also specifically sought to ascertain student perceptions about the topic of immigration prior to the project and determine if community-based work prompts students to become more civically concerned and/or engaged with issues of public policy and concern.

There were two assignments tied to the Toolkit project: a collaborative project proposal and an individual reflective memo. The project proposal required group members to provide a summary of the project collaboratively, including sections such as team member responsibilities, a statement of need, scope of the project, an action plan, and a description of the deliverables. Upon completion of the project, students then individually submitted a formal memo that articulated their contributions, what they learned, the skills employed, and a reflection about the value of project. The assignments and the project itself provided opportunities for research, writing, rhetorical analysis, and reflection. In addition, students also gained practical experience working on a project that could be referenced on their resumes and in writing portfolios. While working on the project, students had to consider public discourse about immigration in order to understand better the context and need for the project.

The second project provided editorial, research, and writing support for *Green Card Youth Voices: Immigration Stories from an Atlanta High School* (*GCV-Atlanta*) in spring 2018. Dr. Tea Rozman Clark, co-founder and executive director of Green Card Voices, a nonprofit based out of Minneapolis, Minnesota, connected with faculty members at Kennesaw State University to build a partnership for the book. The organization was in need of students and faculty who could help facilitate not only the collection of the narratives but also the transcription of recorded interviews of approximately 30 young immigrants (including seven Dreamers), development of essays for publication, research for a glossary of terms, and copyediting of the final manuscript. The organization's mission focuses on "utiliz[ing] digital storytelling to share personal narratives of America's immigrants, fostering tolerance and establishing a better understanding between the immigrant and non-immigrant populations" (Green Card Voices, n.d.).

The students in the course divided into small editorial teams to begin working on the many stages of *GCV-Atlanta*. In contrast to the Toolkit project, a few articles about immigration that included facts about Georgia immigrants and refugees, DACA, and US immigration policy were provided as course readings. In addition, students read narratives from another collection published by the organization, *Green Card Youth Voices: Stories from a Fargo High School* (2017), prior to beginning the project. Dr. Rozman Clark also visited the class and shared information about the genesis and purpose of the essay collections. Though more information was shared about immigration with the class prior to initiating the project because of the need for context and understanding before beginning the transcription and editorial process, the material was carefully selected, and efforts were made to keep the discussions factual, not political. Students were invited to share their interpretations and ask questions, rather than receiving a formal lecture about US immigration.

Reading these materials as a class allowed the students to contextualize the topic of immigration with a common foundation for understanding it. Chris Anson and Kendra Andrews, in their chapter in this collection, "Sleuthing for the Truth: A Reading and Writing Pedagogy for a New Age of Lies," also focused on preparing students before the start of an assignment "to develop a shared vocabulary and framework." While our students started working with the immigrant authors and learned about the topic first through primary research and engagement with community members, their students began an analysis of the media they consume. Each approach ultimately led the students to research more and analyze the sources they typically use to gather information. By creating a foundation from which students could begin to learn more about a topic, both groups of students were able to analyze the information they hear from different outlets. At the end of the *GCV-Atlanta* project, as with the Toolkit, the IRB-approved protocol for this class project would collect data from the students about what they knew about immigration before and after the project as well as the value and impact of working on the project. We hoped to determine whether students felt their experiences with the project, from researching the topic and hearing the immigrant stories firsthand, motivated them to become more civically aware and engaged with the topic of immigration

While working on the essays and publication were the main foci of the community writing and editing project, students had two major assignments for the course that accompanied this work. The first assignment was the final edited and proofread essay that each student worked on from transcription to publication. The grading evaluated the writing, editing, style guide adherence, and general development of the essay. While working on the essays and book manuscript, students also learned to keep an editorial journal, which served as the second assignment. The journal challenged students to keep up with critical details and terms in their journals as well as craft guided reflections through each stage of the project. The journals addressed topics such as ethics of editing, the importance of maintaining authentic voice, and reflections about the value and impact of the project. This assignment created a foundation for how the students could present *GCV-Atlanta* on their resumes; discuss the research, writing, and editing skills developed through the project; and capture information they felt was important about immigration or the project generally. Much like the post-Toolkit research, after the class was completed, students were invited to participate in individual interviews about the impact and value of the project of their academic, professional and civic lives.

Exploring and Understanding the Value and Impact of Community Writing Projects

In crafting the interview questions for the studies, we relied upon considerations of how experience led to the creation of new knowledge and what students learned about immigration through the projects. In *Democracy and Education,* Dewey (1916/2011) recognizes an important facet of what students must to do generate knowledge: "observe for themselves and form their own theories and personally test them. Such a method was the only alternative to the imposition of dogma as truth, a procedure which reduced mind to the formal act of acquiescing in truth" (p. 161). Considering this, the post-project data was collected through small group and individual interviews in the months following the course. The Toolkit data was collected within approximately three months, but the *GCV-Atlanta* interviews were pushed out nearly a year. In addition, the Toolkit had a shorter set of interview questions, whereas the more involved, longer *GCV-Atlanta* project benefitted from what was learned during the first value and impact study and expanded to capture more information from the participating students.

Research questions for both projects included questions that asked students to describe their knowledge about US immigration topics prior to the project and after the project. The interviews also sought to gather information about how students saw the project impacting their lives in three areas: academic learning, professional development and preparation, and civic engagement.

Five of the six students who worked on the Toolkit project agreed to participate in the research; the interviews were conducted face-to-face by Smith-Sitton in the English Department at KSU. Interestingly, all five individuals reported limited or no substantive knowledge about the topic of immigration prior to beginning the project. What was notable about these responses was that two of the five students studied abroad—one in South Korea and one in Spain—yet neither had much interaction with US immigrants and had not given much thought to the issues of immigration policy and the narratives that dominated the news cycles. All five of the students shared that it was difficult to know what was true about immigration before the project, and they found themselves not very engaged with the topic—in fact, all five stated that they did not read or follow the public immigration issues in the news prior to the project.

Upon completion of the project, all five students recognized that while they now understood the subject better, there was still much to learn. Universally, the students reported that working on an authentic project was beneficial to their academic and professional lives as they were more engaged because they knew that it mattered beyond the class, and they all also included the project on their resumes. When asked about how they saw the project impacting their civic interests and/or if they would remain curious and interested in the topic of immigration, two stated they believed they would follow much more closely while three thought they would pay attention more. When collecting the data for the Toolkit project, one of the students, Mac, discussed discomfort with news sources and how the project provided an opportunity to understand things a little better and the way to participate in community work:

> I like to know what is going on and what they are saying [in the media], but it really just makes me uncomfortable .... I don't want to say that something is untrue, but I am skeptical of certain news sources because they may be more political than accurate. Also, this project helped me see that it not just about going to a refugee camp and handing out food or providing medical assistance. I had not really thought about what immigrants experience here. I saw the needs of immigrants and refugees and how others can support and contribute.

Another student, Alice, found herself wanting to learn more about the public policy decisions as a result of the project:

> This project brought [the Muslim ban situation] more to the front my mind than it had been ... and gave me a very different understanding of the situation, especially with the Muslim population. It is important to try to understand. If you are not understanding, you are not solving the problem. I want to know more and understand more so that I can offer more.

Another student, Melissa, described what she found valuable and how the project expanded her knowledge of the sources that can provide information relevant to immigration:

> I learned that there are a lot more resources than I expected [about immigration] and ways to find information ... I did not know about the different organizations and community outreach programs and how they can provide real awareness about immigration beyond what is in the library and the news. I am curious to see how [the organizations] will play a part in the future of the immigration situation and policies in our country.

Through the Toolkit research, we learned that students did not know much about immigration, but the projects helped them become more curious and thoughtful about immigrants and refugees who come here. These students did not seem highly motivated to become more involved in the immigrant and refugee communities, but they felt they gained unique understandings of the situation and a realization of how little they did know ... and how often they avoided the news because they found it misleading and confusing. Two said that they would like to have more discussion in class about the topic of immigration before they started the project because they thought it would have helped them have a better idea of reliable, accurate news outlets, but they all said that reading parts of the Toolkit though the editing and project proposal phases was eye-opening.

When we moved to the *GCV-Atlanta* post-project interviews, we found that the students had much stronger opinions about the human nature of the immigration and the hardships faced by the individuals who resettle in the US. Because this project was focused on the stories of the immigrants and the students not only worked with the essays but also heard the voices of the authors, they seemed more connected to the project itself and passionate about the topic as a result of working with Green Card Voices. The post-project research included eleven individual interviews, each lasting 45–60 minutes. The interviews were recorded and transcribed. The students were asked eighteen questions, providing time for participants to share their perceptions of US immigration before and after the project; the value and impact of the project, specifically the benefits they perceived; and any changes in their understanding about the topic of immigration because of the project.

All of the participants identified the North Georgia community, primarily metro Atlanta as their home and place of residence. While two were from the Midwest—Milwaukee and Chicago—none of the individuals interviewed identified as immigrants nor felt they had more than limited or distant knowledge about immigration. Most made references to being disconnected from the Georgia immigrant community, mostly by description of not knowing immigrants or refugees or just not thinking about the situations of those resettling in the US. In fact, one student admitted that while Georgia is home to approximately one million foreign-born individuals—an estimate that one-in-ten persons is an immigrant—he did not know that the state had a large immigrant community (McDaniel et al., 2017, p. 5). Consistent with the findings in the first study, the participants unanimously concurred that the incorporation of the community engagement project was very rewarding and useful as an academic endeavor, but these participants also shared that they felt *GCV-Atlanta* also had significant professional benefits as well, especially with respect to helping them get jobs in editing and writing. One student attributed the project to his law school acceptance, and another stated the impact of the project on her decision to teach in Central America upon graduation.

The crafting of questions to understand better the ways the project was valuable to the students civically surprisingly revealed every participant found the project taught them about immigration not as a political concern but rather a human concern. One student, Sam, described the impact in this way:

> I think one of the big things for me was the face of immigration, the people that you're actually dealing with that these news stories talk about.... There are real people behind whatever narrative of immigration is pushed on us—that was eye-opening to me.... just being able to keep in mind the human face of immigration and at the end of the day remembering that we're all people. I think that is super important regardless of whatever your civic or political ideologies are.

Like Sam, other students, such as Tamara, were deeply moved by the power of hearing and reading the stories of immigrants, not just what the news reports:

> You can't read the stories of what the people are actually experiencing and not connect on a human level. I feel like you can't read those stories and have no compassion because they are human stories. The kids shared how they wanted to be doctors ... find ways they could help other people, give back.... It makes me mad, frustrated, when you hear things in the news like people come here for purely selfish reasons ... the majority of the people who say those things, you can tell without a doubt that they have very little experience with real relationships with people who are immigrants or refugees.

The study confirmed that these projects changed the perceptions of the students involved and prompted them to learn more about the topic and see the inaccurate and false representations that are present in some of the public narratives. Eleanor explains,

> I wasn't paying a lot of attention. [The project] was more than me just learning any sort of fact of number ... it brought a new level of awareness, maybe a new level of change that could occur just from writing a telling a story. I did not really understand the struggles the immigrants go through ... I feel being able to not only relate but just understand better is important.

This sentiment was echoed repeatedly in the interviews: students were not very political, not interested in the news, and realized they did not understand the complexities of immigration before this project. There seemed to be a general avoidance and distrust of established news sources, but the project made them see how important it is to learn more about what is represented or misrepresented by political leaders and television pundits. Students also shared that by working on these projects with limited political discussions in class, they gained new confidence in their abilities to identify accuracies and inaccuracies in public dialogues and the news. Projects where students are connected directly to communities can allow students to explore contemporary, controversial topics in apolitical ways that provide opportunities to analyze the narratives disseminated through media outlets and become confident critical readers.

Changing the Narratives and Prompting Social Activism through Community Engagement

It is unknown at this point if these students will find themselves becoming social activists opening and assertively pushing back against claims of "fake news" because they are better able to discern facts and falsehoods in the narratives that permeate news sources. What the projects and research confirmed was that this group of seventeen students want to interact with and understand the lives of others in order to uncover the human condition, and the community-based projects prompted students to engage, research, read, listen, and discern new knowledge in their classes. They discovered the complexities of immigration not through a lecture or course text but through collaborative engagement, a practice that Nicholas V. Longo and Cynthia M. Gibson (2016) see as effective for 21st-century students because there is a need to build stronger trust in our institutions to "expand the circle where learning takes place ... implementing an array of curricula and initiatives focused on 'learning' rather than just 'teaching'" (p. 64).

In reflecting on the goals and accomplishments of the projects, the use of community-engaged pedagogies in these courses resulted in engagement, learning, and hard work. Students articulated that they became more critical consumers of news and developed critical reading, thinking, and analysis skills through their experiences. In addition, the students universally expressed the deep value they place on the knowledge acquired through coming face-to-face with not only unfamiliar communities of neighbors but also the topic of immigration. The students made connections between their career interests in writing, editing, nonprofit administration, law, and education (both domestically and abroad) and immigration issues. They also said that their newfound confidence to push through false narratives to find credible sources will be valuable to the communities in which they live and work.

Acknowledgments

The data referenced in this journal was collected under two Internal Review Board Research Projects: "Incorporating Community Writing in Editing Courses: Student Value and Impact," Study #20-127 and "Fostering Multidisciplinary Student and Faculty Collaboration: Community Engagement and Immigration Integration Projects," Study #17-527. While the projects and research described herein were a part of Lara Smith-Sitton's writing courses, Darlene Xiomara Rodriguez, PhD, MSW, MPA and Paul D. McDaniel, PhD serve as essential research partners and colleagues on these immigration-related projects. We also want to express our appreciation for the opportunities provided by Green Card Voices and the Georgia Immigration Research Network, organizations that welcomed Kennesaw State University students to engage with their community-based writing and research projects.

References

Dewey, John. (1916/2011). *Democracy and education*. Simon & Brown.
Dewey, John. (1938//1997). *Experience & education*. Touchstone.
Georgia Immigration Research Network. (2015). Georgia Immigration Research Network. https://girn.kennesaw.edu/.
Graves, L. (2018, February 26). How Trump weaponized "fake new" for his own political ends. *Pacific Standard*. https://psmag.com/social-justice/how-trump-weaponized-fake-news-for-his-own-political-ends.
Green Card Voices. (n.d.). About us: Mission statement. Green Card Voices. https://www.greencardvoices.com/home/about-us/.

Head, A. J., Wihbey, J., Metaxas, P. T., MacMillan, M., & Cohen, D. (2018, October 16). How students engage with news: Five takeaways for educators, journalists, and librarians. *Project Information Literacy Research Institute.* http://www.projectinfolit.org/uploads/2/7/5/4/27541717/newsreport.pdf.

Holmes, Ashley J. (2015). Transformative learning, affect, and reciprocal care in community engagement. *Community Literacy Journal, 9*(2), 48–67. https://doi.org/10.1353/clj.2015.0001

Longo, N., & Gibson, C. M. (2016). Collaborative engagement: The future of teaching and learning in higher education. In M. A. Post, E. Ward, Nicholas V. Longo, & J. Saltmarsh (Eds.), *Publicly engaged scholars* (pp. 61–75). Stylus.

McDaniel, P. N., Rodriguez, D. X., & Kim, A. J. (2017). Receptivity and the welcoming cities movement: Advancing a regional immigrant integration policy framework in metropolitan Atlanta, Georgia. *Papers in Applied Geography, 3–4,* 355–79.

Mould, T. (2018). Introduction to the special issue on fake news: Definitions and approaches. *Journal of American Folklore, 131*(522), 371–378.

Newman, N., Fletcher, R., Kalogeropoulos, A., & Nielsen, R. K. (2019). Reuters Institute digital new report 2019. Reuters Institute. https://reutersinstitute.politics.ox.ac.uk/sites/default/files/2019-06/DNR_2019_FINAL_0.pdf.

One year after the SCOTUS ruling: Understanding the Muslim ban and how we'll keep fighting it. (2019). *National Immigration Law Center.* https://www.nilc.org/issues/immigration-enforcement/understanding-muslim-ban-one-year-after-ruling/.

Rainie, L., Keeter, S., & Perrin, A. (2019, July 22). Trust and distrust in America. *Pew Research Center.* https://www.people-press.org/2019/07/22/trust-and-distrust-in-america/?fbclid=IwAR2tC_ehX7RKhhI22llsLL0-1QiCCwOIBt1glzPAhNQDRGhuGoAhkx945Dk.

Rodriguez, D. X., & McDaniel, P. N. (2018). Immigrant integration toolkit. Georgia Immigration Research Network. https://girn.kennesaw.edu/projects/immigrantintegrationtoolkit.php.

Rozman Clark, T., & Mueller, R. L. (Eds.). (2017). *Green card youth voices: Immigration stories from a Fargo high school.* Wise/Green Card Voices.

Rozman Clark, T., Rodriguez, D. X., & Smith-Sitton, L. (Eds.). (2018). *Green card youth voices: Immigration stories from an Atlanta high school.* Wise/Green Card Voices.

Samuel, A. (2016, November 29). To fix fake news, look to yellow journalism. *JSTOR Daily.* https://daily.jstor.org/to-fix-fake-news-look-to-yellow-journalism/.

Smith-Sitton, L., Rodriguez, D. X., & McDaniel, P. N. (2019). When local community writing initiative crashed into white house public policy—*Green Card Youth Voices: Immigration Stories from an Atlanta High School. Spark: A 4C4Equity Journal,* 1. https://sparkactivism.com/volume-1-intro/when-local-community-writing-initiatives-crashed-into-white-house-public-policy-green-card-youth-voices-immigration-stories-from-an-atlanta-high-school/.

The real story of "fake news." (n.d). In *Merriam-Webster's online dictionary.* https://www.merriam-webster.com/words-at-play/the-real-story-of-fake-news.

Part II. Composition Classroom Practices in the Era of Fake News

6. Factual Dispute: Teaching Rhetoric and Complicating Fact-Checking with *The Lifespan of a Fact*

Danielle Koupf

In 2012, John D'Agata and Jim Fingal published *The Lifespan of a Fact*, a book that presents two texts side by side: an essay and the fact-checking required to publish it. The essay is John D'Agata's piece on 16-year-old Levi Presley's suicide in Las Vegas, denied publication by *Harper's* due to factual inaccuracies and resubmitted to *The Believer* for fact-checking by intern Jim Fingal. Surrounding the draft of D'Agata's essay are Fingal's fact-checks, which appear in black ink when substantiated and in red ink when not. As Fingal identifies more and more factual inaccuracies in D'Agata's piece, a rich dialogue develops, in which D'Agata champions his creative freedom as an essayist and Fingal defends the sanctity of truth as a fact-checker. Allegedly spanning seven years, this dialogue mimics, yet exaggerates, the real-life debate between D'Agata and Fingal, who develop as characters throughout the book in increasing opposition to each other.

The Lifespan of a Fact is a hybrid text in several ways. It is a dialogue between D'Agata and Fingal, and it consists of both an essay draft and the fact-checks of it. Having taught the work in both an introductory literature course and a first-year writing seminar, I also identify a source of multiplicity in its status as both literature and rhetorical criticism. With these labels, I don't mean to establish a false dichotomy between the terms *literature* and *rhetorical criticism* but rather, to celebrate their confluence in this text. For, I argue that, owing to this confluence, the text promotes a productive ambiguity regarding truth, fiction, and reading.

It seems taken for granted that the work is literary both on the back of the book itself (where it is labeled "Literature/Essays") and in Christopher P. Wilson's 2015 article on the book in *Twentieth-Century Literature*. While it is difficult to define *literature*, according to student commentary the book evinces standard elements of fiction, such as characters, setting, plot, conflict, and ambiguity. The dialogue features "Jim" and "John" as antagonists of each other, and the essay draft features D'Agata as writer, Levi as subject, and a host of other characters painting the Las Vegas backdrop. Both the dialogue and the essay draft convey plot, conflict, and only partial resolution. As the essay draft explores ambiguities about Las Vegas and Levi's suicide, the book as a whole complicates seemingly sturdy notions concerning reading, genre, truth, and fiction.

What seems overlooked by critics is the book's concurrent status as a work of *rhetorical criticism* teaching readers about key concepts and disputes in rhetoric concerning audience, context, appeals, and genre. Central to the dialogue are disputes about the genre of D'Agata's draft, the context in which it will appear upon publication, D'Agata's use of rhetorical appeals, D'Agata's assumed audience, and his responsibilities to that audience. Recognizing the work as rhetorical criticism establishes its relevance to the first-year writing classroom as a source for rhetorical education. Yet it is the book's dual identity as *both* literary *and* rhetorical that enables a productive skepticism. While literary education typically exploits ambiguity as an essential learning outcome of reading literature (Chick, Hassel, & Haynie, 2009), I argue that this outcome is desirable too in a rhetorical context. Complicating reading, truth and fiction, fact-checking and fact-bending is important in alleviating binary thinking and recognizing the rhetorical construction of all writing, even facts.

Texts such as *In Cold Blood* by Truman Capote, *The Things They Carried* by Tim O'Brien, *Lying* by Lauren Slater, and *Reality Hunger* by David Shields, along with numerous documentaries and instances of reality television, similarly trouble the distinction between truth and fiction and expose the rhetorical construction of facts and the importance of rhetorical education. However, I suggest that *The Lifespan of a Fact* deserves sustained attention because of its multiple, salient sources of hybridity and its explicit conversation about truth and fiction in various writing genres. Therefore, it holds special promise as a pedagogical text.

In what follows, I first broadly consider how to read *The Lifespan of a Fact* and contend that its stark hybridity offers a prime opportunity for teaching reflective reading. Then, I focus on the content of the book and identify how it supports a rhetorical education and its authors' dispute fundamentally concerns rhetoric. The teaching of reflective reading and rhetorical education are closely connected, as they both involve how texts and readers interact. Overall, *The Lifespan of a Fact* promotes ambiguity around reading—both the physical act of reading and the intellectual processing of what has been read. I contend that this ambiguity is productive because it complicates fact-checking, truth, and fiction, promoting an alternative to binary thinking in which fact and meaning are always contextual. Ultimately, I argue, *The Lifespan of a Fact* encourages students to develop a healthy skepticism in line with Ian Barnard's (2017) recommendations and those advanced by Chris M. Anson and Kendra Andrews in this collection.

To support my reading of this book as a pedagogical text, I draw from student responses written in Fall 2017 and Spring 2018 in sections of first-year writing focused on the theme "Truth and Fiction" at Wake Forest University, a top-30 private university in Winston-Salem, North Carolina with more than 5,100 undergraduates. (Wake Forest University determined that this study does not meet the Institutional Review Board's definition of *research* and is therefore exempt from IRB approval.) I conclude by articulating what students might take from this text to others that they encounter. Similar to Kristina Reardon's contribution to this volume, this chapter proposes that reading *The Lifespan of a Fact* reveals to students the rhetorical framing of all texts, even the facts or the news.

Facilitating Reflective Reading

Readers face an obstacle just in beginning *The Lifespan of a Fact*. Upon opening to the first page, they confront a peculiar question: "How am I supposed to read this book?" Text entirely fills each page. It is Talmudic in appearance, featuring a central text surrounded by heavy annotation. D'Agata's essay draft appears in larger print in the middle of each page. Surrounding it are Fingal's fact-checks, typed in smaller print and appearing in red when Fingal is questioning D'Agata's factual accuracy and in black when he is confirming D'Agata's claims. Each fact-check begins with a quotation from D'Agata's essay, followed by Fingal's remarks and often responses from D'Agata, too. While Fingal's fact-checks adopt a serious, polite tone ("I was hoping you could clarify how you determined that there are thirty-four strip clubs in the city while the source you're using says thirty-one" [p. 15]), the dialogue between Fingal and D'Agata is more colloquial ("Jim, seriously. Chill the fuck out" [p. 66]). The constant shift in language is just one source of disjunction for readers.

Reading the book requires first deciding *how* to read the book, and I argue that this reflective moment facilitates important discussion of reading in the composition classroom. Of course there is no one right approach. One option is to read each page as one might normally read a book written in English: beginning at the upper left corner and working across the page reading left to right. What results is a particularly choppy reading, as the reader must wind their way around the separate components on each page—blocks of fact-checking and essay-writing. A better way to approach the text might be to begin with the chunk of D'Agata's essay on each page, pausing whenever Fingal issues a fact-check, reading his contribution, and then returning to D'Agata's essay. Doing so means constantly interrupting oneself and therefore perhaps finding it difficult to grasp the gist of D'Agata's essay. Another way into the text might be to read all of D'Agata's essay on the page, then consult the fact-checks supplied by Fingal. While this approach is less disruptive, it prevents one from gaining a complete view of D'Agata's essay, making it difficult to follow Fingal's complaints and D'Agata's explanations. What I have opted to do, then, is to read all of each chapter of D'Agata's essay draft, ignoring the fact-checks for the time being; I then return to the fact-checks and read them with the knowledge gained from D'Agata's essay.

However one reads the book, reading *The Lifespan of a Fact* is necessarily, and by design, marked by interruption and disruption. An uncomplicated, linear reading of this book is simply not possible. As students often articulate in response to this book, there is more than one "plot": there is Levi Presley's suicide against the backdrop of Las Vegas, there is Fingal's fact-checking, and there is a debate between Fingal and D'Agata concerning truth and fiction. It is difficult for readers to juggle these competing strands, just as it is difficult for them to attend to the many details Fingal tracks, to abide D'Agata's radical view of truth in nonfiction, and to endure the troubling content of D'Agata's essay draft. Carrying this demanding cognitive load forces readers to slow down and reflect on their reading.

Instructors can use students' questions about and frustrations with reading *The Lifespan of a Fact* to address not only the content of the book but also active reading more generally. Readers who grapple with this text in any capacity must become active readers if they are to make any sense of it; they must choose their way through the morass of D'Agata's essay-writing and Fingal's commentary and corrections. Making visible to students through reflection (whether verbal or written) that they are even making choices when they read this book exposes for them the ways in which so much reading must be active and reflective if it is to be worthwhile. Asking students to extrapolate from the very unusual example of *The Lifespan of a Fact* outward to other texts that similarly require the reader to make choices clarifies that in all reading, particularly on the web where texts such as social media feeds are disjointed and disruptive, readers must actively seek to construct meaning by choosing a way through the text. Perhaps more so than with more traditional or conventional texts, the reader of *The Lifespan of a Fact* constructs a text by choosing a reading strategy, and as a result, one student's reading may differ from another student's reading because they have in a sense constructed different texts, different experiences. While multiplicity in reading experiences can pose a challenge to consistency in instruction, it also proves beneficial in promoting worthwhile discussion of rhetoric and reading, of how readers interact with texts.

Along with reflective reading, Ellen Carillo (2019) recommends enhancing students' reading strategies by "us[ing] models of good reading in the classroom" (p. 150). *The Lifespan of a Fact* models good reading through its extensive annotations. Just observing Fingal's annotations, I suggest, teaches students a bit about good reading. Fingal shows himself to be the kind of good reader that Carillo (2019) imagines. He annotates, he reads actively, and he reads for credibility. In other ways, though, Fingal is a bad reader: he fails to pick up on some of the patterns that D'Agata attempts to achieve with his essay (the importance of the number nine, for instance) and in short, does not see the forest for the trees. Fingal pays too much attention to credibility and thereby misses the rhetorical effects of D'Agata's choices. Thus, this book can engage students in a conversation about how to read essays: the right balance to strike between fact-checking and something like enjoyment, pleasure, mood, effect, and pathos. It affirms that there are multiple ways of reading suited to different rhetorical contexts.

Dramatizing a Rhetorical Education

More than promoting reflection on rhetoric and reading through its design, I argue that in *The Lifespan of a Fact*, the exchange between D'Agata and Fingal fundamentally concerns rhetoric and that its presentation as a dialogue dramatizes a rhetorical education. Thus, the book serves as a useful pedagogical tool for both revealing and reviewing rhetorical concerns such as genre, subject, context, appeals, and audience. I explicate the role of rhetoric in *The Lifespan of a Fact* to support my argument that the book be categorized as rhetorical criticism and used for rhetorical education.

Much of the debate between D'Agata and Fingal hinges on the genre of D'Agata's essay draft and the expectations that this genre carries. D'Agata announces:

> I am not a journalist; I'm an essayist. OK? And this is a genre that has existed for a few thousand years. (Ever heard of Cicero?) So these "rules" that I'm working under are not mine, but rather were established by writers who recognized the difference between the hard research of journalism and the kind of inquiry of mind that characterizes an essay, an inquiry that's propelled by lots of different sources simultaneously—including science, religion, history, myth, politics,

nature, and even the imagination. So there's a bit more freedom in essaying than there is in reporting. (D'Agata & Fingal, 2012, p. 53)

Fingal treats the essay draft as journalism or reporting, a piece to be rigorously fact-checked, given its concern with reality and its use of heavy description and interviews. D'Agata associates his work with art and literature and therefore places it outside the domain of fact-checking. Yet D'Agata's draft is certainly amenable to fact-checking—according to Fingal, "it unleashes a parade of easily verifiable yet clearly manipulated facts in order to make its point" (D'Agata & Fingal, 2012, p. 109)—validating Fingal's position. A work of fiction or poetry can be fact-checked when it includes verifiable information, such as historical detail, challenging D'Agata's contention that literature is not subject to fact-checking. Thus, his argument about the exceptionality of the essay as a genre might be a rhetorical move meant to establish his rule-breaker ethos.

It is not unusual for works of creative nonfiction—the genre to which D'Agata's essay *might* belong—to spark debate about fact and fiction. As Chris Mays (2018) explains, "the genre of creative nonfiction is uniquely complex in its constitution of meaning and of facts, as its authors typically work in the murky waters of subjective experience. Because of this, for observers and participants alike, creative nonfiction is often a site of intense confrontation over the facts its authors represent" (p. 321). In some ways, then, D'Agata's text is not unique, nor is the dialogue between D'Agata and Fingal. The dialogue simply draws attention to the fact that creative nonfiction "is a genre that [...] proclaims its basis in fact despite the use of literary techniques to colorfully render that fact" (Mays, 2018, p. 322). What is unique is the dialogue's appearance in a book, allowing all to see what happened behind the scenes of publication—sort of. It must be assumed that the dialogue has been significantly edited to make it not only presentable to readers but also interesting to read. The book itself is a rhetorical construction, designed for a particular context, not a faithful reproduction of the email exchange.

I see D'Agata's draft as a hybrid text, suitable for fact-checking yet open to creativity, given the vagaries of memory and the fact, which Fingal concedes, that "there aren't any 100 percent reliable sources" anyway (D'Agata & Fingal, 2012, p. 111). D'Agata and Fingal reveal the fluidity of genre. D'Agata variously defines the essay as an "attempt" and an "experience" (D'Agata & Fingal, 2012, p. 108–111), lending it that "bit more freedom" he claims above. Yet he never clarifies just how much freedom he is afforded by defining the genre this way. Readers might be willing to grant him a bit of freedom, but D'Agata intentionally bends small details and claims readers won't care. When, for instance, Fingal finds flaws in D'Agata's account of all the events that supposedly took place on the day Levi died, D'Agata responds:

> I don't think readers will care whether the events that I'm discussing happened on the same day, a few days apart, or a few months apart. What most readers will care about, I think, is the meaning that's suggested in the confluence of these events—no matter how far apart they occurred. The facts that are being employed here aren't meant to function baldly as "facts." The work they're doing is more image-based than informational. Nobody is going to read this, in other words, in order to get a survey of the demographics of Las Vegas or what's scheduled on the community calendar. Readers can get that kind of information elsewhere. (D'Agata & Fingal, 2012, p. 17)

Both D'Agata and Fingal model rhetorical analysis: they think in terms of audience and the expectations readers will bring to the piece given their identification of its genre and their familiarity with D'Agata's previous work (D'Agata & Fingal, 2012, p. 110). Yet D'Agata's analysis of his audience seems flawed.

In fact, his attitude toward the reading public comes across as elitist and unfair. Early on, he expresses disdain for his audience:

> I'm tired of this genre being terrorized by an unsophisticated reading public that's afraid of accidentally venturing into terrain that can't be footnoted and verified by seventeen different sources. My job is not to re-create a world that already exists, holding up a mirror to the reader's experience in hopes it rings true. If a mirror were a sufficient means of handling human experience, I doubt that our species would have invented literature. (D'Agata & Fingal, 2012, p. 22)

Later, he places unfair expectations upon his audience: "I've been giving readers winks and nods for my entire career, Jim. I've edited anthologies, I've written essays, I've given lectures, I've taught courses ... all about this issue. At some point the reader needs to stop demanding that they be spoon-fed like infants and start figuring out on their own how to deal with art they disagree with" (D'Agata & Fingal, 2012, p. 110). D'Agata has cultivated a certain ethos: he's an established essayist, a professor of nonfiction at the Iowa Writers' Workshop, and the editor of a trio of anthologies on the essay and its history. Yet Fingal has a point when he reasons that some readers may not "know what they're getting into" when approaching D'Agata's work—he thus proposes adding a disclaimer (D'Agata & Fingal, 2012, p. 109), a suggestion that my students have echoed. D'Agata and Fingal's dispute rests on different assumptions concerning the audience who will read D'Agata's essay.

While at times D'Agata seems to place undue emphasis upon his reputation, at other times, he disrupts expectations for reliability and credibility. He thus presents a complex, perhaps contradictory, view on ethos. When Fingal asks, "So now, even though it's clear that there aren't any 100 percent reliable sources, can you agree with me that people should at least be able to hope for reliable intentions?" D'Agata responds, "Yeah. But I'm not a politician, Jim. Nor am I [a] reporter. And I'm also not the reader's boyfriend or daddy or therapist or priest or yoga instructor, nor anyone from whom they should be seeking a trustworthy relationship. Just because there are some parts of our culture in which we need to demand honesty and expect reliable intentions doesn't mean that it's appropriate for us to expect that from every experience we have in the world" (D'Agata & Fingal, 2012, p. 111). Of the rhetorical appeals, D'Agata seems to value pathos most, in contrast to Fingal, whose attention, as fact-checker, is largely attuned to logos and ethos. D'Agata hopes to achieve for readers "an experience," one for which cultivating a certain mood and tone is necessary (D'Agata & Fingal, 2012, p. 111).

Fingal questions whether the subject matter and context of the essay draft permit the manipulations that D'Agata admits to crafting. The two men disagree about the subject of the essay: for Fingal, it's about Levi, while for D'Agata, it's about Las Vegas, with Levi representing an idea about the city (p. 108). Yet Fingal argues that this essay will become the "authoritative" piece of writing on Levi's death (D'Agata & Fingal, 2012, p. 107); he shows concern for the context in which the essay will appear and how it will circulate. He admits, "there still seems to be something strange about doing this sort of thing with someone like Levi, who was just a teenager, after all, just a kid in Las Vegas—not a cultural figure or an icon whose life is for the taking and can be radically manipulated and reinterpreted" (D'Agata & Fingal, 2012, p. 108). While D'Agata proposes that facts become "trifling" in the face of Levi's eventual suicide, Fingal suggests, "you're giving them [the facts] meaning by calling attention to them" (D'Agata & Fingal, 2012, p. 107). The dialogue ponders whether the gravity of the situation demands special accuracy, highlighting the fraught relationships among such rhetorical concepts as subject matter, context, and author.

When students posted their initial responses to the book on an online forum, they picked up on these rhetorical nuances. Responses indicated that students recognized distinctions between D'Agata and Fingal's relationships to the rhetorical appeals and to audience. For instance, Brad reflected that D'Agata prefers pathos in writing while Fingal prefers logos, and Isabel questioned the purpose or goal of D'Agata's writing. But more central to students' responses, first in forum posts and later in difficulty papers, was a challenge choosing sides in the debate. Their responses identified ambiguity in the text concerning both how to read the physical page and how to respond to it intellectually. Writing about *The Lifespan of a Fact* became a prime opportunity for combining students' developing rhetorical awareness with their reflections on reading.

Difficulty Papers: Writing about Rhetoric and Reading

I followed the forum posts with what Mariolina Rizzi Salvatori and Patricia Donahue (2005) call "difficulty papers." Writing a difficulty paper engages students in the metacognitive work of describing how they have chosen to read a text, why they are reading it in that way, and what consequences result from such a reading. My assignment instructed students to do the following:

> First, describe how *The Lifespan of a Fact* is different from other texts you've encountered. Then, identify any difficulties you are experiencing while reading it and propose at least one strategy for overcoming these difficulties. Choose one or more challenging passages and read them carefully with your difficulty strategies in mind to reach a better understanding. I don't expect you to reach full understanding but to make some progress. Try to walk your reader through your reading of the passage(s) you've chosen. Finally, pose any lingering questions or difficulties you are experiencing, and be ready to share them during class discussion.

Difficulty papers, like the reflective reading journals that Carillo (2019) recommends, help make reading visible. Salvatori and Donahue (2005) explain, "As students put their difficulties in writing, as they write them out, they give themselves a chance to acknowledge the complexity of reading, which, if not *captured through writing*, would easily slide away" (p. 5). As Carillo (2019) writes, "If we are committed to teaching our students to become better readers, we must find ways of making reading as visible as writing so we can work as deliberately on reading as we do on writing" (p. 149). Salvatori and Donahue (2005) show through sample difficulty papers that recounting one's reading experience and wading through difficulties not only enhance students' reading but their writing too. Bringing those difficulty papers into classroom conversations is an important way to reflect as a class on our reading strategies and the different resulting texts that we as readers construct. Difficulty papers engage students with uncertainty, a key element of this text and of reading in a post-truth age.

Students often report uncertainty choosing a side in *The Lifespan of a Fact*, which I suggest owes to the ambiguity that it promotes as a dual rhetorical and literary work. This pedagogical result contrasts with the ways in which critics have responded to the book. As Wilson (2015) explains,

> Rather predictably, most reviewers of *Lifespan* simply dug in around the entrenched positions the essayist and fact-checker had already staked out. To

> one camp—usually positioning themselves as resolute defenders of the journalistic profession—D'Agata seemed little more than a "preening" apostle of postmodern "truthiness," his facile factoids held in check only by the valiant intern. Conversely, D'Agata's renegade pugnacity gave heart to those—not uncommonly aficionados of memoir and creative nonfiction—who felt that the archives of memory and experience were hardly so empirically solid to begin with. (p. 484)

While many students reported that the book generated ambiguity for them, one difficulty paper, written by a student named Jackson in Spring 2018, promotes a particularly salient sense of uncertainty. In providing excerpts from Jackson's paper, I demonstrate how reading this book can facilitate a more nuanced approach to argumentation in line with Carillo's (2018) and Barnard's (2017) recommendations. Rather than promote a binary view of truth and fiction, *The Lifespan of a Fact* complicates student thinking on these matters in favor of something messier and more chaotic, which can lead to the recognition that even facts are rhetorically constructed.

In response to our "post-truth" moment following the 2016 presidential election, rhetoric and composition scholars such as John Duffy (2017) have championed the effectiveness of the first-year writing classroom in teaching "constructive, fact-based public discourse." They have aligned themselves with facts—with Fingal's position. In contrast, Ian Barnard (2017) rejects a binary analysis of facts and "alternate facts" in our current climate. He reminds academics that facts are rhetorical, writing that:

> The facts you produce are necessarily shaped by the questions you ask and the investigations you undertake to produce those facts. And even then, facts don't speak for themselves. They are necessarily articulated, interpreted, and mediated in a variety of ways. This isn't a bad thing—it is what it is. However, liberal and even some radical intellectuals, politicians, and activists continue to peddle the sanctity of "facts," as if facts can somehow be cordoned off from the contexts that produce, disseminate, interpret, and receive them. (Barnard 2017)

Barnard calls facts "fluid" yet resists succumbing to endless relativism. Instead, he calls into question the binary thinking that D'Agata and Fingal dramatize throughout *The Lifespan of a Fact* and that Wilson claims its critics reproduce. Binary thinking, as presented in "those generic and persistent pro/con essay assignments that imply that there are only two positions on any given issue, and that the composer's job is to come down on one or [the] other side," discourages "nuance and complexity" and, Barnard argues, "suppress[es] ideas and ideologies that challenge and subvert the neo-liberal status quo." "To claim or assume that there are only two positions on 'facts' (pro or con, progressive or Trump)," Barnard reasons, "is precisely to enforce the manipulation of reality in the service of self-interest that the defenders of facts claim to be contesting." Though *The Lifespan of a Fact* may seem to reproduce the binary that Barnard eschews, I suggest that in response to the book, students such as Jackson tend to embrace non-binary thinking in favor of something more nuanced, complex, and ultimately, unsettled—exactly the goal of the difficulty paper assignment.

Jackson begins his difficulty paper by plainly disclosing his uncertainty about whose side to take: "The think [*sic*] I have found most difficult in *The Lifespan of a Fact*, so far has been deciding whether John has an obligation to report his findings from his interviews and facts in a more professional journalistic matter, or if it is okay for him to slightly fictionalize and adjust quotes so that his essay has more literary substantiality." This uncertainty continues throughout the paper as Jackson simultaneously acknowledges the opposition that D'Agata and Fingal present and refuses to engage in binary thinking himself—instead embracing something messier. He recognizes that the two men possess "diametrically opposed philosophies" yet calls their debate "a manifestation of the internal indecisiveness that I find myself experiencing." He tries to reason out the differences between journalism and essay, mostly as articulated by D'Agata. His writing follows a meandering discovery process, something that a difficulty paper allows for more than a position-based assignment (the kind that Barnard critiques):

> I don't think journalistic articles are written to expose something about the human experience to readers. Rather, they are utilitarian. Most journalistic work involves tracking down sources and discovering what really happened as accurately as possible. But perhaps a journalistic article on this subject wouldn't be enough to teach us anything about suicide or the human experience. An essayist writes when he or she has a certain insight that they feel should be shared. However, journalism does not lend itself to any opinions or insight the author might have, which is why Jim can't seem to understand why John is twisting quotes or possibly fabricating interviews.

Jackson then turns to the question of audience, asking "But would readers make the same mistake Jim makes and assume that this is journalism, and be misinformed about the true motives for a teens suicide, and is it immoral for John to fictionalize this event as a tool for demonstrating an idea that he developed before he was even informed about the incident[?]" I contend that the winding nature of this sentence, its status as a run-on, confirms that true thinking is happening here, that Jackson is balancing multiple, competing possibilities at once; in other words, he's grappling with ambiguity. This trend continues as Jackson poses a hypothetical scenario:

> Let's assume that John discovers that Levi Pressley [*sic*] had been diagnosed with schizophrenia a year prior to his suicide and his parents had dismissed and denied the diagnosis to save them embarrassment from friends and family. Would John report on this fact if it didn't fit in with his pre-developed thesis? Or would he ignore this and continue to portray Levi as an ideologically misguided youth, resulting from being raised in a godless violent city that tourist[s] view as a modern inferno to purge their deepest desires?

Jackson's uncertainty is amplified in his response to this hypothetical scenario, where he mixes hedging and intensifiers, uncertainty with certainty: "*I think* that would *pretty obviously* be immoral, but there is *definitely* a *gray area* between what it is okay to change about the actual story so that it fits in with an essay, and outright fabricating" (emphasis added). As the paper continues, Jackson never resolves his uncertainty, just picks away at it. For instance, he questions why he finds "Jim" so disagreeable, while at the same time, he justifies his behavior: "I have realized that fact checking is a tedious job that takes a certain kind of perfectionist to do, and I can't figure out if I just hate Jim's job or have a dislike for Jim."

This difficulty paper, while remarkable in expressing its uncertainty, is representative of a larger trend I've observed in teaching this book: students read it and are capable of holding multiple competing ideas in their minds at once. The book thus offers students an alternative to either/or thinking in spite of its seeming portrayal of such thinking in the debate between D'Agata and Fingal. Binary thinking is often unreflective and representative of a knee-jerk reaction rather than careful time spent with a text or question. Dwelling in uncertainty, which this book and difficulty papers support together, promotes more integrative thinking. While I don't deny the value in taking strong positions, I suggest that there is value in uncertainty too. As Jackson's difficulty paper has demonstrated, there is particular value in writing about one's uncertainty and thus developing more complex thinking.

Conclusion: Pedagogical Lessons from The Lifespan of a Fact

While D'Agata and Fingal are opposed throughout the book, at its conclusion Fingal reaches some realizations that challenge his previous sense of security regarding the sanctity of truth and the value of fact-checking. As Fingal completes his review of D'Agata's essay draft, he begins talking to himself: red ink surrounds a blank box where the essay draft had been, and D'Agata drops out of the conversation altogether. Fingal questions the reliability of the coroner's report on Levi's death and Levi's parents' own account of Levi's last interactions—two sources that seemed reliable until now. Fingal gestures toward the pointlessness of facts and fact-checking upon writing that even if he could definitively report what happened to Levi that day, Levi would still be dead: "Which of these sources can we trust as 'the' authority if they all have demonstrated in one way or another the potential of inaccurately representing what actually happened that night? And at this point, does it even matter? [...] I'd have done my job. But wouldn't he still be dead?" (D'Agata & Fingal, 2012, p. 123). Particularly in presenting this realization at the book's conclusion, *The Lifespan of a Fact* endorses skepticism toward anything that claims to capture the authoritative account of an occurrence.

Fingal reminds readers that writing is just a representation, not a 100% accurate reproduction, of the truth. His findings affirm Mays's (2018) conclusion:

> [W]hile there is merit in holding authors accountable for basic community standards for honesty or for fidelity to the subjects of their writing, it is also valuable to recognize that there can never be absolute accuracy in the complex world rendered by writing. Indeed, the act of writing itself is the creation of an unstable and malleable context in which absolute accuracy is impossible, even though writing also, paradoxically, creates the conditions—genres—in which such an absolute can be ostensibly assessed. (p. 337)

Completing *The Lifespan of a Fact* thus provides an opportunity to teach students that the act of writing places the facts in a gray area where they become framed by subjective experience and reinterpretation. Writing is a representation, not a reproduction, as my students have often acknowledged when lamenting how difficult it can be to transfer their thoughts onto paper. As the title *The Lifespan of a Fact* implies, facts have duration: they are rhetorically constructed in and for certain contexts, they have limits, and they do not exist in a vacuum. A fact represents the truth only until proven otherwise, as more information becomes available.

The Lifespan of a Fact and Mays (2018) remind us that all writing is a rhetorical construction, even the writing of facts. Readers must learn to question what authors are trying to do with the "facts" that they present, thus combining rhetorical education with information literacy. More than placing students in an endless quandary regarding reliability, reading *The Lifespan of a Fact* reaffirms the value of rhetorical education. In dramatizing a rhetorical education, I argue, the book both gives students the tools to conduct rhetorical analysis and challenges them to use it to enact skepticism about even that which seems categorically true.

Particularly when paired with a difficulty paper, *The Lifespan of a Fact* promotes essential written processing of the reading experience, as it both physically and cognitively unfolds. Upon completing *The Lifespan of a Fact*, students can approach new texts—even the news or the "facts"—with the tools for reading and rhetorical analysis that they have gained from this reading experience.

References

Barnard, I. (2017). The fluidity of facts. *Anastamos*, (2). https://anastamos.chapman.edu/index.php/portfolio-item/the-fluidity-of-facts/

Carillo, E. C. (2018). *Teaching readers in post-truth America*. Utah State University Press.

Carillo, E. C. (2019). Navigating this perfect storm: Teaching critical reading in the face of Common Core State Standards, fake news, and Google. *Pedagogy, 19*(1), 135–159.

Chick, N. L, Hassel, H., & Haynie, A. (2009). "Pressing an ear against the hive": Reading literature for complexity. *Pedagogy, 9*(3), 399–422.

D'Agata, J., & Fingal, J. (2012). *The lifespan of a fact*. Norton.

Duffy, J. (2017, May 8). Post-truth and first-year writing. *Inside Higher Ed*. https://www.insidehighered.com/views/2017/05/08/first-year-writing-classes-can-teach-students-how-make-fact-based-arguments-essay

Mays, C. (2018). "You can't make this stuff up": Complexity, facts, and creative nonfiction. *College English, 80*(4), 319–341.

Salvatori, M., & Donahue, P. (2005). *The elements (and pleasures) of difficulty*. Pearson.

Wilson, C. P. (2015). When noir meets nonfiction. *Twentieth-Century Literature, 61*(4), 484–510.

7. Fighting Fake News with Critical Reading of Digital-Media Texts

Lilian W. Mina, Dakota Mills and Shifat Niha

"I hear a lot of versions of, well, they [college students] don't read any more, you know. Their attention spans are so short from reading tweets and Buzzfeed articles that they don't know how to read longer texts" (Amicucci, 2019).

"I hear a lot of complaints about students not reading (or not reading well) because they are too lazy to read long texts due to their consumption and interaction with social media" (Gagich, 2019).

These were responses that I received to a Facebook post discussing typical complaints about college students' reading skills. If you work in academia, which I assume you do, more probably than not you have heard your colleagues voice similar concerns. Chances are you too have had your share of frustration at college students' reading skills (or lack of to be more accurate) in your classes. Most academics seem to agree (for once for a change) that current college students don't seem to have adequately rigorous or critical reading skills. Academics also seem to agree (ok, on a second thing) that students' consumption of digital and social media content is to blame for these sub-par reading skills. Yet, is this really true? Or is the problem that "Reading is not what it used to be .... Students don't have poor reading skills; they have different reading skills" (Buford, 2019). My colleague Buford's comment on the Facebook post captures my argument: reading at the turn of the second decade of the 21st century is not what most of academics were trained on or would like to teach, and the reading skills, albeit questionable or uncritical, students bring to our classes mandate adopting a different approach to conceptualizing and teaching reading in college.

In spring 2019, I taught a sophomore writing-intensive Honors Seminar around the theme Seeing the Unseen. I designed the course around one major goal: students should be critical readers of the digital texts they encounter and consume all the time. Like most English professors, I was aware of the changing, sometimes deteriorating, reading skills of college students in my classes. Not only do college students lack the critical reading skills that enable them to critique and evaluate digital texts and online sources, they don't question the authenticity of visual materials presented as the ultimate truth (McGrew et al., 2017). From doctored images to chopped viral videos that project one perspective of events and situations, college students are left lacking the cognitive and digital tools that they can use to critique, analyze, research, and reach unbiased conclusions for themselves.

More than two decades ago, Sorapure et al. (1998) raised important questions about the knowledge "images and graphic design convey" and how students can assess these resources (p. 410); they emphasized the need to "expand our conception of literacy" to best prepare students for using the web in their research. Things have dramatically changed since that argument was made to the degree that Miller (2016) suggested that "digital reading will be the norm" and the change to digital medium is "irreversible" (p. 153).

Fast forward to 2017 when Horning noted that as online materials are increasingly multimodal, there is a question about students' information literacy skills and their ability to evaluate these materials. In his study of students' digital reading skills, Keller (2014) found that students who were used to consuming digital texts struggled with unfamiliar websites not only because of their different interface and design, but mostly because the type of text required different reading strategies with which students weren't familiar. Furthermore, Carillo (2017) argued that as students continue to read digital and multimodal texts, their reading habits and practices are altered in ways that may not always be suited for learning critical thinking and active reading.

In this chapter, I aim to reimagine and reconceptualize the role of the English Composition professor to claim the role of "master of resourcefulness" (Miller, 2016, p. 155) who prepares college students to be informed citizens in a digital world through exploring the concepts of criticality, authenticity, and credibility in more nuanced ways. I discuss my course design and the multiple assignments, daily activities, and selection of reading texts, with text broadly defined to include alphabetic texts, images, memes, comics, videos, and (interactive) websites. Furthermore, two students from my class share their responses to the role I played and my pedagogy before I conclude the chapter with implications for teaching and research.

Playing the Master of Resourcefulness Role: Course Design

While designing my course, I wanted students to become "successful participants in a global society" who are able to "recognize the bias and privilege present in the interactions" (NCTE, 2019). I agree with Wuebben (2016) that professors should "study, teach, and be worried about" (p. 68) viral texts and shareable content if we're keen on connecting our classrooms to the digital world where students live, read, obtain their information and knowledge, and develop their worldviews.

To achieve my overarching goal, I designed the course on two major concepts: critical (digital) reading and rigorous research. Miller (2016) envisioned that the professor should be a "quality-control manager" (p. 154) who "models how to think in the face of an endless torrent of information" (p. 155). I wanted this role to evolve in this age of digital disinformation that comes to us in all modalities and media and shades of truth to include teaching students to be critical thinkers who are able to verify and evaluate the quality and authenticity of digital content they encounter. I enacted this design by selecting thought-provoking readings, steering classroom discussions through critical questions, and engaging students in activities that would push them out of the shallow-reading and thinking comfort zone. In addition to reading-based class discussions and activities, the course included four major requirements (illustrated in Figure 7.1) that combined critical thinking and research. Due to space limitation and in order to stay focused on the purpose of this volume, I'll discuss how I incorporated critical digital reading and how students used their newly-developed skills to engage in rigorous research in the course.

Six-Word Stories: At any point in the class, I'll ask you to write a six-word story on the reading, the discussion, class activity, or anything else. Near the end of the semester, you'll use these stories to create a word cloud. You'll give a two-minute presentation about your stories and what they reveal about your learning experience in the course.

Autoethnography Reports (4x): As the course description states, you will scrutinize your own doubts and skepticisms about various topics. Using autoethnography (we'll learn about that, don't worry) you will examine these doubts and write four three-page reports about them throughout the semester. These reports can come in genre and medium you prefer: journal entry, narrative, research report, podcast, a short video clip.

Response to Guest Lecturers (3x): Four professors will guest lecture in our class on different topics pertaining to seeking the truth about your doubts. I expect you to engage in each lecture by taking careful notes and asking thoughtful questions. You will use these notes later to write a three-page critical response to three of these lectures.

Final Group Project: In groups of four, you will research a topic of interest based on the course theme. Your goal is to debunk one major doubt to public audience. The project requires substantial research that incorporates library and ethnographic (we'll learn about that) research. The final product will be a multi-genre report that includes a minimum of three distinct genres, one of which is movie/video clip.

Figure 7.1 Course Major Assignments

Critical Digital Reading Skills

Building on Miller's (2016) argument that "digital reading will be the norm" (p. 153), it was imperative for me to teach students reading in its broad meaning to include reading alphabetic texts, images, videos, websites, and design elements. Critical reading of these texts in various modalities entails training students to not accept what they "see" and to reject the common belief that "I won't believe it until I see it" because what you see isn't necessarily true. From photoshopped images to cropped videos, the truth is blurred and harder to identify. Insisting on using print materials in class disadvantages college students, and stubbornly advocating for the value of print over digital reading creates a digital divide between students and professors because as Miller says digital reading is "irreversible" (p. 153).

We started the semester by reading the Oatmeal's comic Backfire Effect (n.d.). In reading and discussing that digital comic, students learned that they should question everything they read, see, and hear and that if they caught themselves questioning one piece of news but not the other, it was most probably because of their bias for or against an idea. Not only did that reading set the tone for our class discussions for the following 15 weeks, more importantly, it was a good opportunity to introduce students to digital reading skills and how to navigate a digital comic, thus preparing them for the more diverse digital texts that we read and examined later as we ventured to discuss viral videos, media bias, and the authenticity of digital texts.

Viral Videos. I had planned to start the critical digital reading journey by reading and discussing the first part of McComiskey's (2017) book as a springboard to expose students to the phenomenon of information overload that resulted from the ease of publishing using digital technologies. The goal was to discuss how this information overload is embodied on social media platforms where the ease of publishing occurs through sharing, commenting, and posting content all the time. Keller (2014) noted that the variety of "form and content" of texts can be a problem because readers may not know how to effectively and critically read these various forms of media (p. 3). I further problematize the variety of content and form by bringing the multi-layered problems of fake and junk news, emotion-provoking content, emotionally enticing clickbait advertising, and deceiving media (images and videos) to the conversation. These problems emerged in the last few years, most notably since the 2016 presidential campaign and elections, and with an intense hyper-partisan political climate leading to the 2020 presidential race, I wanted to read and discuss McComiskey's book with students. Interestingly, in the weekend before our class discussion, the videos of the Lincoln Memorial incident went viral on social media.

The video of a confrontation between Nick Sandmann, the Covington Catholic High School student, and Nathan Phillips, the Omaha leader, at the Lincoln Memorial went viral. In a matter of hours, the three-minute video stimulated angry responses across all social media platforms, and millions of social media patrons shared the video with similar statements of disgust and condemnation of the high-school student because he wore a MAGA (Make America Great Again) red hat and "appeared" to mock and challenge the Indian American leader.

After about 24 hours, a much longer video surfaced, depicting a wholly different perspective than the one that triggered those angry responses the day before. The viral circulation of these two videos presented a kairotic and opportune moment to discuss critical digital reading skills. After seeing millions fall susceptible to the short viral video for various reasons, I knew that students in my class weren't immune to what Wuebben (2016) described as popularity metrics (e.g., the number of likes and shares). He argued that these metrics affect the reader's perception and evaluation of the viral materials. A 2015 *Harvard Business Review* report attributed the wide and quick circulation of certain videos to their appeal to the viewers' dispositions and emotions, or what Jenkins et al. (2013) described as "deep audience engagement" with the content that motivates them to share that content (p. 4).

I used Wuebben's (2016) question "how do the popularity metrics ... shape our reading practices and metacognition evaluations of the digital composition process?" (p. 67) to guide that class discussion of viral videos and how students should guard themselves against these popularity metrics by using critical reading and thinking skills. I argue that these critical digital reading skills are key for students who rely almost entirely on social media for their learning and worldviews, and thus need to learn how to assess the authenticity and credibility of the content that invades their social media spaces.

I asked students to read Bogost's (2019) article on viral videos in *The Atlantic*. Bogost used the two Lincoln Memorial incident videos as examples, thus connecting that kairotic moment to the social media phenomenon of viral videos. When we started the class discussion of the two readings, I asked students to think of this combination of questions: What sets the stage for the viral moment in other videos? What combination of factors may have created a viral video that turned out to be not the complete truth? My goal was to get students to critically question the wide circulation of content and to have the "power to read through views, likes, and other digital symbols of approval" (Wuebben, 2016, p. 68). I aimed for them to see that the main reason any digital content becomes viral has to do with who gets the first interpretation of an event or an incident out to the world and how these interpretations set the scene for viral content, pushing critical thinking and searching for alternative views to the periphery of our thinking. I wanted to use the viral Lincoln Memorial chopped video as an example of the other content that gets shared widely and as a springboard to "appreciate the rich, layered processes of communication in the digital age" (Wuebben, p. 68). For example, not only was that three-minute video cut of a much longer recording that presented other perspectives, it rapidly got boiled down to a still image of Sandmann and Phillips staring at each other, with the image zoomed on the former's facial expression that was interpreted as challenging and mocking the latter. The image was interpreted as Sandmann confronting the Omaha leader, thus triggering much condemnation of the student, and cascading the effect to condemning his school, religion, race, and political views.

After a heated class discussion, I wanted to extend the concepts of popularity metrics and how they affect and cloud judgment to other viral content student have seen on various social media platforms. It was time for students to apply what they've discussed and practiced on their own. This application element ensures the transfer of these new skills and practices to students' everyday life when they are not guided by a professor in a class activity. Students' task was to find another video or news item that went viral and to discuss that content using the concepts they learned from Bogost's (2019) article. I gave them some questions to reinforce the class discussion and to give them a toolbox that they can use in future encounters with such viral content:

- How are different groups portrayed and what does it mean for you?
- Which lifestyles, values, and points of view are represented—or missing?
- How might different people interpret this message?
- How would you articulate a response to problematic representations and advocate for better ones?
- How does this affect your own daily media use?

This activity, according to NCTE's (2019) very recent position statement on defining literacy in the digital age, engages students "with texts that vary in format, genre, and medium" in order for them to develop "new perspectives and insights" into viral content, thus expanding "their understanding of the world." As students embarked on this activity, they "critically analyze[d] a variety of information and ideas from a variety of sources" to not only validate the questionable content that arrives unsolicited to their social media newsfeeds, or what Lawrence (this volume) calls information that finds us, but to also challenge it by unearthing the truth of such content.

Media Bias. Unlike viral content that students may not solicit to view because it comes to their digital doorsteps, media and news sources are more significant because students select to watch or reach the content these media outlets produce. Discussing media bias then was more serious because it would be about students' own choices of media sources, which may make many students uncomfortable or put them on the defensive about their choices. While students may claim that they don't spend much time on social media or that they don't get affected by the content they see shared on these platforms, asking them to think more critically about their trusted sources of information is different because that would bring them face to face with choices that were presumed as trustworthy and unbiased.

I asked students to make a list of the top five sources they used to obtain news, and to list their go-to sources for analysis, interpretation, and commentary on news. I then asked students to plot their sources on the Media Bias chart (n.d.). I could hear lots of gasps and see lots of frowns as students went down their lists and found where their sources belonged on the chart, realizing that their sources were not anywhere close to the middle of the chart. That meant that their sources were mostly biased and either far-right or far-left leaning. I asked them to take a few minutes to write down their responses before reporting back to class. I wanted students to have a safe place to process and channel their feelings about their own media choices before engaging in a discussion of these choices and their interpretation.

Many students attempted to challenge the validity of the Media Bias Chart and questioned its own bias. Even though I could see that their response was an act of resistance to the interpretation of their media choices, I welcomed that challenge as a sign of critical thinking to encourage students to do more with that chart and their findings than just challenge them back. I showed them a video that explains the research behind its creation. I wanted that tension to be another learning moment for them and to see that while the Chart may not be perfect, it was based on research and big data sources to minimize its bias or false plotting of news sources.

As always, I aimed for students to see what media bias meant and how it shapes their perspectives and beliefs. The application aspect involved a Bias Detection activity adapted from the Media Bias Chart website that students completed in groups. In her chapter in this volume, Canfield offers a longer assignment that aims for students to "demonstrate their understanding of malicious propaganda versus effective persuasion." Because all educational materials on the website have been recently put behind a pay wall, I used a screenshot of the prompt that I have saved to my computer Figure 7.2 below.

> 1. Choose one recent political news story (past two weeks but nothing from the last two days to ensure the story has had time to spread to various media sites)
> 2. Compare how the news story was reported across at least three different sources of the ones you usually use:
>   o Headlines
>   o Language
>   o Graphics
>   o Fact reporting/omitting
> 3. Was there consistency in communicating that news story across these platforms? If not, what differences could you notice?
> 4. In your opinion, why did these differences take place?
> 5. Were any special phrases/words repeatedly used in reporting the news story?
> 6. What were the media (images, videos, other) used in communicating the news story on the different sites?
> 7. What are your conclusions about media bias from this short activity?

Figure 7.2: Activity Prompt on Bias Detection in News Sources. Source: Author

That activity allowed students to see for themselves the media bias in highlighting the news details that are compliant with their agenda and political and social affiliation. Students didn't stop at the name of the media outlet no matter how reputable or trusted (by students) that media platform was. This activity was also an example of "hubris" or "having excessive trust in one's ability to accurately pass judgment on an unfamiliar website" (McGrew et al., 2017, p. 9). Students thought that because they trusted websites, they developed an abundance of confidence in those websites whether they were media outlets, pages and groups they follow on social media, news shared by their parents or trusted elders (e.g., pastors and teachers), they thought they were immune to falling for fake news and invalid information. After that activity, students shared that it was an eye-opening experience for them and that they needed to be more cautious about accepting anything they see at face value even if shared by someone or an entity they trusted.

As students reported on the outcome of their activity, they referenced our prior discussion of viral content, expressing varied opinions on the authenticity of the visuals (images and videos) used in news reports and analyses. Their concerns made me realize that students would remain vulnerable in the face of edited visuals regardless of where they see them, social media platforms or media outlets. The heated discussion of media bias and students' argument for or against the authenticity of visuals on media websites were an organic connection to the third element of critical digital reading skills.

Digital Content. Carillo (2019) drew our attention to the daily challenge all social media and internet users in general face: visual content. On the one hand, the tradition has been to trust what we "see" because it's probably true, which isn't true any longer due to image, meme, and video manipulation software programs that have repeatedly altered reality into fake visual content. On the other hand, visual content is widespread on all digital platforms: blogs, *Instagram*, *YouTube*, *Facebook*, and millions of other digital spaces and services. The wide spread of this visual content increasingly poses cognitive, temporal, and technical challenges on viewers of this content. According to Carillo, these two problems require a different set of skills to be able to navigate a different landscape of information and how it is disseminated. I further argue that relying on dated strategies and skills won't help Gen Z students become digitally literate citizens.

The Citizen Evidence Lab is "an online space to share **best practices, techniques and tools for authenticating user-generated content** for human rights defense" (bold in original, Koettl, n.d.). Originally created by Amnesty International, the website includes a toolbox section with lots of tools and detailed strategies to help visitors authenticate visual materials they view on the web. After navigating the website and toolbox with the students using the class projector, I asked them to get in groups and to find a questionable image or video footage to authenticate using two tools from the toolbox. To make the activity (illustrated in Figure 7.3) more exciting, I told students that they could start with a picture from their own devices to see how the tools work.

Not only was this activity a big hit among students, it helped me achieve multiple objectives: (a) to give students handy tools they can use to authenticate any questionable visual content they encounter and (b) to bridge the blurry boundaries between everyday digital practices and academic research. According to the aforementioned NCTE statement, a precursor to students becoming "empowered learners" is to be able to "analyze and evaluate the

---

Using two tools from the Citizen Evidence Toolbox, analyze data for one image and one video that you had doubts about.

- What's the image/video about?
- Where did you first see it?
- What doubts did you have about it? Why?
- What data were able to reveal about that image or video using these tools?
- Did you find anything that confirmed your doubts?
- How easy was the process?

Figure 7.3: An Activity Prompt to Authenticate Visual Content Using Citizen Evidence Lab. Source: Author

multimedia sources that they encounter" and to "examine the credibility and relevancy of sources they consume." Analysis and evaluation of sources is a fundamental component of the research process (Howard & Jamieson, 2014) that shouldn't be restricted to scholarly or non-scholarly sources used in a typical research paper assignment. Therefore, extending our conversations about credibility and authenticity of media and social media materials to credibility of sources for their research projects was a logical next step that followed our numerous discussions and activities around the credibility and authenticity of digital sources.

This broad range of skills and tools that students learned and practiced repeatedly in class represented the first foundation of my course: critical digital reading skills. The second foundation was a rigorous academic research process that allows students to build on and extend their newly-learned critical digital reading skills to academic research practices.

Academic Research Skills

Howard and Jamieson (2014) acknowledged that students in the 21st century "seem no wiser about how to find or use information than were their pre-Internet predecessors" (p. 239). The problem might be what Keller (2014) found in his research on digital reading skills. Keller found that some students struggled with unfamiliar websites that included unfamiliar type of texts that required a different set of reading skills that students didn't possess. Consequently, Keller emphasized "the value of teaching digital reading" (p. 109)

As you can see in Figure 7.1, students were researching common ungrounded ideas that are widespread in their communities. Each research team had to address one false idea among these communities. Due to the nature of topics students were researching, they were likely to use both scholarly and non-scholarly sources. After spending time discussing information literacy and hands-on activities on using the university library database, it was time to venture to the more difficult task of finding credible non-scholarly sources on the Web.

I used the CRAAP (Currency, Relevance, Authority, Accuracy, and Purpose) test designed by Sarah Blakeslee from California State University, Chico ("CRAAP test," 2020) to engage students in the nuanced meaning of credibility of online sources of information. The sheet includes a list of questions under each criterion, and students had to use multiple criteria and questions to examine the credibility of a website. The CRAAP test and similar tools have been criticized by a number of scholars for their assumed simplicity.

For example, McGrew et al. (2017) strongly critiqued the use of checklists of questions and points that students may use to check the validity and trustworthiness of materials and websites. Their criticism centers around the simplicity of these checklists that doesn't match the nuances of materials produced and circulated on the web. They also critiqued the way such checklists are used in the classroom, assuming that teachers stop at checking boxes or asking students to answer simple questions. This is not completely true because their critique implies that teachers do not engage students in extended discussions of the questions on these checklists. In reality, many teachers use these checklists as the springboard to engage students in more critical practices that allow them to develop critical awareness of vetting websites and information floating on their social media accounts for trustworthiness and accuracy. I don't use the CRAAP test checklist as a simple yes/no check of a website; rather, I use it to open a conversation with students that take them outside of that website, or what the authors call lateral reading (p. 8), and to read various sources that discuss the same information so that they can see for themselves how biased or invalid some websites can be.

Students embraced the CRAAP test and started applying it in order to select trustworthy and reliable sources for their projects. I'd argue that having been through the prior coursework and developing the mindset that the internet is full of junk information has been instrumental in getting students to question the authenticity and value of sources for research purposes. In other words, students were transferring their previously-learned skills of critical digital reading and were becoming "critical, savvy producers and consumers" of digital content because they've learned to "analyze information for authorial intent, positioning, and how language, visuals, and audio are being used" in that content (NCTE, 2019). In other words, students were on the right path to become digital literate citizens who have "the ability to use information and communication technologies to find, evaluate, create, and communicate digital information, an ability that requires both cognitive and technical skills" (Carillo, 2019, p. 1).

Reading students' multi-genre projects at the end of the semester was excitingly reassuring that students have grown during this 15-week course to be better readers and critical thinkers who were able to research and address a public misconception with informed and considerably unbiased knowledge. However, I wanted to hear more from students about their learning experience and their response to my role as "master of resourcefulness" (Miller, 2016, p. 155) during the course of the semester. Rather than assuming my pedagogy worked or didn't work, I liked for students to practice their newly-acquired critical thinking skills and to evaluate my approach and pedagogy from their perspective. I invited a few students to contribute their responses to this chapter as co-constructors of knowledge and Dakota Mills and Shifat Niha accepted my invitation. For the sake of fairness and to avoid pressuring students in any possible way, Dakota and Shifat were asked to keep a journal with their thoughts and responses to their classroom experience and to share these responses after final grades had been submitted.

Dakota Mills: My Six-Word Story of Fake News

The HONR 2757 course routinely geared us towards questioning the beliefs and preconceived notions of ourselves and others to expose misinformation. This, in my understanding, has been a three-step process to provide us the tools and experience to accomplish such a task. Entailed in this were: in-class teachings on how to examine the integrity of information, autoethnographies examining our beliefs, and responses to lectures examining expert's beliefs. The culmination of all this learning and understanding took the form of a six-word story presentation (see Figure 7.1 above).

First and foremost, I used the words "fake news" (the focus of much of the class) to show the similarities between the motivation of arbitrators of fake news and individuals who speak falsely. These similarities being that it pushes a desired narrative and can enhance their current position, whether monetarily or socially. I also used the word "stupidity" to address the negative ramifications of fake news, as it creates a misinformed and polarized society. Next, I used "CRAAP Test" and "Citizen Evidence" to show the two tools we used to vet our sources. Citizen Evidence has been primarily effective, as it has allowed me to vet videos for accuracy by searching different media that have published them. This is the first lesson this class taught me: I actually possess the ability to vet videos myself. This has certainly benefited me as I have found many fake videos that I had believed at first glance. I have even begun to use outside of my university studies, vetting videos which I have come across on YouTube and social media sites.

My presentation continued by speaking of a lecture by an expert in the field of psychology. Because this lecture took place well into the semester, I had already been given the experience and tools necessary to distinguish between fake news and opinion. While much of what the lecturer said was quite factual and true, I was able to utilize these new skills to discover some falsity in her lecture. This was the basis of my critical response to the lecture and was honestly quite surprising. Beginning at a young age, students are taught to trust their instructors and the information that they give; the second lesson this class taught me was that I cannot trust those in authority purely based on their ethos.

The last portion of my presentation covered my autoethnographies, which covered the negative ramifications of assumptions. This was closely linked to the subject of fake news. By examining my own beliefs and preconceptions I was able to not only reflect on my past factual ignorance, but I also exposed current ill-founded beliefs that I held. This was the third lesson that this class taught me: the problem of misinformation was not only outside of myself.

Misinformation is a huge problem in our society, and it is vital to root it out in order to maintain social stability. This class has greatly increased my ability to do this, which will benefit me through the rest of my studies and continue to do so in my personal life. By teaching the class how to perceive misinformation, we gained a valuable tool; by necessitating that we write papers critical of the information of experts, we gained valuable experience; and by requiring us to apply this to our own beliefs and preconceptions, we gained the ability to recognize misinformation regardless of our own biases. This method of educating us, teaching us to apply it to others, and showing us how to apply it to ourselves is truly a great learning method, favorable over the others that I have been exposed to in my university.

Shifat Niha: A Story of Bias, Research, and Truth

HONR 2757 was a successful course for me. The design of the course focused mainly on research which helped me to strengthen my academic skills not only academically, but some lessons improved my personal experiences as well. During the semester, the class went over various topics related to bias, skepticism, and research. Some parts of the lectures were so intriguing to me that I will remember them for a long time. For example, I found it very interesting to know about confirmation bias and how it subconsciously affects our thoughts. It was surprising to know how researching, which is supposed to be impartial, can be also biased without us noticing. One of the major things for me in this course was learning how much our perspective matters in our social media experience, and how it can actually improve our critical thinking.

As a college freshman, I did not have much academic research experience. Before, while doing similar works, I would usually choose my topic, pick a side, and then look for evidence to support my hypothesis. I mostly ignored any counter-arguments, simply because I thought they were not important since I already had evidence to support my opinion. As I was learning more, I realized that the way I did my research was completely one-sided. I was sunk in my own beliefs and did not bother to look at the story from different sides. I remember one of the guest lecturers' words, "Self-research is not being self-absorbed". While I was doing the autoethnography assignment for this course, I actually understood what these words mean. Every story has a different side other than the one I can see, and I should consider the other perspectives to verify the truth. Even my personal experiences can be biased if I only look at it from my point of view.

This brings me to the most important lesson for me in the course—social media bias. We spent a good bit of time on the topic, and it really helped me to understand proper way to do critical thinking both for academic and personal research. Opportunists use these platforms to trigger users' biased thinking of political or religious issues. Nowadays, internet is the source of news for most people, including myself. Usually I get most of the current events through online news outlets, and my friends and families on social media. Learning about the filter bubble in social media was surprising, because I realized that my choices are not only affecting me but also the people I am connected to and vice versa. After knowing about how social media algorithm works to provide us the most viewed but not the most trusted news, I became more cautious and do some thinking before reacting to anything online.

I remember we talked about the CRAAP test to verify the credibility of sources. I started to notice the authors and the source's purpose before accepting the information. I believe this has definitely improved my research skills. The final group project actually tied up most of the topics together. While working on the project, the group members stayed unbiased and equally analyzed both supporting and contradicting evidences on the topic.

During the whole semester, what we practiced in HONR 2757 is to think outside of the box. We were encouraged to do critical thinking and analysis of the topics. The course contents really helped me to develop better research skills that I applied on other course materials as well, and received satisfying outcomes. Overall, the course helped me to understand the difference between research and confirming one's biases and the proper way of verifying the truth.

Conclusion

Keller (2014) discussed students' rhetorical moves on social media and other websites. He describes these behaviors as examples of "fast rhetoric" (p. 95), or rhetoric that responds to acceleration and speed and aims to better circulation of the content created or shared on these platforms. Even though he agreed with Faigley's argument for teaching slow rhetoric and asserts its benefits for students, he wondered at the missed opportunities of teaching and engaging students in fast rhetorics. Based on my experience teaching this course, I argue that insisting on teaching and valuing one form of rhetoric (slow) and intentionally overlooking the other (fast) form our classes isn't a sound pedagogical decision. The fast rhetoric is what students engage in all the time once they step outside our classrooms as both Dakota and Shifat confirm. By not talking to students about that rhetoric, we are leaving them unprepared and unequipped to properly deal with and practice fast-rhetoric skills. Engaging them in fast rhetoric, though, means that we are meeting them where they are, at the sites where they practice that rhetoric, and use these practices as a site of teaching and learning. This is what I've tried to do in this course by engaging students in looking closely at their fast-rhetoric social media practices (shares, comments, clicks, perceptions) and asking them to think more carefully and critically about these practices.

Teaching that course has been such a rewarding experience for me with lots of future pedagogical implications. I had to be responsive to students' needs and flexible about my lesson plans while teaching the course. Taking advantage of kairotic moments and connecting them to the course discussions, as what happened with the Lincoln Memorial incident viral videos, pushed me out of the comfort zone of my meticulously prepared course syllabus and schedule to embrace and welcome the chaos of political life into my pedagogy.

Building opportunities for immediate and delayed application of the concepts, skills, and tools we explored in the course was another invaluable lesson. As a writing professor, I'm always intentional in having practice and application times built into the fabric of my classes. In addition to the immediate application activities I discussed earlier, I used the response to guest lecturers assignment as a site for students to practice critical thinking. As Dakota mentions in his narrative, students were encouraged to disagree with what guest professors said and to support their counterargument with strong evidence that they collected through online search.

This transfer and repurposing of skills in various contexts suggests an important direction for future research: transfer of critical digital reading skills. Keller (2014) extensively discusses how the repurposing of prior knowledge can be useful in new contexts and argues that with the changing landscapes of literacy, our goal should extend to "helping students gain versatile, dexterous approaches to both reading and writing" that they can adapt and use in variety of contexts (p. 9). His argument opens the door to researching how the transfer of critical digital reading skills students develop in one class or context can be transferred and made useful in a new one. The anecdotal evidence from my class can be substantiated through empirical research that examines the transfer of these versatile critical digital reading skills beyond the classroom where they were learned and practiced.

Similarly, Carillo (2015) suggested two levels of transfer of reading skills: transfer from reading to writing in the same course, mostly to the assignment following a given reading, and transfer from reading in a first-year writing class to reading in other courses and in the disciplines. This multi-directional transfer is another candidate for future research that examines transfer between reading and writing in and outside a specific course, and critical digital reading in one course to other reading practices in and outside the classroom.

References

Amicucci, A. (2019, November 7). I hear a lot of versions of, "Well, they don't read any more, you know. Their attention spans are [Comment]. Facebook. https://bit.ly/2P3g7MZ

Bogost, I. (2019). Stop trusting viral videos. Retrieved from https://bit.ly/2P3g-7MZhttps://www.theatlantic.com/technology/archive/2019/01/viral-clash-students-and-native-americans-explained/580906/?fbclid=IwAR0qf4388f31cBuyT5l-ra9qqpPmQyXzRzTHv9V3HB2K-LiZBxNSzg6y3PWw

Buford, M. (2019, November 7). I'm not sure it makes sense to assume that any particular class can force any particular student to read. [Comment]. Facebook. https://bit.ly/2P3g7MZ

Carillo, E. C. (2015). Creating mindful readers in first-year composition courses: A strategy to facilitate transfer. *Pedagogy: Critical Approaches to Teaching Literature, Language, Composition, and Culture, 16*(1), 9–22. doi:10.1215/15314200-3158573.

Carillo, E. C. (2017). A place for reading in the framework for success in postsecondary writing: Recontextualizing the habits of mind. In N. N. Behm, S. Rankins-Robertson, & D. Roen (Eds.), *The framework for success in postsecondary writing: Scholarship and application* (pp. 38–53). Parlor Press.

Carillo, E. C. (2019). *MLA guide to digital literacy*. The Modern Language Association of America.

CRAAP test. (2020, January 29). In *Wikipedia*. https://en.wikipedia.org/wiki/CRAAP_test

Gagich, M. (2019, November 7). I hear a lot of complaints about students not reading (or not reading well) because they are too lazy to [Comment]. Facebook. https://bit.ly/2P3g7MZ

Horning, A. S. (2017). Enhancing the framework for success: Adding experiences in critical reading. In N. N. Behm, S. Rankins-Robertson, & D. Roen (Eds.), *The framework for success in postsecondary writing: Scholarship and applications* (pp. 54–68). Parlor Press.

Howard, R. M., & Jamieson, S. (2014). Researched writing. In G. Tate, A. R. Taggart, K. Schick, & H. B. Hessler (Eds.), *A guide to composition pedagogies* (pp. 231–247). Oxford University Press.

Jenkins, H., Ford, S., & Green, J. (2013). *Spreadable media: Creating value and meaning in a networked culture*. New York University Press.

Keller, D. (2014). *Chasing literacy: Reading and writing in an age of acceleration*. Utah State University Press.

Koettl, C. (n.d.) Citizen evidence lab: About & FAQ. Retrieved from https://citizenevidence.org/about/

Koettl, C. (2017). Citizen evidence lab: Toolbox. Retrieved from https://citizenevidence.org/toolbox/

McComiskey, B. (2017). *Post-truth rhetoric and composition*. Logan, UT: Utah State University Press.

McGrew, S., Ortega, T., Breakstone, J., & Wineburg, S. (2017). The challege that's bigger than fake news: Civic reasoning in a social media environment. *American Educator, 41*(3), 4–9. Retrieved from https://www.aft.org/ae/fall2017/mcgrew_ortega_breakstone_wineburg

media, a. f. (2019). Media bias chart 5.1. In (5 ed.): ad fontes media.

Miller, R. E. (2016). On digital reading. *Pedagogy: Critical Approaches to Teaching Literature, Language, Composition, and Culture, 16*(1), 153–164. doi:10.1215/15314200-3158717.

National Council of Teachers of English. (2019). Definition of literacy in a digital age. Retrieved from http://www2.ncte.org/statement/nctes-definition-literacy-digital-age/

Sorapure, M., Inglesby, P., & Yatchisin, G. (1998). Web literacy: Challenges and opportunities for research in a new medium. *Computers and Composition, 15*, 409–424.

The Oatmeal. *You're not going to believe what I'm about to tell you*. Retrieved from https://theoatmeal.com/comics/believe_clean

Vision statement: Why some videos go viral. (2015). *Harvard Business Review*, 34–35.

Wuebben, D. (2016). Getting likes, going viral, and the intersections between popularitymetrics and digital composition. *Computers and Composition, 42*, 66–79. doi:10.1016/j.compcom.2016.08.004.

8. Critical Science Literacy in the Writing Classroom: A Pedagogy for Post-Truth Times

ELLERY SILLS AND DANIEL KENZIE

Higher education today faces a potent threat: the phenomenon of post-truth politics. Defined by Oxford Dictionaries as "relating to or denoting circumstances in which objective facts are less influential in shaping public opinion than appeals to emotion and personal belief" (Post-truth, 2016), post-truth has challenged students' abilities to identify and evaluate information. In an era where social media frequently circulates so-called "fake news" into the public discourse, it can seem that "everything is true and nothing is true," since "an explanation of climate change from a Nobel Prize-winning physicist looks exactly the same on your Facebook page as the denier of climate change on the Koch brothers' payroll" (Remnick, 2016). In the midst of this credibility crisis, students can struggle to discriminate between facts and "alternative facts." This is a particular threat for literacy education; as Ellen Carillo (2018) unsettlingly questions, "In a culture that does not agree on the principles of evidence and rationality or on facts, how does one teach reading, writing, and thinking?" (p. 5). Clearly, post-truth is something that we, as educators, need to confront and challenge directly.

The question is how. Writing for *Inside Higher Education*, John Duffy (2017) argues that teaching argument in first-year writing courses can instill virtues of "honesty, accountability, fair-mindedness, and intellectual courage" (para. 5). Pointing to policy statements such as the *Framework for Success in Postsecondary Writing* and the *WPA Outcomes Statement*, Bruce McComiskey (2017) claims that educators "need to double-down on the values we have already articulated and published" (p. 43). In each case, the refrain is similar: educators should keep doing what they do best when teaching writing and argument. While we agree, we also believe that a robust response to post-truth requires extending our pedagogies past familiar traditions and into new territory.

In this chapter, we offer one such approach: the incorporation of *critical science literacy* (Priest, 2013; Gigante, 2014) into our writing classrooms. Susanna Priest presents critical science literacy as meta-knowledge of "'how science works' as a set of social practices and social institutions" (p. 139) and the "effective navigation skills" (p. 138) needed to act on that knowledge, as opposed to familiarity with accepted facts and scientific method. In her discussion of science writing pedagogy, Gigante connects critical science literacy to rhetorical training in writing, given the former's capacity to "sensitize students to different audiences and expose them to the moral concerns that arise in various situations" through "case-specific analysis" (p. 22). This parallel also applies to reading, as Priest herself discusses multiple reading behaviors: considering funding sources and potential biases, looking for multiple expert sources in a news story, checking the reputation and peer review process of a journal, and other cues beyond the data and methods themselves that even expert readers need to evaluate sources.

Moreover, both Priest and Gigante are concerned with making experts' tacit knowledge about how science works explicit, an aim that overlaps with efforts to make tacit behaviors of expert readers explicit. Horning (2011) argues that expert readers are "meta-readers [who] bring specific kinds of awareness and an array of skills" to reading a text: meta-textual awareness of organization and structure; meta-contextual awareness "of where the text comes from and how it fits into the larger scheme of things"; and meta-linguistic awareness of the text's language (p. 5). Similarly, Priest (2013) describes meta-knowledge necessary to "identify valid scientific truth claims," such as "recognizing that the conduct of science is a social process" and "understanding the assertion that some uncertainty always surrounds specific scientific claims" (p. 139). For more on how wrestling with uncertainty enriches students' reading practices, see Koupf, in this volume.

Our current moment makes the need to elaborate on critical science literacy in relation to writing and reading especially urgent. Priest (2013) suggests that what science literacy looks like in the context of abundant information and blurred distinctions between entertainment, news, and advertising is "overdue for further thought" (p. 140). We believe that our own efforts to attend to circulation in scientific texts can contribute to this further thought. Reading researchers like Ellen Carillo (2019) have warned against the persistent "reverence for texts" in educational literacy standards, a text-centric approach that "is especially worrying in a digital culture that already encourages a passive model of reading" (pp. 141, 145). In contrast, by examining the material-epistemic networks in which textual claims are embedded, our adoption of critical science literacy aims to bring a greater meta-contextual awareness of scientific texts to the fore.

We begin this chapter by assessing existing literature on post-truth and its relationship to science denial. As this literature indicates, post-truth politics and science denial pursue similar rhetorical strategies, namely, "a strategic use of indifference to truth" (Gudonis, 2017). We then establish how critical science literacy addresses science denial and, by extension, post-truth politics. Finally, we explore how pedagogical approaches to critical science literacy can be adapted to broadly different contexts and still share common goals in combating post-truth politics. In our different educational contexts (science writing and first-year writing, respectively), we jointly emphasize building a richer vocabulary for problematic information, attending to questions of circulation, and negotiating scientific (un)certainty claims. After outlining our practices in these contexts, we address their relevance for critical science literacy, as well as broader critical literacy goals, in the conclusion.

Science Denial, Post-truth, and Critical Science Literacy

Lee McIntyre (2018) writes that science denial precedes and informs post-truth. As he argues, science denial is "a road map for understanding post-truth," since decades of corporate-funded contrarian claims about tobacco's links to cancer, pollution, global warming, vaccination, and other scientific issues created a "blueprint" for current post-truth political and rhetorical practices (pp. 17, 22). In addition, both involve the challenge of experts by "legions of nonexperts who happen to disagree with them" (p. 17). Post-truth politics and science denial pursue similar rhetorical strategies, namely, the manufacturing of doubt and controversy over well-documented and verifiable realities. In this light, it makes sense to use counterstrategies designed to challenge science denial—such as critical science literacy—to address post-truth issues in the classroom, as well.

Pascal Diethelm and Martin McKee (2009) define denialism as "the employment of rhetorical arguments to give the appearance of legitimate debate where there is none, an approach that has the ultimate goal of rejecting a proposition on which a scientific consensus exists" (para. 5). They highlight five characteristics of denialism: the identification of conspiracies, the use of fake experts, selectivity, impossible expectations of what research can deliver, and the use of misrepresentation and logical fallacies. Deception and the "weaponization" of contrarian claims for ideological purposes are paramount. Conservative political consultant Frank Luntz's 2002 advice to

Republicans that "you need to make *the lack of scientific certainty* a primary issue" to stymie public consensus about climate change is a case in point (as quoted in Latour, 2004b, p. 226). Such tactics represent an effort to manufacture a scientific controversy, presenting a dissenting, denialist minority as "heroes in an unfolding scientific revolution, oppressed by mainstream scientists who are ideologically deaf to their appeals" (Ceccarelli, 2011, p. 198). Denialism distorts science into a power struggle, with two equally strong and compelling sides.

Post-truth, in this light, constitutes an extension of denialism: the employment of arguments to give the appearance of legitimate debate about reality where none exists. McComiskey (2017) calls post-truth "a state in which language lacks any reference to facts, truths, and realities," making language "a purely strategic medium" (p. 6). Although some scholars like Ari Rabin-Havt (2016) equate post-truth with simple deception and lying, Gudonis (2017) suggests that its "strategic use of the indifference to the truth" makes it distinctive (p. 146). While liars show great concern for the truth in their deceptive strategies, "the purveyor of post-truth makes no attempt to justify their comments or provide any corroborative evidence" (pp. 145–146). According to McIntyre (2018), post-truth also signifies a sharply partisan environment, in which picking a team can take priority over considering evidence, and disinformation can spread in broad daylight. Thus, for example, Donald Trump can tweet in 2012 that "the concept of global warming was created by and for the Chinese in order to make U.S. manufacturing non-competitive" with no corroborating evidence, and this claim is accepted by his followers at face value, with 24,831 retweets and 14,654 likes (Jacobson, 2016). Without visible counterarguments to address such claims, they can go entirely unchallenged.

Critical science literacy offers a means of addressing science denial—and, by extension, post-truth politics—in the writing classroom, in part by situating contrarian views that rely on efforts to manufacture scientific controversy. Priest (2013) suggests, for example, that attending to "social" factors, such as contrarians' political and economic interests in pursuing their claims, can help illuminate when and how contrarians lack credibility. The perspective offered by critical science literacy reveals these dynamics by encouraging readers and writers to look beyond what is evident in a text itself. Priest (2013) and Gigante (2014) rightly advocate for science majors to become more critically literate in order to contribute to the larger public's literacy. We agree but present our courses (taught at two different institutions) as efforts to improve critical science literacy for both science majors and non-majors at multiple levels.

First, Daniel Kenzie describes how a three-unit sequence in his upper-level writing course for science majors addresses social dimensions of science by having students build their vocabulary for problematic information, trace the circulation of information about a topic, and negotiate how to gauge and convey levels of certainty. Then, Ellery Sills describes lessons and practices from a unit on popular science documentary (with specific attention to the 2006 documentary *An Inconvenient Truth*) in his first-year writing course. In this unit, students use Latourian vocabulary of *matters of fact* and *matters of concern* to trace the circulation of public arguments surrounding the documentary. For both courses, we emphasize key objectives of critical science literacy, such as understanding how science works, understanding science as a social process, and understanding that uncertainty always surrounds scientific claims.

Writing in the Sciences

Over multiple semesters, I have prioritized critical science literacy in light of post-truth concerns by scaffolding relevant themes and lessons across assignments in a course called Writing in the Sciences. The main assignments are not centered around post-truth on their face, so the themes and lessons I discuss should be adaptable to a range of assignment sequences. My overarching goal has been to push the class beyond a traditional understanding of what scientific information is, how it is produced, and the spaces where it lives and moves. Writing in the Sciences fulfills a campus-wide upper-division writing requirement for juniors and seniors at my Midwestern, land-grant research university. Students major in varied fields, such as biology, chemistry, geology, natural resources management, horticulture, and psychology. While some students plan to become researchers, many plan to enter applied professions with some relationship to scientific research. I have used a four-project sequence: career materials (such as a resume and cover letter), an analysis of science accommodation (ASA) in which students locate a public report of a scientific finding and analyze how information was adapted from the original scholarly report, a literature review, and a feature article for a public audience. I will focus on the second, third, and fourth of these projects, as relevant threads are built over the course of this sequence.

At the start of the ASA, our textbook, *Writing in the Sciences* by Penrose and Katz (2010), lays the groundwork for recognizing the social and communicative dimensions of science before Fahnestock's (1998) classic article "Accommodating Science: The Rhetorical Life of Scientific Facts" elaborates on how scientific information is transformed for public audiences. As the literature review involves synthesizing scholarly research for a scientific audience, this unit elaborates further on "how science works," including topics such as scholarly peer review, debates over scientific publishing and predatory journals (Green & Speed, 2018), the role of academic organizations, and how to read IMRaD reports purposefully for their implicit and explicit arguments. Then, students are encouraged to write their feature articles on the same topic as the literature review as they delve further into public communication. Below, I discuss three major themes that develop over the course of this assignment sequence to cultivate critical science literacy: building vocabulary, tracing circulation, and negotiating uncertainty.

Building Vocabulary

Terms like "fake news" are limiting because they set up a binary: news is either "fake" or not. Similarly, "bias" is only so useful because a source is either "biased" or not (or can perhaps be attributed with degrees of bias). Such binaries are only so useful for addressing post-truth concerns because they flatten differences among misleading information sources that are important to how we respond to them. For students to have a more sophisticated understanding of problematic information, they need a richer vocabulary. To that end, my students read the *Lexicon of Lies*, an overview published by the Data and Society Research Institute of different types of problematic information (Jack, 2017). The *Lexicon* defines and distinguishes misinformation, disinformation, propaganda, and gaslighting, among others, while describing complexities of how this information circulates and how information is labeled with one category or another. Students also read an article about Discovery Channel mockumentaries suggesting that the National Oceanographic and Atmospheric Association (NOAA) covered up the existence of mermaids (Thaler & Shiffman, 2015). Thaler and Shiffman suggest that such programs undermine trust in institutions and lend credence to campaigns such as climate change denial that benefit from that slip in trust.

In class, we apply language from the *Lexicon* to classify provided texts, while discussing the limitations of any categories and the often-subjective nature of what counts as what. As Priest (2013) suggests, innocent mistakes and intentional fraud can often be separated by a fine line, and public judgments often draw on inferences of character and motive beyond scientific evidence. In class, we watch Vox's coverage of a *Shark Week* segment suggesting the prehistoric shark Megalodon may still exist, which was controversial for many of the same reasons as the mermaid programs (Stromberg & Fong, 2014). In addition to discussing which kind of problematic information the segment is and what those terms capture about the show, the class also considers whether they would choose to run it. While students disagree about the best decision, their discussion demonstrates that any decision about specific problematic presentation involves a mix of factors related to audience, genre, ethics, economics, and the law. Building vocabulary for these factors and for rhetorically varied types of problematic information means developing a concrete framework for both meta-textual and meta-contextual awareness of that information.

Tracing Circulation

Once students have built a vocabulary for problematic information, they begin to consider how it circulates through media. During the feature article unit, student groups work in class to look up popular reports on their topics and consider where these reports are being circulated; which institutions, authorities, or communities promote or believe it; what the motivations of those actors might be; students' own reasons for trusting these sources or not; and how algorithms might be at work to promote or hide certain content (for more on "how information finds us," see Lawrence, 2020, this volume). These questions add to traditional ways of evaluating sources by reconstructing what philosopher Gloria Origgi (2018) calls the "reputational path" of a piece of information, including "the intentions of those who circulated it" and "the agendas of those authorities that leant it credibility." Such analyses draw critical attention toward "the social network of relations that has shaped that content and given it a certain deserved or undeserved 'rank' in our system of knowledge" (Origgi, 2018, para. 9).

Tracing this reputational path in groups allows students to see how this circulation plays out with multiple topics, including those with varying levels of controversy or political baggage (student topics span a wide range, such as biofuels, antibiotic resistance, coconut oil, and plastic pollution). After interrogating possible sources for their project and their own relationships to those sources, students then justify their own rhetorical strategies based on their observations about their topics' information ecology. This accounting of circulation is increasingly necessary in an environment with fewer resources going into formal journalism (Priest, 2013) and information relying on lay users to contribute to its spread, making it important for scientists, journalists, and the public to be circulation-literate. This activity also supplements a close reading of cues within individual texts with a wider reading that puts those texts in dialogue with others.

Negotiating Uncertainty

One of Priest's (2013) elements of critical science literacy is understanding the idea that some uncertainty always accompanies scientific claims. Students begin to explore uncertainty in the science accommodation unit by classifying levels of certainty in claims, often directly comparing similar claims between their scholarly and popular sources. As one assigned reading, a page about climate change science by the Union of Concerned Scientists (2010), puts it, "To most of us, uncertainty means not knowing. To scientists, however, uncertainty is how well something is known" (para. 2). Fahnestock (1986) borrows Latour and Woolgar's (1979) statement types to classify levels of certainty, where level 1 statements are outright speculation and level 5 statements are so accepted as fact that they are left unstated. Fahnestock demonstrates that claims tend to become more certain when accommodated for a public audience, because scientists increase their credibility with each other by carefully situating and hedging their claims, while public audiences are more impressed by bolder claims. This analytical point gives students a hypothesis to test out with their own research articles and popular reports, tracking the level of certainty of individual claims and interpreting the reasons and impact of those wording choices. This focused reading of fine-tuned word choice promotes meta-linguistic awareness (Horning, 2011) of disciplinary values behind qualifying language, as well as the "active, purposeful reading" (Davies, 2017, p. 177) needed to fully engage with scientific texts.

The feature article unit has students transfer the "skills in analysis" they developed while reading for certainty levels to "skills in application" (Horning, 2011, pp. 7–8). As students prepare their articles, class discussions address how most topics are a mix of aspects with differing levels of certainty. Uncertainties can be productive or misleading depending on how they are deployed, and there are tradeoffs between being transparent about uncertainties versus simplifying truth claims for public audiences requiring careful language choices. Readings include the Union of Concerned Scientists page, which delineates aspects of climate change for which there are particular levels of certainty, and a *New York Times* piece (Revkin, 2012) covering Walker and Walsh's (2012) rhetorical research into Rachel Carson's *Silent Spring*. Walsh and Walker suggest Carson used uncertainty productively to invite public participation, rather than sow doubt. At the same time, numerous well-documented examples show how uncertainty can be co-opted in the move from the technical to the public sphere to cast doubt on good science.

Once we discuss these readings as a group, students are asked to apply the ideas to their project with questions such as, "Based on your literature review, how would you describe the level of technical certainty on your topic?" and

"How do you plan to communicate the certainty level to a public audience in your feature article?" Key to this discussion is the idea that a larger phenomenon can accord a high level of certainty, while a causal relationship between that phenomenon and a specific event (such as climate change and a specific storm) is trickier. This point is especially important for the feature article, since narrative involves dramatizing specific events. Thus, students not only develop a nuanced idea of uncertainty, but get practice making concrete decisions about conveying uncertainties.

Science Documentary, Bruno Latour and the First-Year Writing Classroom

In spring 2017, I taught a first-year writing (FYW) course, the second semester of a full-year composition sequence, at a land-grant research university in the Southwest. This course was organized around the theme "Believing is Seeing: Documentary, Rhetoric, and Public Engagement," presenting documentary film as a new way to consider researched writing: as a public engagement with the world. One unit of this course emphasized the popular science documentary as a way of addressing critical science literacy and scientific argumentation (both verbal and visual). During this unit, students rhetorically analyzed the climate change documentary *An Inconvenient Truth* (Guggenheim et al., 2006) by drawing from science studies scholarship, particularly the work of Bruno Latour. Introducing Latour provided a vocabulary that presents science as a social process, illuminated the role of networks and circulation in scientific appeals, and revealed "uncertainty as an ingredient of crises in the environment" (Latour, 2004a, p. 63).

Students viewed *An Inconvenient Truth* in order to complicate their understanding of what constitutes a scientific argument. *An Inconvenient Truth* largely films former Vice President Al Gore's delivery of a well-honed slide show on climate change, interspersed with personal interviews with Gore and images of ongoing ecological catastrophe. Rather than presenting the documentary as a purely factual account of climate change, the course engaged in a network tracing of the film's arguments and climate change deniers' counterarguments, effectively immersing itself in the wider public debate about the film's factual accuracy. This debate included considerations of whether "factual accuracy" is the most relevant criterion for judging the film's truthfulness and credibility, and if not, what criteria we should be using instead.

The work in the unit consisted of four parts: (1) Reading rhetorical and science studies scholarship, especially Latour; (2) screening and discussing *An*

Inconvenient Truth; (3) tracing the networks of scientific truth claims from, and surrounding, the film; and (4) writing a rhetorical analysis that considers the film in relation to these networks.

Reading Latour

Reading excerpts of Latour's (2004b) "Why Has Critique Run Out of Steam?" informed our subsequent discussion of scientific uncertainty and network tracing, as well as providing a vocabulary to interrogate contrarian scientific truth claims. Latour (2004b) addresses scientific uncertainty when pointing to Luntz's emphasis on the "lack of scientific uncertainty" surrounding climate change (as quoted in p. 226). For Latour, Luntz's framing belies a fundamental distortion in what scientific uncertainty entails. In discussing this article with my students, I connected it with the critical science literacy objective that uncertainty always surrounds scientific truth claims. I stressed that an artificially maintained controversy over global warming persists to this day, with the polemical deployment of "facts" on either "side" of the controversy, both wielding absolute professions of "certainty" (on behalf of the scientific consensus on climate change) and "uncertainty" (on behalf of the minority of climate denialists).

A vocabulary that avoids this impasse, however, includes Latour's notions of *matters of fact* and *matters of concern*. Matters of fact are rhetorical constructions that purport to be "[t]he indisputable ingredients of sensation and experimentation" (Latour, 2004a, p. 244). The word that gives away the game is *indisputable*; because matters of fact will not admit to interrogation and shut down public debate, Latour (2004b) deems them shallow descriptions of scientific issues, "very polemical, very political renderings of matters of concern" (p. 232). Matters of concern, on the other hand, are not immune from dispute. Because they gather an assemblage of human and nonhuman actants in addressing an issue of vital *concern*, they necessarily invite questions of scientific and deliberative uncertainty. In our case, discussing climate change, as critically literate student-citizens, required us to examine scientific claims circulating urgently throughout the wider public sphere; moreover, it required us to consider that these claims may be better described as *matters of concern*, rather than *facts*. This Latourian vocabulary offered a starting point for students' network tracing.

Discussing and Network Tracing An Inconvenient Truth

Jenny Rice (2012) describes network tracing as a practice that "requires one to reflect on the relational processes and linkages that form a network"

(p. 171). By using network tracing for arguments in the film whose accuracy has been challenged, we could reconstruct these factual appeals as matters of concern. In addition, network tracing privileged students' meta-contextual reading awareness (Horning, 2011). Instead of limiting students' analysis to a single text (*An Inconvenient Truth*), I asked them to analyze particular claims that then circulate across texts. Attending to this circulation allowed students to see *An Inconvenient Truth* "as part of an on-going conversation about key issues or ideas," achieve a better understanding of each claim, and evaluate these claims against the supporting or competing claims found in other texts (Horning, 2011, p. 5).

To illustrate this affordance of meta-contextual awareness, I will focus on one scientific appeal from *An Inconvenient Truth*, whose "afterlife" we traced: the connection Al Gore draws between warming oceans and the increase of stronger storms, such as Hurricane Katrina in 2005. In discussing this appeal with my students, I encouraged them to explore the larger assemblages within which this appeal worked. First, we read the decision for the British court case *Dimmock v. Secretary of State for Education & Skills* (2007). This case involved a legal action against the UK's Department for Education for planning to distribute copies of *An Inconvenient Truth* to secondary schools in order to educate students about climate change. In the decision, Justice Burton determined that there were nine factual "errors" in the film that marked it as a political film subject to the requirement of balance; one of these errors, Justice Burton claimed, is that "Hurricane Katrina and the subsequent devastation in New Orleans are ascribed to global warming. It is common ground that there is insufficient evidence to show that" (para. 31).

This court case introduced students to the larger debate over the film's factual accuracy. In terms of the film's circulation, they were able to see how the question of scientific uncertainty was being negotiated. In the documentary, uncertainty about the relationship between global warming and any particular weather event nonetheless gave rise to an assertion about the relationship vis-à-vis Katrina. In the court case, on the other hand, this same uncertainty led Justice Burton to conclude that the assertion was an "error."

Next, we read a variety of documents related to *An Inconvenient Truth* and the British court case: news reports and editorials from the left-leaning *Guardian* and the right-leaning *Daily Mail*, climate science blogs, and arguments made by The Heartland Institute, a climate change denialist think tank. On the one hand, climate scientists such as oceanography professor John Shepherd claimed that "[t]o refer to 'nine scientific errors' is itself a considerable misrepresentation of the facts" (Shepherd & Rapley, 2007, p. 4). The Heartland Institute, on the other hand, asserted that *An Inconvenient Truth* is "riddled with misleading exaggerations and factual errors" (Taylor, 2007). Students were thereby exposed to the polemical circulation of competing assertions as "facts" in a wider, artificially maintained controversy over global warming.

This kind of network tracing allowed students to trace the legal, political, and scientific bodies *gathered* by Al Gore's scientific truth claim about Hurricane Katrina, and they learned to identify the interests and ideological affiliations of several of the parties involved. For example, they learned that Stuart Dimmock, who brought the suit against the Secretary of State and is described as a concerned parent, was a candidate for the UK New Party, "a small anti-regulation, low-taxation political party whose Chairman, quarry owner Robert Durward, was a co-founder of the Scientific Alliance, a UK-based lobby group which challenges the scientific consensus on climate change" (Mellor, 2009, p. 137). In addition, they learned that The Heartland Institute was previously funded by Phillip Morris to challenge the links between smoking, secondhand smoking, and lung cancer, thus rendering its credibility highly suspect. This is what Venturini (2015) calls connecting "statements to debates" in the network tracing of controversies, or "controversy mapping" (p. 79).

Writing the Rhetorical Analysis

In writing their rhetorical analyses, students were expected to connect the scientific truth claims of *An Inconvenient Truth* to the larger debate surrounding climate change. They were asked to address the circulation of arguments supporting and challenging the film in relation to vocabulary from our readings (including Latour), issues of scientific uncertainty, and their own network tracing. Students generally acknowledged that accuracy claims have not "settled the matter" of global warming in any practical or political sense. Their network tracing frequently helped them articulate that the science of global warming was more nuanced than the popular debate around the film frequently evidenced. They also frequently identified the impoverished credibility of global warming denialists, based on these critics' weaker networks and conflicts of interest. Certainly, some students disputed the science of climate change entirely and attempted to find credible networks to support their claims (with limited success). However, other students recognized that the language of *concern* might do rhetorical work that the language of *facts* could not. In this way, students learned how Latourian vocabulary, network tracing, and a clear understanding of scientific uncertainty could help them to "navigate a world full of competing truth claims about science" (Priest, 2013, p. 144).

Conclusion

Although the contexts of our FYW and writing in the sciences courses differed, these courses shared common goals in cultivating critical science literacy and addressing post-truth. They also shared common strategies in building new vocabulary for reading scientific texts, tracing the circulation of these texts and their claims, and negotiating scientific uncertainty. In this conclusion, we will discuss the implications of these strategies for students' critical science literacy, their understanding of science denial and manufactured controversy, and their broader literacy practices.

First, in introducing vocabulary that foregrounds identifying problematic information, we offered students a more nuanced perspective on both scientists' rhetorical practice ("how science works") and its co-option by denialist interests. Dan's explicit focus on problematic information using the *Lexicon of Lies* moved students beyond binaries of "true" or "fake." Ellery's Latourian vocabulary of *matters of fact* and *matters of concern*, similarly, eschewed absolute claims of "certainty" or "uncertainty" and instead attended to the relative degrees of instability in constructing scientific facts. In each case, we worked toward a broader meta-textual and meta-contextual framework for scientific *ethos*.

Second, in tracing the circulation of scientific texts, we invited students to challenge the "reverence for texts" Carillo (2019) warns against. In tracing the "reputational path" of scientific arguments, Dan's students gained more sophisticated skills in evaluating the wider social ecologies of scientific sources. Ellery's students, likewise, used network tracing to interrogate factual appeals across texts, thereby aiding their meta-contextual awareness.

Finally, in addressing how uncertainty always surrounds scientific claims, we helped students to distinguish appropriate and inappropriate deployments of uncertainty in the public sphere. While denialists often point to scientific uncertainty as a cause for controversy and perpetual impasse, teaching students about different levels of scientific uncertainty promoted a meta-linguistic awareness of disciplinary values and a meta-contextual awareness of the misuse and abuse of uncertainty in popular arguments. Uncertainty became a "site of public participation," rather than a magic formula for banishing uncomfortable subjects (Walker & Walsh, 2012).

Given the challenges that post-truth poses to higher education and to democracy, educators must use every weapon at their disposal to combat it.

In this chapter, we have suggested that our adoption of critical science literacy is one such weapon. By working through the social dimensions of science, the rhetorical circulation of information and images, and analyzing and practicing the translation of technical uncertainties for public audiences, students prepare to be professionals and citizens capable of evaluating truth claims and promoting the common good. This kind of preparation makes critical science literacy a pedagogy for post-truth times.

References

Carillo, E. C. (2018). *Teaching readers in post-truth America*. Utah State University Press.

Carillo, E. C. (2019). Navigating this perfect storm: Teaching critical reading in the face of the Common Core state standards, fake news, and Google. *Pedagogy, 19*(1), 135–159. doi:10.1215/15314200-7173805.

Ceccarelli, L. (2011). Manufactured scientific controversy: Science, rhetoric, and public debate. *Rhetoric & Public Affairs, 14*(2), 195–228.

Davies, L. J. (2017). Getting to the root of the problem: Teaching reading as a process in the sciences. In A. S. Horning, D. Gollnitz, & C. R. Haller (Eds.), *What is college reading?* (pp. 161–181). The WAC Clearinghouse and University Press of Colorado. http://wac.colostate.edu/books/atd/collegereading

Diethelm, P., & McKee, M. (2009). Denialism: What is it and how should scientists respond? *The European Journal of Public Health, 19*(1), 2–4. doi:10.1093/eurpub/ckn139.

Dimmock v. Secretary of State for Education & Skills. (2007). EWHC 288 (Admin) (10 October).

Duffy, J. (2017, May). Post-truth and first-year writing. *Inside Higher Education.* https://www.insidehighered.com/views/2017/05/08/first-year-writing-classes-can-teach-students-how-make-fact-based-arguments-essay

Fahnestock, J. (1986). Accommodating science: The rhetorical life of scientific facts. *Written Communication, 3*(3), 275–296.

Gigante, M. E. (2014). Critical science literacy for science majors: Introducing future scientists to the communicative arts. *Bulletin of Science, Technology & Society, 34*(3–4), 77–86.

Green, J., & Speed, E. (2018). Critical analysis, credibility, and the politics of publishing in an era of "fake news." *Critical Public Health, 28*(2), 129–131.

Gudonis, M. (2017). How useful is the concept of post-truth in analyzing genocide denial?: Analysis of online comments on the Jebwadne massacre. *Zoon Politikon, 8*, 141–182. doi:10.4467/2543408xzop.17.006.9265.

Guggenheim, D., David, L., Bender, L., Burns, S. Z., Skoll, J., Chilcott, L., Ivers, J., Strauss, R., Weyerman, D. (Producers), & Guggenheim, D. (Director). (2006). *An inconvenient truth* [Motion picture]. United States: Lawrence Bender Productions. https://www.amazon.com

Horning, A. S. (2011). Where to put the manicules: A theory of expert reading. *Across the Disciplines, 8*(2), 1–18. https://wac.colostate.edu/docs/atd/articles/horning2011.pdf

Jack, C. (2017). *Lexicon of lies: Terms for problematic information.* Data & Society. https://datasociety.net/output/lexicon-of-lies/

Jacobson, L. (2016, June). Yes, Donald Trump did call climate change a Chinese hoax. *Politifact.* https://www.politifact.com/truth-o-meter/statements/2016/jun/03/hillaryclinton/yes-donald-trump-did-call-climate-change-chinese-h/

Koupf, D. (2020). Factual dispute: Teaching rhetoric and complicating fact-checking with *The Lifespan of a Fact.* In E. C. Carillo & A. S. Horning (Eds.), *Teaching critical reading and writing in the era of fake news.* Peter Lang.

Latour, B. (2004a). *Politics of nature.* Harvard University Press.

Latour, B. (2004b). Why has critique run out of steam?: From matters of fact to matters of concern. *Critical Inquiry, 30*(2), 225–248.

Latour, B., & Woolgar, S. (1979). *Laboratory life: The construction of scientific facts.* Princeton University Press.

Lawrence, D. (2020). How information finds us: Hyper-targeting and digital advertising in the writing classroom. In E. C. Carillo & A. S. Horning (Eds.), *Teaching critical reading and writing in the era of fake news.* Peter Lang.

McComiskey, B. (2017). *Post-truth rhetoric and composition.* Utah State University Press.

McIntyre, L. (2018). *Post-truth.* MIT Press.

Mellor, F. (2009). The politics of accuracy in judging global warming films. *Environmental Communication, 3*(2), 134–150.

Origgi, G. (2018, March). Say goodbye to the information age: It's all about reputation now. *Aeon.* https://aeon.co/ideas/say-goodbye-to-the-information-age-its-all-about-reputation-now

Penrose, A. M., & Katz, S. B. (2010). *Writing in the sciences: Exploring conventions of scientific discourse* (3rd ed.). Longman.

Post-truth. (2016). *Oxford Dictionaries.* https://en.oxforddictionaries.com/definition/post-truth

Priest, S. (2013). Critical science literacy: What citizens and journalists need to know to make sense of science. *Bulletin of Science, Technology & Society, 33*(5–6), 138–145.

Rabin-Havt, A. (2016). *Lies, incorporated: The world of post-truth politics.* Anchor.

Remnick, D. (2016, November). Obama reckons with a Trump presidency. *The New Yorker.* www.newyorker.com/magazine/2016/11/28/obama-reckons-with-a-trump-presidency

Revkin, A. C. (2012, September). How Rachel Carson spurred chemical concerns by highlighting uncertainty. *The New York Times.* https://dotearth.blogs.nytimes.com/2012/09/27/how-rachel-carson-spurred-chemical-controls-by-highlighting-uncertainty

Rice, J. (2012). *Distant publics*. University of Pittsburgh Press.
Shepherd, J., & Rapley, C. (2007, October). *Al Gore versus Mr Justice Barton: A personal evaluation*. http://www.cpi.cam.ac.uk/gore/pdf/Al%20Gore%20versus%20Mr%20Justice%20Barton1.pdf
Stromberg, J., & Fong, J. (2014, August). Is Megalodon real? *Shark Week*, debunked. *Vox*. https://www.vox.com/2014/8/12/5994479/shark-week-debunked
Taylor, J. (2007, December). Gore film is partisan, riddled with errors, U.K. court rules. https://www.heartland.org/news-opinion/news/gore-film-is-partisan-riddled-with-errors-uk-court-rules
Thaler, A. D., & Shiffman, D. (2015). Fish tales: Combating fake science in popular media. *Ocean & Coastal Management, 115*, 88–91.
Union of Concerned Scientists. (2010, March). Certainty vs. uncertainty: Understanding scientific terms about climate change. https://www.ucsusa.org/resources/understanding-scientific-terms-about-climate-change
Venturini, T. (2015). Designing controversies and their publics. *Design Issues, 31*(3), 74–87.
Walker, K., & Walsh, L. (2012). "No one yet knows what the ultimate consequences may be": How Rachel Carson transformed scientific uncertainty into a site for public participation in *Silent Spring*. *Journal of Business and Technical Communication, 26*(1), 3–34. doi:10.1177/1050651911421122.

9. The Resurgence of the Pacific Northwest Tree Octopus: How Instructors Can Use New Media to Increase Students' Awareness of Fake News

JESSICA SLENTZ REYNOLDS AND STEPHANIE JARRETT

In the 1990s, Lyle Zapato created a website (still extant) that presented the world with the elusive Pacific Northwest Tree Octopus (Zapato, 2018). This internet hoax found its way into literacy classrooms and was used as a strategy to teach students to question the reliability of the internet (Leu et al., 2011). In an increasingly open and accessible digital world, there are many opportunities for tree octopuses to hide among the vast amounts of information available to students in postsecondary contexts. This frequent access to information with limited knowledge on how to examine and assess text may inhibit a student's ability to "participate fully and appropriately in the broad range of social and professional digital communities available to them" (Blaj-Ward & Winter, 2019, p. 880). As we begin the third decade of the 21st century, many traditional college students do not remember a world without smartphones, fast internet, or instant communication. This is a time where students are more likely to get their news and homework help from social media sites and Google, rather than from their instructors. Brumberger (2011) referred to these students as "digital natives," or "millennial learners who have grown up with ... new technologies ... connect with friends and family through social networking, text messaging, and other technology-mediated approaches" (p. 19). These are also the students referred to throughout this chapter.

Reading and writing instructors from all levels are now tasked with preparing students, these digital natives, to interpret, analyze, and apply rhetorical strategies to texts well beyond traditional modes of communication. People have decoded nontraditional texts prior to the 21st century. However, no other generation has been inundated with the surplus of information, both real and fake, and almost always digital, as those born after 1995. Because of the rapid influx of both real and fake news, reading and writing instructors need to teach students transferable strategies they can apply to texts in and out of the classroom.

In this chapter, readers will find two interconnected units that were implemented in a postsecondary Integrated Reading and Writing (IRW) course. The focal purpose of these units was to create a semester project to introduce students to think of text beyond a traditional or academic sense and provide them with transferable strategies for application to make meaning within the context of their own lives. Following the completion of the project, students were asked to complete a written reflection on their reading and writing processes. These reflections demonstrated an increase in students' abilities to recognize, analyze, and synthesize information in the era of fake news.

This chapter also offers readers a look into our data collection process, our analysis, findings, and implications for future research. We provide practical tools and resources to implement in the classroom, and we hope to inspire others to continue to research students, media, and the evolution of reading and writing instruction within the 21st century. Finally, we seek to inform readers that literacy instruction can be viewed as an act that transcends formal education and offers students a chance to develop necessary rhetorical skills that have shown to be essential in today's fake news landscape.

Instructional Context

For this chapter, we studied a developmental reading course that implemented an IRW model. The course was taught by one of the authors of this chapter. The course sequence and major projects for the course were developed by both authors of this chapter. Though developmental reading courses are more prevalent in community colleges, the class we focused on took place at a 4-year, emerging research institution in central Texas. This university has a population of nearly 40,000 students and is classified as a Hispanic Serving Institution (HSI) with 39% of its population identifying as Hispanic. However, over 50% of the class population we refer to in this chapter identified as Hispanic.

As practitioners in the field of developmental education, we witness the struggle students often endure when faced with the literacy expectations of higher education. The majority of faculty assume students are prepared for college-level reading and writing, and students assume they enter college knowing how to read and produce college-level material. Consequently, both parties are distraught when their expectations are not met. Developmental reading instructors often play the mediator in this sometimes problematic scenario. Specifically, we often find that developmental reading instructors must simultaneously provide students with basic college-level literacy skills while helping them enter and engage with what Gee (2015) refers to as Academic D/discourses (an overview of the significance of Gee's use of an upper— or lower-case "D" is below). Currently, developmental reading instructors are tasked with the responsibility of helping students better understand the rapid whirlwind of information they are consuming and processing with every glance at the screen. These instructors must also evolve from experts in their disciplines to experts in exploring and engaging with new media.

Epistemological Components of Integrated Reading and Writing Instruction

Provoked by the basic writing "crisis" Shor (1997) addressed regarding racial and social injustices in education, specifically within writing instruction, Goen and Gillotte-Tropp (2003) argued students enrolled in developmental reading courses would benefit from instruction that combines reading and writing. Tierney and Pearson (1983) supported this approach by asserting that reading and writing are both acts of composing. Components of the writing process are not limited to producing text, but also play a crucial role in consuming text (Tierney & Pearson, 1983).

A central focus for developmental reading instruction addresses students' abilities to transfer knowledge and literacy skills to effectively communicate within specific groups (Bartholomae & Petrosky, 1986; Goen & Gillotte-Tropp, 2003; Lea & Street, 2006). Another facet of the IRW model follows Alexander's (2005) assertion that to get students to engage with reading and writing, educators should encourage lifelong literacy by making their coursework and readings engaging and interesting. Bartholomae and Petrosky (1986) suggested reading instructors use their courses to help students uncover their voices in academia, and that reading and writing courses "cannot begin by telling students what to say and must provide a method to enable students to see what they have said—to see and characterize the acts of reading and writing represented by their discourse" (p. 7). Essentially, Bartholomae and Petrosky emphasized how postsecondary literacy courses can give students a voice in academia they were unaware they possessed.

Integrated Reading and Writing in the 2010s

To continue to achieve what Bartholomae and others presented as fundamental principles of developmental reading in a post Y2K world, instructors need to get creative. Not only do instructors need to cover student learning outcomes and adhere to state mandates, but they must immerse themselves into discourses that can be uncomfortable, but essential, to serve students. Film and television have been used in courses for decades and are just a fraction of what constitutes new media. Now, smartphone apps like Twitter, Instagram, TikToK, and SnapChat are the places students go for news and to keep up with friends and family. Knowing this vital information about students makes it essential to integrate new media literacies, along with critical literacy, within reading and writing intensive courses.

When access to information was limited and the internet was not as widely available, critical literacy development was dependent on the interactions and the context in which they occurred. Critical literacy, as defined by Shor (1999) influences the questioning of power relations, discourses, and identities in the world around us and therefore "challenges the status quo in an effort to discover alternative paths for self and social development" (p. 2). In a time when students have immediate access to information, it is more important than ever to discuss the global, local, economic, and political perspectives that inform every aspect of media available to students. One prime example of this phenomenon was apparent during the 2016 presidential election.

Following the 2016 presidential election, the term "fake news" became a commonly used phrase in popular culture. As consumers of text, people are inundated with news that may or may not be accurately representing or depicting information. Sometimes, even the most expert readers fall victim to the falsities that fake news offers. In her chapter in this volume, for example, Angela Laflen suggests that fake news stories can often emulate the look and titles of professional sources. To increase students' abilities to identify fake news, like the aforementioned Pacific Northwest Tree Octopus, instructors should integrate course components that support the critical analysis of text. However, these components do not need to only represent traditional academic texts, as Chris Anson and Kendra Andrews point out in their chapter in this volume about students' informal research. Similarly, components of the course discussed in this chapter motivate students to critically analyze texts within their various communities and social contexts, to question how everyday texts shape identity, and to recognize implicit power dynamics imposed by these texts.

Academic and Personal Identities: A False Dilemma

To explain how students' various communities and affiliations influence the multiple facets of their language and literacy processes, we refer to Gee's (2015) term D/discourses. To clarify, the term Discourse (with a capital D) signifies a recognized group of people, identified by language, interactions, beliefs and values (Gee, 2015). Whereas discourse (lowercase d) is an emphasis on the specific lexis used within Discourses (Gee, 2015). According to Gee (1990), assimilation within a Discourse community, "is a socially accepted association among ways of using language, thinking, feeling, believing, valuing, and of acting that can be used to identify oneself as a member of a socially meaningful group or 'social network', or to signal (that one is playing) a socially meaningful 'role'" (p. 143). This concept becomes increasingly important in a developmental classroom setting, as students who are deemed "developmental" can experience unique struggles when attempting to integrate into the literacy expectations of higher education.

However, we complicate Gee's assertions because one of the key objections for the project provided in this chapter is to promote a crossover of D/discourses. We do not want students to think their academic and personal D/discourses are dichotomous. The exchanges they have between friends and family do not need to be separated from their exchanges with peers and professors. The project provided in this chapter sought to provide a connection between students' multiple identities through using information relevant to them, like popular media, to promote the growth of a new identity. The project's goal was to help students develop a new identity that synchronously supported and represented students' personal and academic growth.

To connect students' current digital identities to their emerging academic identities, instructors can utilize current media to develop students' abilities to recognize, analyze and synthesize current media. Consequently, the development of students' academic literacy can forge a common and critical discourse that is centered around their lives within popular media to support their personal, academic growth and critical consciousness (Morrell & Duncan-Andrade, 2002). Therefore, our goal for this project was to utilize popular media to help students transfer knowledge and make connections between their preexisting literacies to academic literacies. Overall, we wanted to facilitate nontraditional instructional approaches that offered students multiple ways to develop fundamental rhetorical skills. Students, then, could apply these skills to better navigate digital landscapes influenced by fake news.

Project Implementation

We implemented two major units into one IRW course to create a semester project that demonstrated how the integration of social media, music, film, and television can help students learn college-level reading and writing skills and, in turn, transfer these skills to academic texts. The epistemological choices within this specific IRW model are supported by current college composition practices and new media studies (George, 2014; Gifford Brooke, 2014; Stahl & Armstrong, 2017; Thaiss & McLeod, 2014; Zimmerman et al., 2018). After the completion of the project, we found the integration of students' social D/discourses (Gee, 2015) can lead to an increase in students' understanding and engagement with processing information in and out of the classroom.

Legislative Impact

Fall 2017 brought new changes for developmental education in Texas (Texas Higher Education Coordinating Board [THECB], 2018). A state mandate determined that 75% of students enrolled in developmental education must earn their developmental credits through a corequisite model (THECB, 2018). The Texas Higher Education Coordinating Board (2018) explained the corequisite model as "[allowing students] to enroll in the entry-level college course but requires co-enrollment in a developmental education course/intervention designed to support the student's successful completion of the college-level course" (n.p.). Our institution chose to align IRW with freshman-level history.

Therefore, instructors of this course were now tasked with helping students make connections across disciplines, introduce them to academic literacies, and most importantly, give them the necessary tools to be active readers and writers in contexts outside of academia. Horning and Kraemer (2013) proposed that developmental reading should break away from a traditional skill and drill model. Like Horning and Kraemer's epistemological view of developmental reading, we knew we wanted a course design that emphasized a holistic and current approach to teaching college-level reading and writing. We started designing the course just shy of one year following the 2016 presidential election, an election where social media was considered a major influence on the election's outcome. The rapid influx of news, both real and fake, in students' lives led us to feel accountable toward helping them understand the great responsibility they hold as consumers and producers of information. We felt compelled to help students understand how their consumption of information, typically via smartphones, and in turn their production of information, impacts their identities, lives, communities, and futures.

The following tables are assignment descriptions for the unit criteria for developing digital natives' academic literacy through the investigation of multiple sources. Table 9.1 presents the criteria for an expository unit. Table 9.2 presents the criteria for an argumentative unit. The argumentative unit interconnects with the expository unit.

Table 9.1:   Expository Unit

Expository Unit

Purpose: Traditionally, students find history courses in college to be an unexpected challenge. In high school, students can often excel in history class by remembering facts and dates. However, college history courses challenge students to explain the significance of historical events through the perspective of significant figures (people) who experienced an era or event firsthand. Therefore, this assignment asks you to analyze just **one** aspect of the Civil Rights Movement and can be viewed as an introduction to **how** to read and write effectively for a history course.

Assignment Instructions: Since the Civil Rights Movement is an era consisting of a multitude of significant figures and historical moments, you will choose a specific population, organization, or event from the Civil Rights Movement as the focus of your project—think of this as your topic. Once you have selected your topic, you will need to start looking for a primary source (a firsthand account of your topic), a secondary source (what someone else has said about your topic), and a song (an artistic interpretation of your topic). You will then analyze these sources with the help of your instructor, your classmates, and the textbook, *Understanding Rhetoric*. By the end of this unit, you will complete a 3–5 page essay explaining your topic through an analysis of your three different sources. This essay will be in APA format.

To-Do: While we will spend class time to work on these projects, anything you do not complete in class will need to be completed on your own time.
- Select your topic and find sources
- Bring a variety of sources to class
- Narrow down sources to one primary source, one secondary source, and one song
- Start analyzing and synthesizing sources using *Understanding Rhetoric*, Issues #2, #3 and #5
- Continue synthesizing sources using *Understanding Rhetoric*, Issues #2, #3 and #5
- Outline project, APA help
- Bring a draft of your project to class for peer review
- Submit final project

The task then evolved into utilizing current sources of media to analyze information in relation to developing students' critical consciousness (see Table 9.2).

Table 9.2: Argumentative Unit

Argumentative Unit

Purpose: The term "fake news" is a commonly used phrase in our current culture. As consumers of text, we are inundated with "news" that may not be accurately representing or depicting information. Sometimes, even the most expert readers fall victim to the falsities that fake news offers. As producers of text, we may repeat these inaccuracies through Tweets, Facebook posts, or just by talking with our friends. Fake news goes beyond poor journalism or a lack of ensuring accuracy of a story. Those who produce fake news have intentions and goals (political, economic, and social) to persuade their audience, and as consumers of text, we need to be able to decipher what is true and what is not.

Instructions: Your job for this last unit is to continue exploring your selected topic from our expository unit; however, now you are going to look at your topic's place in current society. Once you have a topic selected, you will find 3–5 fake news stories that are inaccurately portraying your topic. Since we are now experts at analyzing images, you may also use images and videos as sources of fake news. Once you have analyzed your sources, you will need to make an argument addressing the following: 1) why society is falsely portraying your topic in the media, 2) what are the repercussions of this false depiction to society as a whole, 3) the other side of the argument: why would people think it is acceptable to portray your topic in a fallacious way, and finally, 4) consider both sides of your topic—what needs to be done so that others can successfully decipher what is true and what is not in regard to your topic.

Project Requirements

You will include:
1. A presentation consisting of the following parts:
   - A title page for your presentation
   - Historical overview of your topic using your sources from the previous project (if you don't want to use that topic, we need to talk)
   - An overview of how your topic is still seen in today's society (use new sources: music, credible online news sources, videos from the internet)
   - An argument (your thesis) for how your topic is falsely portrayed in the media and what needs to be done for people to understand the "real" side of your topic
   - "Fake news", or false representations of your topic and an in-depth analysis of each source (3–5 examples/sources)
   - The other side of the argument: why some people believe the false depictions of your topic? Also, simply saying, "They are dumb" is not an option.

Table 9.2: Continued

- Connect back to the argument to how consumers of information are being "tricked" by fake news, explain what consumers need to look for, and how we, as a society, can solve this problem
- Last slide: References citing any source you used in the presentation

2. A written reflection addressing the following questions:
   - Why did you select your topic? What about this topic was interesting to you?
   - How did completing this assignment make you a more cautious consumer or producer of information?
   - After completing this assignment, do you view your topic in a different way? Do you view the media in a different way? Why or why not? Explain.

Findings from Students' Reflections

Students were asked to complete project reflections for metacognitive purposes. We looked at these reflections as artifacts within a case study (Yin, 2009) and approached them as data sources. The reflections were graded based on participation. That is, the students knew their answers did not influence the grade they earned on the project. The following questions were used to elicit a discussion on what students gained from the project.

1. Why did you select your topic? What about this topic was interesting to you?
2. How did completing this assignment make you a more cautious consumer or producer of information?
3. After completing this assignment, do you view your topic in a different way? Do you view the media in a different way? Why or why not? Explain.

Following the completion of the project, specific questions were provided to encourage students to reflect on their perceived ability to responsibly consume and produce information in the era of fake news. Our intention was not to direct students to reflect on what we believe was important, but to steer them away from personal anecdotes on how they felt about the project.

Unfortunately, we did not collect preliminary data prior to introducing the project. At the time, we did not realize the impact this project would have on the students in the course. Moreover, the students' reflections were also not considered a data source until after the completion of the course;

therefore, IRB approval was requested retroactively. Though we are aware that self-reported data may be biased since it is often 'based on interpretation, perception, and misunderstanding' (Gerlaugh et al., 2007, p. 1), the students' interpretations of what they achieved by completing the project represents a newfound understanding that information they consume, especially from online forums, is not always fully truthful, and sometimes, presented to perpetuate political and social divisiveness within our society. Additionally, the students' reflections demonstrated an awareness that perhaps consumers of text, including themselves, sometimes lack rhetorical skills that are critical for consuming and interpreting information, especially as many people use social media as their main source for news and information. To analyze the students' reflections, we utilized emergent coding which is a qualitative approach designed to match language and ideas in textual data allowing for the emergence of organic concepts (Saldaña, 2016). The demographics of the class consisted of 16 students, including 11 self-identified females and five self-identified males. All students ranged between ages 18–20. Two students identified as Asian, three as African American, nine as Hispanic or Latino, and three as White.

Perceived Paradigm Shift

Topics from the expository unit seamlessly transferred to the argumentative unit. For example, students who wrote about the Chicano Movement during the Civil Rights Movement researched the perception of immigration in the 21st century. Another student produced a historical analysis on women's rights which led them to investigate how current media's representation of birth control and abortion impacts health insurance policies. The most common topic chosen by students was a comparison between racist propaganda from the 50s and 60s and current anti-Black Lives Matter media and racial stereotypes. The overarching theme that emerged from an analysis of the students' reflections was this explicit development in students' critical consciousness.

Most students discussed what we refer to as a perceived paradigm shift in the way information is consumed and interpreted. The students' reflections often presented a change in positionality in terms of consuming and producing information. As seen in the following excerpt, students realized they need to avoid reading passively, even if what they are reading is for leisure.

Below is an excerpt from one student's reflection:

> After completing this assignment, I believe I have learned to be cautious when encountering information. I need to check the credibility and the logistics of the

information that is set before me. Some information can have some truth in it and also have a lie in it. I should not just believe everything I see, I need to check the information for myself before I choose to believe it or not. I also need to be careful about what information I put out there in the world.

This was a common response from multiple students and aligned with the course's intent of identifying power relations, shaping students' identity, and supporting their growth of self and social development. Many students reflected on how the consumption of incorrect or "altered" information not only made them question the reliability of internet sources, but also made them question themselves as potential contributors of false information.

Consuming and Producing Information

Throughout the course, we applied rhetorical strategies to both academic and non-academic texts. Twitter was a common non-academic text we referred to for these exercises due to its accessibility of both factual and false information. The more practice and experience students had with rhetorically examining text, the more they noticed how abundant fake news was on their Twitter feeds and within other media they relied on throughout their daily lives.

In response to how the project impacted their view of the media, one student wrote:

> It definitely made me view media differently, I now consider whether whoever Tweets something is a credible source or who they are out to target, and I realize that most people's Tweets are nonsense or simply their opinion. Many of them grab a fact or two to make their Tweets look credible but in reality, they use those facts to make it seem like their word matters and nobody else's does. It truly seems that in social media people are completely ignorant and only their point matters. I knew that social media was a place people can speak up for what they believe in but never that they'd be so ignorant doing so.

This student's reflection demonstrates a new awareness of both consuming and producing text. This supports Tierney and Pearson's (1983) statement that reading and writing are both acts of composing and that components of the writing process are not limited to just producing text, but also play a crucial role in consuming text.

In terms of producing information, students developed self-awareness for how they contribute to the era of fake news. One student expressed concern for the role they play when sharing information online, "when posting on social media or commenting, I have to make sure that what I write and publish is accurate, true, and far from fake news." Another student stated, "it makes me more cautious of what I post and who sees what I post. False news is not okay, and you have gullible people that actually believe these fake claims and ads." Another student noted the biases that can be present through online modes of communication. The student recognized how social media can propagate false information and perpetuate stereotypes that may be harmful to marginalized groups. The student proclaimed, "You have to be an individual thinker and know what's true and what's just there to entertain others and make a certain group of individuals look bad." By acknowledging the ever-increasing amount of unreliable and biased information found online, and understanding how this phenomenon culturally impacts society, students started reevaluating not just how they read, but also how they present information, particularly on social media.

Transfer of Knowledge

By completing this project, students showed an understanding of how to apply reading and writing approaches that are generally thought of as academic to types of texts that are traditionally considered nonacademic (e.g. Twitter). Students reflected on applying rhetorical strategies to texts they encounter within both academic and nonacademic contexts. Additionally, students started noticing how rhetorical appeals and the use of illogical fallacies are often used to persuade audiences, for better or worse. This realization led many students to not only notice rhetorical appeals in others' texts, but also in their own. The rhetorical situation became embedded in their way of thought. One student wrote:

> Completing this assignment made me learn how people create fake news, what strategies they use to make other people believe them, and how to identify these [strategies]. This assignment helped me to be a better producer of information by teaching me how to identify false and true sources, which is beneficial for when I use them to support my arguments.

Exposing students to common rhetorical strategies provided the opportunity for students to evolve into more critical readers. Additionally, this project provided students an opportunity to transfer critical thinking skills between D/discourses. Students demonstrated the ability to apply rhetorical strategies to both popular culture and to more traditional texts, like compreheding course assigments and composing original arguments for other courses.

Implications and Next Steps

Developmental reading instructors often face major setbacks where IRW or other accelerated versions of the course, like the corequisite model, are implemented. Though research shows that students today are completing their developmental coursework faster as the developmental sequence decreases, students aren't necessarily demonstrating an increase in college-level skills (Hodora & Jaggars, 2014). Accelerating students through developmental coursework results in students accessing college-level classes faster, but sometimes results in low performance in college-level courses (Hodora & Jaggars, 2014).

Additionally, besides textbooks produced for developmental reading instruction, IRW instructors do not have access to materials that are explicitly designed for such a course (Kalamkarian, Raufman, & Edgecombe, 2015). IRW instructors are left to independently produce and implement materials and strategies that connect reading and writing seamlessly. However, many instructors are approaching their class preparation with two different course designs in mind, an additive approach and an integrative approach. An additive approach involves combining course components from standalone classes. This approach often leads to reading supplementing writing or writing supplementing reading (Bickerstaff & Raufman, 2017). However, an integrative approach uses few components of standalone reading and writing courses and incorporates more metacognitive strategies, text-based writing, and integrates literacy skills and strategies into the course's content (Bickerstaff & Raufman, 2017).

In short, instructors of accelerated developmental reading courses endure two major dilemmas: the students in their courses often struggle at excelling in college-level courses, and as educators, instructors often lack materials to help students make connections from developmental reading to college-level work and beyond. Projects like the one we describe in this chapter are a response to these issues. Instructors need to make all courses relevant to students, but in developmental reading courses, they must also provide a foundation of literacy for students that they can carry with them in future courses, within their personal lives, and eventually, to the workforce.

Finally, the project's outcomes were consistent with the original intent of utilizing popular media to develop students' critical analysis processes. More specifically, by using popular media, students were able to build their college-level reading and writing skills and transfer these skills to texts found in their everyday contexts. The positioning of fake news as a genre of text allowed students to relate culturally, which in turn, helped facilitate the notion that inquiry and critical analysis does not just take place in academic settings.

Since students were able to generate interpretations, as well as make inferences between popular media and academic texts throughout this project, future research could explore how these students' new analytical skills are influencing their preexisting sociocultural contexts. For example, if students are learning to interpret and analyze the nuances and norms of popular culture, how is that influencing interactions with their preexisting cultural contexts? Referring to Gee (2015), do students start overlapping D/discourses once they recognize that they, essentially, use the same rhetorical strategies within various contexts, just in different ways? Our hope is that this project helps students understand that using rhetorical strategies and maintaining an analytical approach to processing information is fundamental in all parts of their lives—not just in academic contexts.

As a culture we are undoubtedly experiencing a resurgence of hypothetical tree octopuses. Those of us teaching reading and writing, regardless of educational level, are at the frontlines witnessing this phenomenon. In this chapter, we offered a brief look at the implementation of a semester project where we explored students' reading and writing processes within their personal, digital, and academic contexts. Our findings echo prior literature suggesting that when current media is integrated into academic contexts, it leads to an increase in students' understanding and engagement with processing information in and out of the classroom (Gee, 2015). Our findings also suggest that following the completion of the project, students questioned power relations, discourses, and their previous identities influencing their self and social development (Shor, 1999). Consequently, we also found that students were able to transfer academic, rhetorical strategies to popular media, which is vital for anyone navigating information in the era of fake news.

References

Alexander, P. A. (2005). The path to competence: A lifespan developmental perspective on reading. *Journal of Literacy Research, 37*(4), 413–436.

Bartholomae, D., & Petrosky, A. (Eds.). (1986). *Facts, artifacts and counterfacts: Theory and method for a reading and writing course.* Boynton/Cook.

Bickerstaff, S., & Raufman, J. (2017). From "additive" to "integrative": Experiences of faculty teaching developmental integrated reading and writing courses. (CCRC Working Paper No. 96).

Blaj-Ward, L., & Winter, K. (2019). Engaging students as digital citizens. *Higher Education Research & Development, 38*(5), 879–892. doi:10.1080/07294360.2019.1607829.

Brumberger, E. (2011). Visual literacy and the digital native. An examination of the millennial learner. *Journal of Visual Literacy, 30*(1), 19–47. doi:10.1080/23796529.2011.11674683.

Gee, J. P. (1990). *Social linguistics and literacies: Ideology in discourses* (2nd ed.). Taylor & Francis.

Gee, J. P. (2015). *Social linguistics and literacies: Ideology in discourse* (5th ed.). Routledge.

George, A. (2014). Critical pedagogies: Dreaming of democracy. In G. Tate, T. Rupiper, K. Schick, & B. Hessler (Eds.), *A guide to composition pedagogies* (2nd ed., pp. 77–110). Oxford University Press.

Gerlaugh, K., Thompson, L., Boylan, H., & Davis, H. (2007). National study of developmental education II: Baseline data for community colleges. *Research in Developmental Education, 20*(4), 1–4.

Gifford Brooke, C. (2014). New media pedagogy. In G. Tate, T. Rupiper, K. Schick, & B. Hessler (Eds.), *A guide to composition pedagogies* (2nd ed., pp. 177–193). Oxford University Press.

Goen, S., & Gillotte-Tropp, H. (2003). Integrated reading and writing: A response to the basic writing 'crisis.' *Journal of Basic Writing, 22*(2), 90–113.

Hodara, M., & Jaggars, S. S. (2014). An examination of the impact of accelerating community college students' progression through developmental education. *The Journal of Higher Education, 85*(2), 246–276.

Horning, A., & Kraemer, B. (2013). *Reconnecting reading and writing*. Parlor Press.

Kalamkarian, H. S., Raufman, J., & Edgecombe, N. (2015). *Statewide developmental education reform: Early implementation in Virginia and North Carolina*. New York, NY: Columbia University, Teachers College, Community College Research Center.

Lea, M. R., & Street, B. V. (2006). The 'academic literacies' model: Theory and applications. *Theory into Practice, 45*(4), 368–377. https://www.jstor.org/stable/40071622

Leu, D. J., McVerry, J. G., O'Byrne, W. I., Kiili, C., & Zawilinski, L., Everett-Cacopardo, Kennedy, C., & Forzani, E. (2011). The new literacies of online reading comprehension: Expanding the literacy and learning curriculum. *Journal of Adolescent & Adult Literacy, 55*(1), 5–14. https://www.researchgate.net/publication/228409747_The_New_Literacies_of_Online_Reading_Comprehension_Expanding_the_Literacy_and_Learning_Curriculum

Morrell, E., & Duncan-Andrade, J. M. R. (2002). Promoting academic literacy with youth through engaging hip-hop culture. *English Journal, 91*(6), 88–92. http://ncte.org/library/NCTEFiles/Resources/Journals/EJ/0916-july02/EJ0916Promoting.pdf

Saldaña, J. (2016). *The coding manual for qualitative research*. SAGE.

Shor, I. (1997). Our apartheid: Writing instruction and inequality. *Journal of Basic Writing, 16*(1), 91–104. https://wac.colostate.edu/docs/jbw/v16n1/shor.pdf

Shor, I. (1999). What is critical literacy? In I. Shor & C. Pari (Eds.), *Critical literacy in action* (pp. 1–30). Boynton/Cook.

Stahl, N. A., & Armstrong, S. L. (2017). Re-claiming, re-inventing, and re-reforming a field: The future of college reading. *Journal of College Reading and Learning, 48*(1), 47–66. https://www.tandfonline.com/doi/abs/10.1080/10790195.2017.1362969?journalCode=ucrl20

Texas Higher Education Coordinator Board [THECB]. (2018). HB2223 implementation. http://reportcenter.thecb.state.tx.us/agency-publication/miscellaneous/faq-hb-2223-tsi-de/

Thaiss, C., & McLeod, S. (2014). Writing in the disciplines and across the curriculum. In G. Tate, T. Rupiper, K. Schick, & B. Hessler (Eds.), *A guide to composition pedagogies* (2nd ed., pp. 283–300). Oxford University Press.

Tierney, R. J., & Pearson, P. D. (1983). Toward a composing model of reading. *Language Arts, 60,* 568–580. https://www.researchgate.net/publication/49176034_Toward_a_composing_model_of_reading

Yin, R. K. (2009). *Case study research: Design and methods* (4th ed.). Sage.

Zapato, L. (2018). Help save the endangered pacific northwest tree octopus from extinction. https://zapatopi.net/treeoctopus/

Zimmerman, M., Skidmore, S. T., Chuppa-Cornell, K., Arrington, T., & Beilman, J. (2018). Contextualizing developmental reading through information literacy. *Journal of Developmental Education, 41*(3), 2–8. http://ncde.appstate.edu/publications

10. Teach from Our Feet and Not Our Knees: Ethics and Critical Pedagogy

Jeaneen Canfield

I approached my first Advanced Composition class with great anticipation, imagining deep conversations, sophisticated writing, and meaningful discussions. Indeed, these characterized students' interactions, but surprisingly, many students were not eager to conduct an in-depth, critical interrogation assignment that would help them become critically aware of the information they were consuming. They seemed to deem information credible if it was published and accessible in any form on the web, and they seemed to approach information solely from their personal biases. This concerned me, particularly in the aftermath of the 2016 presidential election. When writing instructors accept Bazerman's 2016 premise that "people contend for the control of those ideas" (p. vii) shaping and forming societies, we are able to examine those communicative practices that polarize people and subdue democratic debate. Since Henderson and Braun (2016) bring attention to the important task writing instructors have to strengthen "deliberative democracy" (p. 5) in response to the impact of manipulative propaganda, I decided my students' hesitation toward critical interrogation was worth investigating.

My institution is an R1, state-funded, 4-year university in the South-Central region. In the second four weeks of this course, I designed a unit to foster students' growth in research and critical interrogation of news reports and to promote productive critique of information. Students first selected a current, politically-debated issue and one news source. Conducting research into archived issues, they examined, analyzed, and evaluated how that source reported on the issue. Learning outcomes for the unit included that students demonstrate their understanding of malicious propaganda versus effective persuasion (fake news versus reliable news) by composing an essay evaluating news reporting.

While students were leaving class one day, I overheard two students discussing their concerns about the upcoming assignment. One student was wondering why they were not able to just write a paper about their beliefs on a topic, rather than the required analysis/evaluation. The conversation provoked me to ask myself this question: Considering my pedagogical goals to prepare students for active citizenship, what about this assignment will help me achieve those goals? This reflective question prompted me to seek IRB approval to examine emerging data and understand how I might promote students' literacy growth in critical thinking and writing. In this chapter, I explore the data through the lens of the following questions: What are the ways a focus on ethics productively informs writing pedagogy? Further, how might propaganda scholarship influence critical pedagogical strategies, thus enhancing writing assignments?

Kristie Fleckenstein (2010) argues that "the kind of literacy pedagogy teachers practice directly affects the kind of citizenship that their students practice" (p. 13), and I considered my assignment in terms of the literacies I was practicing and seeking for my students. What I am advocating here is nothing new for composition instructors. Lazare's 1992 work clearly outlines a framework for approaching political texts and controversial issues, and he urges instructors to "restore the study of composition to its classical role as the center of education for citizenship" (p. 203). Conversations in our current political climate command our attention as we see rhetorical communication misused at almost every turn. Given the present situation then, revisiting Lazare's schema can inform an ethics framework for a critical literacy assignment. By reimagining critical pedagogy, writing instructors have an ethical responsibility to encourage students to become ethical writers as they learn to critically examine current societal issues and power relationships—to interrogate the cultural and ethical practices informing rhetorical communication.

The critical pedagogy I imagine considers what we already know from composition theory and combines it with what we can glean from scholars who study propaganda. Merging these concepts allows us to ask students to consider ethics as an essential factor of productive news source evaluation. To explicate this understanding of critical pedagogy in 21st-century writing instruction, I divide this chapter into two parts. First, I offer a framework for ethics in writing classrooms. Second, I describe and examine my assignment and the ensuing data from a case study that was part of a larger data set. I conclude by discussing broader implications and thus (re)imagine ethical considerations within 21st-century critical pedagogy.

A Framework for Ethics in Writing Pedagogy

For my students to become critically aware of the information they were consuming, I wanted them to start by examining the production of the information, similar to what Forte describes in this collection as rhetorical ecology. I wanted students to deepen their knowledge of ethics, thereby empowering them to evaluate information based on ideological considerations. To illustrate how ethics and ideology are related, I recall the work of James Berlin (1996/2003) who explained that language use is influenced by the ideological power relationships within the societal context. This indicates that language is a social construct binding people together and is influenced by ethics. In the 1990s, there was a growing concern for ethics in writing instruction. For Katz (1992), the dilemma was how do composition instructors perpetuate an ethic of expediency in the classroom? The move he advanced was to be purposeful in our pedagogical choices, to call students to question. Writing instructors were encouraged by Lazere's (1992) work to consider a four-point schema for an ethical approach in teaching critical engagement with politically-charged texts. Sipora (1999) asserts that ethics means behavior codes are reflexively examined, and Jan Swearingen (1999) argued for a pedagogical ethic fostering dialectical treatment of dichotomous issues and thus equip students to expand their own identities. More recently, McComiskey's 2017 exposition of post-truth rhetoric in the aftermath of what he calls "the Trump effect" (p. 44) calls us toward a pedagogy that resists "unethical qualities of rhetoric" (ibid). And in a recent special issue of *Rhetoric Society Quarterly*, collected essays explore impacts of demogoguery's rhetoric (Skinnell and Murphy, 2019), and urge "rhetoricians to reinvest in what is one of the signature issues of our political moment" (p. 231). Indicative of our long historical concern with ethics, scholars strongly call us to remain committed to the ethical roots embedded in rhetorical studies. I suggest the following framework to encourage pedagogical approaches that foreground ethics in writing studies.

Rhetorical Practice

Sound rhetorical practice involves, as Crowley and Hawhee (2012) explain, three specific and distinct moves: listen, consider, respond. These moves slow down the communication process and allow for thoughtful consideration and deliberation. Contrary to this is the technique characterized by a sensationalized, attention-grabbing heading that provides a link to another article or website, which continues the lure of clicking to find out more ("clickbait"). There is no time for careful listening nor considering because link-clicking moves the consumer from place to place rapidly. Information is distributed via the "Share" button and carried out in an instant.

The "clickbait" nature of fake news eliminates the intentional progression of the aforementioned three moves: which is what fake news depends on (Jowett and O'Donnell, 2017; McComiskey, 2017). Writing instruction benefits from rhetorical practice characterized by these three moves to listen, consider, and respond. Students, therefore, thoroughly consider and examine all contributed voices before composing their responses, thus developing productive consumption and production schemes. Data from this case study seem to suggest that instructional strategies characterized by the framework encourages students to practice a thorough critical interrogation of information and its sources.

Propaganda versus Persuasion

There are frequent accusations levied against news reporters and sources, and the term "fake news" has surged since 2016. According to Derakhshan and Wardle (2017) in their *CNN* Op-Ed piece, the term is overused, causing it to become meaningless because it does not correctly identify the complexity of the communication problem. Interestingly, the debate has also come to include discussions distinguishing between *propaganda* and *persuasion*.

In its most basic interpretation, *propaganda* is not always maliciously manipulative. For the purposes of my class, though, we employed the term in its negative context. Jowett and O'Donnell (2015) explain propaganda as a deliberate, systematic, and manipulative communication form. Further, manipulative propaganda is a deliberate link between "institutional ideology and objective" (p. 4) where the propagandist operates from selfish motives in the sense of "I win—you lose" stance. *Persuasion*, on the other hand, is a communicative act providing new information or new perspectives regarding an issue, and the persuader adopts an "I win—you win" stance—where "[b]oth parties ... mutually [benefit from the persuaded change]" (p. 44). Lesson activities provided occasions for students to practice employing these terms so that they were able to clearly communicate their critique.

Ethical versus Non-Ethical

Drawing from Aristotle's *Nicomachean Ethics,* rhetoricians understand ethics as behavior rooted in the value of promoting what is good for the whole community—what benefits the constitutive whole (inclusivity). Elsewhere in this volume, West-Puckett, Shepley, and Gray explain that ethics involves more complexity than absolute binaries; it evaluates how a decision or action benefits the contextual community. This understanding of ethics can inform assignments and activities that encourage students to examine power dynamics of voices represented within a text. Bringing terms like "good" and "bad" back to the continuum is what McComiskey (2017) strongly calls instructors to practice. Framing "good" and "bad" through the lens of inclusivity encourages conversations about dominant voices and ignored voices, thus promoting a productive critique of information.

The order of steps within this suggested ethics framework encourages students to slow down their engagement with information and thoroughly examine it. They next look for traits within the reporting that help them identify it as either propagandic or as persuasive; then they can determine the ethical value of the news source.

Critical Interrogation Assignment

Context

The study was conducted in a south-central university categorized as an R1 institution, serving domestic and international, as well as traditional and non-traditionally-aged students. The course was a 3000-level course, primarily serving juniors or seniors. In general, students are English majors, but any student needing an additional humanities credit might also enroll. In the semester of my study, there were fifteen students: eight self-identified females, one self-identified trans student, and four self-identified males. There were two seniors, twelve juniors, and one sophomore. Ten of the students were English Education majors, two were English-professional writing majors, and the remaining three were other majors needing a humanities credit. The student for my case study was a junior at the institution, majoring in English Education. She was from an upper-class, metropolitan community in a neighboring state and had plans to return there to pursue her teaching career. She frequently recalled her secondary education, describing it as "premier." I mention this point because it seemed to influence the student's expectations for course assignments, as well as her engagement with in-class activities. She often stated there was nothing new for her to learn, and this was evidenced in her open critique of the critical interrogation assignment.

My over-arching learning objective for students in this class was that they would be able to engage critically with texts and thus demonstrate writerly growth in 21st-century literacy practices. For this specific assignment, I wanted my students to understand the difference between rhetorically sound *persuasion* and manipulative *propaganda,* as well develop a sophisticated conceptualization of other key terms such as *analysis, critical interrogation, fake news,* and *ethics.* I drew from Aristotle's *Nichomachean ethics* and guided students toward a working definition of "ethics." Reading assignments were from the following scholars: J. Murray (2010), Kirsch (2016), Herrick (2018), and Jowett and O'Donnell (2015). Informed by these readings, students critically interrogated a current political issue and evaluated a news source, employing the key terms to help with their analyses and discussions. Ethics operated as an analytic concept for their critical interrogation, and framed the assignment itself.

The assignment asked students to do two things: (1) select a current, political issue and a news source, and (2) evaluate the reliability of the news source. More specifically, students chose a current political issue and a news source (print or visual or audio) reporting on their selected issue. Informed by assigned readings, class discussions, and research into the news source's database, students analyzed the communicative functions and interrogated the effectiveness of the issue's representation. A four-question heuristic (described later) guided their inquiry. After discussing the heuristic, I further clarified the assignment, reminding students that the main point was for them to thoughtfully analyze the compositional/rhetorical strategies news source used to convey its message. I also emphasized this critical interrogation was *not about* the issue, but rather *about how* this news source presented/reported/broadcast the issue and whether or not they believed the source to be reliable.

After handing out the assignment sheet, we brainstormed a list of sources students might consult for information. They next selected a news source, such as *The Washington Post* or *CBS Nightly News* or something similar, and researched to find articles reporting on their selected political issue. Activities and mini-lessons were scaffolded to help students develop productive thinking and composing skills, as well as a growing meta-awareness of their 21st-century literacy practices. Through my understanding of multimodal texts (Kress, 2004), and non-discursive texts (Murray, 2009), I designed in-class lessons and activities where students explored and analyzed digitally-formed communicative texts.

The unit began with a discussion about how students currently consume information. The general consensus was that they receive current event/political information in a highly visual medium via digital devices (none of the students regularly read a printed newspaper). This was an interesting moment in class discussion because students had initially stated that digital compositions seemed "less academic" and would probably not be taken seriously. When students saw that (through our class-generated list on the board) none of them consulted print news, but rather podcasts or digital news apps, there was a shift in their attitude toward this assignment. Establishing this common ground, therefore, created an opportunity for class discussions and activities to develop students' curiosity about the reliability of digital news texts. Furthermore, considering current conversations regarding writing instruction in a post-truth era (McComiskey, 2017), and demagoguery rhetoric (Roberts-Miller 2005), I adjusted daily lessons and activities to guide students' thinking and engagement with information available to them in digital platforms.

An important aspect of this assignment was that I offered a four-question heuristic to develop students' close reading and subsequent analysis of the way news sources report on a particular political issue. The guiding questions are as follows:

- What are the specific techniques employed by the medium as it reports the issue?
- In what ways does the medium effectively tend the rhetorical situation?
- Based on your working definition of "ethics," how ethical is the representation of the issue? Why?
- Would you describe the medium's message as "propaganda" or as "persuasion?" Why?

These questions asked students to thoughtfully consider how a news source reported information and thus determine whether or not it might be considered a reliable source of information. The students' responses throughout the course of this 8-week module included discussion posts, reflective blog posts, and a complex argument paper addressing the four-question heuristic with a multimodal translation of the formal paper. At the close of the semester, I examined the students' responses—their critical interrogation—and looked for evidence of their critical literacy growth. Of the fourteen consenting students, all demonstrated similar levels of understanding and literacy growth. For the purposes of this chapter, I have selected one student (Clara) as a case study representative of the overall critical literacy growth. This student also experienced an epiphanic moment during her final presentation that marked a shift in her self-awareness as a consumer of information.

The first discussion prompt asked students to draw from assigned readings and compose a brainstormed frame by thinking through and briefly responding to the four points on the heuristic. Clara's responses are evidenced below:

Specific reporting techniques?
- "Tons of citations, links to articles are constantly included throughout the article, bringing in a different mode of communication. This also gives the reader the opportunity" (unfinished by student).
- "Anecdotes. She brings up her own abortion as a means to argue her point"

Rhetorical Situation?
- "This article is not a simple 'yes or no,' [sic] it is specifically arguing to stop referring to abortion as a difficult decision, as it is her opinion that this rhetoric is sexist and comes with certain implications."

Ethical representation?
- "I believe it to be ethical, but I know a lot of people would take this article the 'wrong' way, misinterpreting the author's actual argument."

Propaganda or Persuasion?
- "The writer's argument of her topic is persuasive. She is obviously biased, but because she doesn't explicitly argue" (unfinished by student).

Clara's response does not include any reference to the assigned reading material, which would have helped her more clearly explain the "why" of her discussion regarding the ethical representation, as well as whether or not the reporter's article is persuasive or propagandic. I was concerned that my expectations were not as clear as I wanted. I then became curious about how Clara would answer a reflective discussion prompt at the project's conclusion. Below is the prompt and Clara's response.

Discussion #6: "A Critical Gaze Inward: My Evolving Literacies"
For this final post—and there are **no** peer responses required—please address the following prompt:

As you consider this past semester (literacy sponsorship, digital composing practices, multimodal composing, discursive versus non-discursive composition/rhetoric, and collaborative writing), thoughtfully explain the ways your perceptions about composition, about reading/writing, about 21st-century literacy have evolved or have not evolved.

For full credit on this post, you will want to incorporate information from the course readings—these may be short references, but be sure to remain true to the author's contextual and intended meaning. (suggested length = approx. 200 words.)

> "I thought I knew enough about my composing practices, as I think of myself as a good writer. Since the beginning of this class, I have learned that there is so much more to composition. Whether that be evident in multimodal composition, writing an article collaboratively, or the difference between discursive and nondiscursive, I feel that my opinions and perceptions of composition have expanded immensely. I came in having a very good understanding of a lot of these concepts, I just didn't have names for all the things I was doing. Learning specifics about composition will help me be a better teacher when the time comes, as well as a better student until I can be a teacher."

Although the prompt plainly states the students are to "incorporate information from the course readings," again, as in her previous discussion post, Clara's post contains no reference to any of the assigned readings. She seems to be operating from her prior knowledge, instead of engaging with and incorporating new knowledge from the scholarly reading material. The absence of evidence that Clara's critical literacy was developing as a result of her engagement with new information concerned me when I examined and evaluated her critical interrogation paper. Below, I include the concluding paragraph from her critical inquiry:

> "[The] *Washington Post* seems to be in support [of one side of the argument], but then publishes another piece in which the argument is completely the opposite ...[its] representation of abortion, in this case, is not ethical, as the publication flip-flop [sic] on each others' [sic] opinions ... Overall, the *Washington Post* lacks a definite opinion on the abortion topic. By publishing multiple different opinions on the topic, the WP creates an uncomfortable reading experience for the audience. Even so, the *Washington Post's* motto, posted on every page of their site reads, 'Democracy Dies in Darkness' (Harris). So, it could be argued that *Washington Post's* goal is to create a site with diverse biases in order to inform its readers of a variety of opinions toward the topic. This argument is evident in that the *Washington Post* clearly states each author's biases, as well as the respective section for each piece. However, it still provides a confusing and ineffectively communicated view from the medium. Because of this, it can be discerned that the *Washington Post* is not a viable news source."

The student only quoted from the researched articles she found on *The Washington Post's* website, which is evident here in the concluding paragraph. The important take-away for me is that Clara's thinking has not been impacted by the readings discussing any of the key terms, including "ethics" and "propaganda" and "persuasion." This troubles me because if students do not engage with the course readings, then they will potentially not grow beyond the knowledge they with which entered higher education. The good news is, though, this student had a turning point on the very last day of class when she presented her critical interrogation project.

The course final asked students to translate their critical inquiry paper into a multimodal composition and present it to their peers. Students could choose to compose a multimodal project based on Shipka's (2013) discussion of material analogue as multimodal or on Ball et al.'s (2018) discussion of digital multimodal projects (e.g., webpages, animation projects). I also explained that there would be time for audience questions and that students should plan accordingly. When Clara closed her presentation with the statement, "Because the *Washington Post* lacks a definite opinion on the topic of abortion, I conclude it is not a viable nor ethical news source," one student immediately raised her hand and asked how Clara came to that conclusion based on what we had learned that semester regarding ethical news reporting as fairly representing various points of view. Clara paused before responding and admitted her peer was correct and that she was just now realizing how concepts from the assigned readings were applicable—even referring to specific readings. She admitted she had expected her news source (*The Washington Post*) to reflect her shared "liberal views," but that she was disappointed to find it seemed to include opposing viewpoints. She concluded by stating that she seemed to have been unethical in her evaluation of the news source, and she wished she had spent more time on her interrogation and engaged with the readings better.

Her response indicates a couple of interesting points. First, Clara had read most, if not all, of the assigned readings. Second, she felt the negative impact of her poor time management skills and lack of deliberation. Below is Clara's reflection on her translation project and paper, including evidence of her growing self-awareness:

> "Another big thing I would want to change if given the chance is my paper itself. I [sic] procrastinating self did not give myself enough time for either assignment, and my grade suffered because of it."

Her statements above further support my conclusion about her feelings regarding the time she spent on the project. But the question from her peer is interesting because it pushed her to pause and reflect on her project and to recognize the flaws within her own writing that tended toward an unfair, biased, and unethical evaluation of *The Washington Post*. Clara's assumption about her news source lacked thoughtful investigation. She approached the assignment, instead, with an evaluation already in her mind ("I expected it to be liberal") and was disappointed to find it did not match her presupposition. Her reaction to her peer's question revealed her sudden realization that she was operating from her personal bias without self-interrogation. This is the cognitive move for which I was hoping.

The peer's questions and Clara's responses demonstrated that students were distinguishing between manipulative *propaganda* and effective *persuasion*, thus beginning their journey toward becoming ethical consumers and producers of information. While I do not claim that this student completely represents all of the students (there were some who exhibited more pronounced literacy growth earlier in the semester), there were similar trends in most of the other students' responses. Clara's data, therefore, was indicative of a larger issue where all fourteen students experienced a specific moment of self-realization later than I had expected, and it prompted me to examine my assignment and the activities surrounding it, searching for ways to foster my students' critical literacy growth earlier in the semester.

Assignment Critique

Considering the three-step framework discussed earlier, I now turn to examine the lesson sequencing to determine effective scaffolding and instruction. Students were encouraged to engage with politically-charged texts and issues in a dialectical and recursive manner. For students to acquire critical literacy, they need a working vocabulary of terms they can use to explain their critique. In Clara's case, her responses early in the semester did not reflect her working knowledge of "ethics" or "propaganda," nor did she demonstrate awareness of *The Washington Post's* attention to its audience. While I realize that students bear significant responsibility to carefully read all assignment guidelines, I also want to limit the potential for misunderstanding as much as I can. My proposed changes, then, are based on the points emerging from Clara's data as they represent her and my other students' delayed cognitive shift.

My first point of critique is over the arrangement of the instructions on the assignment sheet. The four-question heuristic was inserted in the middle of the assignment description/explanation. This creates a sense of disorganization and potentially causes students to miss important connections between the assignment's scaffolding steps; therefore, I reorganized the way I explained the assignment. I describe the assignment requirements, explain the detailed steps where students are to choose (1) a current political issue, (2) and news source reporting on that issue, and (3) analyze the rhetorical strategies used by the news source. I remind students this is not an analysis of the issue; rather it is an analysis and evaluation of the way the issue is presented/reported/broadcast. It is after the complete explanation of the assignment that I provide the four-question heuristic. I also switched the question about "propaganda" and "persuasion" with the question about "ethics," and I adjusted the third bullet (formerly the fourth). The heuristic now looks like this:

- What are the specific techniques employed by the medium as it reports the issue?
- In what ways does the medium effectively tend the rhetorical situation?
- Would you describe the medium's message as "biased propaganda" or as " rhetorically-effective persuasion?" Why?
- Based on your working definition of "ethics," how ethical is the representation of the issue? Why?

I have noted in my teaching journal how the assignment arrangement now offers a better cognitive flow of information for the students. In fact, this arrangement seems to encourage students to deliberate over their interrogation because each question provides details leading to the next question. It also guides the students to think about propaganda and persuasion in more nuanced ways.

My second critique of the assignment is the discussion prompts did not seem sufficient to guide students' thinking growth because the prompts lacked connection to my three-point framework. For example, rather than a discussion post simply asking students to briefly comment on the heuristic points, students need to identify any patterns of propaganda, or the lack thereof, and then comment on specific strategies they believe the news source utilizes to inform its target audience. Students also need more opportunities to discuss and deepen their understanding of "ethics." An adjustment to my previous course plan, for example, would include a class structure where we examine ethical considerations of how credit card companies lure consumers into high-interest debt. A follow-up class blog post would have students find their own example of unethical advertisement and explain how the ad could be modified to reflect a more ethical approach. These types of activities can guide students toward the specific details they need to use as evidence when addressing the heuristic for their formal paper.

Pedagogical Considerations

Through a framework such as the one I have described here, writing instructors can design lessons and activities that encourage students to move beyond surface-level interpretation and thoughtfully analyze a text's genesis and subsequent paths toward the desired outcome. Students are also positioned to consider how they might frame their own production of information. As Gries (2019) argues, writing classes are spaces where students can come to believe they are "viable agents in this complex, organic process" (p. 336) of the complex assemblage of life. They can practice the type of deliberation Roberts-Miller (2019) advocates because they do not mindlessly accept the information. Students also gain a sense of agency since they are exercising their abilities to doubt and to question. Their critical literacy is characterized by a sense of Fleckenstein's (2010) hope because they are "finding ways of speaking *and* ways of seeing that bring about a good outcome" (p 148, italics in original), and the good outcome is an evaluation of the news source as reliable or not, and thus ethical for the constative whole.

Another important aspect useful for conducting a critique framed by ethics is to ascertain how the credibility of the speaker and the message is supported by others. Who are the supporters? What sorts of issue do these supporters also promote? In this fashion, ethics becomes more complex than merely "what's good for all." It also entails a thorough examination into the implied *ethos* of the information. Ascertaining *ethos* means a consumer of information must slow down the rate of consumption, to allow time for deliberate consideration ("Rhetorical Practice" above). Instead of conducting a quick scan of the information, students can be asked to re-read information to encourage a deep understanding of the material. Teachers must also provide sufficient time for deliberative reading and guide students to plan ahead by providing scaffolding activities that work with sections of the news articles. This can help mitigate habits, such as Clara's, to hastily read at the last minute and thus conduct a shallow evaluation of information.

Consumers of information participate in a productive interrogation of a source when they identify voices included in the information and voices left out. Thoughtful consideration allows readers to pause and identify the voices they hear in a text and then think about other voices they expected to hear but do not. Readers are exercising a form of agency that keeps them from mindlessly following the "charismatic leader" voice represented in an unfairly-biased text. In other words, manipulative propagandic information will ignore opposing views and voices; it promotes a singular voice as the only trusted source, characterizing Roberts-Miller's (2019) "charismatic leadership" (p. 237) where the speaker is the sole source of the vision for the good of the whole.

Finally, students, as information consumers and producers, need to be able to explain what they have learned by researching the speaker/supplier of the information, the supporters of the information, and come to an informed defense for their assessment of the news source. Through a deepened understanding of manipulative *propaganda* and effective *persuasion,* students gain vocabulary skills aiding them to clearly articulate their critique of news sources. Through rhetorical practice, distinguishing between manipulative *propaganda* and effective *persuasion,* student-consumers become more equipped to evaluate the ethical value of information, which are important critical literacy skills in and beyond school.

Conclusion

To agree with McComiskey that a problem exists for American citizens in this *post-truth era* because "there has been a shift in the way that public audiences consume unethical rhetoric" (p. 3) is to also agree there is an ethical responsibility facing writing instructors. Similarly, an article in *The News Literacy Project (2020)* advocates for a news literacy that equips readers to distinguish between legitimate and misleading news. This is not a new concern, as indicated by Lazare's scholarship decades ago; however, the urgency is that with the amount of developing information so readily available, there is a need for citizens to be equipped and prepared to productively critique the information. Student writers must deliberate and think through the deluge of information they receive and be given opportunities to write with hope toward productive change.

If writing instructors value good thinkers and writers over good writing as an end product, then it is safe to conjecture we need a set of core values to propel action. In other words, we need a code of ethics from which to operate. Clara's case reflects a tendency to approach information from personal, unexamined biases, and that is what I, and others in this plight, work against. While I want my students to become confident thinkers and writers, I also want them to be aware that a confident writer is not necessarily an ethical writer, and a confident reader is not necessarily an ethical reader. This affords an opportunity to engage in dialectic interactions and encourage students to compose critical writings. In this way, I answer Henry Giroux's 2013 call to educators when, in his Conference on College Composition and Communication address, he stated educators must "teach to transform—not from your knees, but from your feet!" The composition classroom is a place rich with opportunities to empower students to become productive citizens who are equipped to critically and deliberately produce and consume information. In short, I contend that we have an ethical responsibility to teach students how to critically engage with information in the 21st century: we must teach from our feet and not from our knees. And who better to do that than composition instructors?

References

Aristotle. *Nicomachean ethics.* (W. D. Ross, Trans.). The Internet Classics Archive. http://classics.mit.edu/Aristotle/nicomachaen.html (Original work published 350, B.C.E.).

Ball, C. E., Sheppard, J., & Arola, K. L. (2018). *Writer/designer: A guide to making multimodal projects* (2nd ed.). Bedford/St. Martin's.

Bazerman, C. (2016). Foreword. In G. L. Henderson, & M. J. Braun (Eds.), *Propaganda and rhetoric in democracy: History, theory, analysis* (pp. vii–x). Southern Illinois University Press.

Berlin, J. (2003). *Rhetorics, poetics, and cultures: Refiguring college English studies.* Original work published 1996. Parlor Press.

Crowley, S., & Hawhee, D. (2012). *Ancient rhetorics for contemporary students* (5th ed.). Pearson.

Derakhshan, H., & Wardle, C. (2017). Ban the term 'fake news.' *CNN Opinion*. https://www.cnn.com/2017/11/26/opinions/fake-news-and-disinformation-opinion-wardle-derakhshan/index.html. Updated 3:12pm ET, Mon November 27, 2017.

Fleckenstein, K. (2010). *Vision, rhetoric, and social action in the composition classroom*. Southern Illinois University Press.

Giroux, H. (2013, March 13–16). *Writing the public good back into education* [Featured Speaker]. Conference on College Composition & Communication, Las Vegas, NV, United States.

Gries, L. E. (2019). Writing to assemble publics: Making writing activate, making writing matter. *College Composition & Communication, 70*(3), 328–355.

Henderson, G. L., & Braun, J. J. (2016). Introduction: A call for renewed attention to propaganda in writing studies and rhetoric. In G. L. Henderson, & J. J. Braun (Eds.), *Propaganda and rhetoric in democracy: History, theory, analysis* (pp. xx–xx). Southern Illinois University Press.

Herrick, J. A. (2018). *The history and theory of rhetoric: An introduction* (6th ed.). Routledge.

Jowett, G. S., & O'Donnell, V. (2015). *Propaganda & persuasion* (6th ed.). SAGE Publications.

Katz, S. B. (1992). The ethic of expediency: Classical rhetoric, technology, and the holocaust. *College English, 54*(3), 255–275. Stable https://www.jstor.org/stable/378062

Kirsch, S. J. (2016). Democracy and disclosure: Edward Bernays and the manipulation of the masses. In G. L. Henderson, & J. J. Braun (Eds.), *Propaganda and rhetoric in democracy: History, theory, analysis* (pp. xx–xx). Southern Illinois University Press.

Kress, G. (2004). Gains and losses: New forms of texts, knowledge, and learning. *Computers and Composition, 22*, 5–22. doi:10.1016/j.compcom.2004.12.004.

Lazere, D. (1992). Teaching the political conflicts: A rhetorical schema. *College Composition and Communication, 43*(2), 194–213.

McComskey, B. (2017). *Post-truth rhetoric and composition*. Utah University Press.

Murray, J. (2009). *Non-discursive rhetoric: Image and affect in multimodal composition*. Southern University New York Press.

Murray, J. (2010). Composing multiliteracies and image: Multimodal writing majors for a creative economy. In G. Z. Giberson, & T. A. Moriarty (Eds.), *What we are becoming* (pp. 217–224). http://www.jstor.org/stable/j.ctt4cgppw

National News Literacy Week. (2020). *The News Literacy Project*. Retrieved January 28, 2020, from https://newslit.org/news-literacy-week/

Roberts-Miller, P. (2005). Democracy, demagoguery, and critical rhetoric. *Rhetoric and Public Affairs, 8*(3), 459–476. doi:10.1353/rap.2005.0069.

Roberts-Miller, P. (2019). Demagoguery, charismatic leadership, and the force of habit. *Rhetoric Society Quarterly, 49*(3), 233–247.

Shipka, J. (2013). Including, but not limited to, the digital composing multimodal texts. In T. Bowen, & C. Whithaus (Eds.), *Multimodal literacies and emerging genres* (pp. xx–xx). University of Pittsburgh Press.

Sipiora, P. (1999). Ethics and ideology in the English classroom. In F. G. Gale, P. Sipiora, & J. L. Kinneavy (Eds.), *Ethical issues in college writing* (pp. 39–62). Peter Lang Publishing.

Skinnell, R., & Murphy, J. (2019). Rhetoric's demagogue/demagoguery's rhetoric: An introduction. *Rhetoric Society Quarterly, 49*(3), 225–232.

Swearingen, C. J. (1999). The hermeneutics of suspicion and other doubting games: Reclaiming belief in the writing and reading and the reading of writing. In F. G. Gale, P. Sipiora, & J. L. Kinneavy (Eds.), *Ethical issues in college writing* (pp. 155–181). Peter Lang Publishing.

11. News as Text: A Pedagogy for Connecting News Reading and Newswriting

KRISTINA REARDON

> The most important thing I learned was that bias can be unintentional and sneaky. It is really important to always question if things were written as stated facts or opinions.
> —*First Year Writing Student*

When they enter the first-year writing classroom, students do not always know when—never mind how—to question if things were written as facts or opinions, as the first-semester freshman notes above. The problem is not confined to students alone. As Dana Gioia wrote in the preface to his executive summary for the National Endowment for the Arts' study *To Read or Not Read*, that reading in general is declining across the American populace, and that, "as Americans, especially younger Americans, read less, they read less well" (2007, p. 3). While Gioia's study concentrates on literary reading, his caution that these developments "have demonstrable social, economic, cultural, and civic implications" (2007, p. 3) feel particularly relevant even a decade on, when we consider students' news reading abilities in the fake news era. The recent Stanford History Education Group's study of more than 7,000 student responses to civic online reasoning exercises found that middle school, high school, and college students alike were "easily duped" when evaluating information passed along through social media channels (Evaluating information, 2016, p. 4).

In *A Writer's Guide to Mindful Reading* (2017), Ellen Carillo urges students to see reading and writing as active, meaning-making processes. She encourages students to create meaning as they read, not simply find it, stressing that texts do not hold a hidden message that students are meant to uncover. Particularly in a journalistic context, creating meaning through the reading process involves negotiating one's understanding of the world with one's understanding of the way new developments in the world are represented in writing. While there may seem at first much more to unpack in a poem or novel than in a breaking news story, the news offers a rich space for students to come to terms with their own assumptions about the world and how those assumptions are shaped by the way that journalists, both professional writers and citizen reporters, present information that they find credible. As Danielle Koupf notes in her chapter, "fact and meaning are always contextual." And when we conceive of even hard news stories as narratives, we open interpretive possibilities that can lead students to productively question sources, ordering of information, and the representation of ideas. In Carl T. Bergstrom and Jevin West's provocatively titled fall 2019 course, "Calling Bullshit: Data Reasoning in a Digital Word," students are taught to "remain vigilant for bullshit contaminating [their] information diet." A news-as-text model of teaching provides students with the tools to do just that, embracing an attitude of skepticism that parallels Koupf's argument that students must attend to the "rhetorical construction of all writing, even facts."

A news-as-text pedagogy involves inviting students to become more critical readers of news by reading mindfully, critically, and carefully—but also by trying their hand at writing news as well. Literacy instructors, Michael Bunn among them, have long advocated teaching students to read like writers, with an eye on the rhetorical and stylistic moves that authors make in producing texts under consideration (2013). Coupled with an attention to the sort of meaning creating that Carillo proposes, such methods can help students develop their deep reading. Yet in their introduction to *Deep Reading* (2017), Patrick Sullivan et al. note that many first-year writing programs focus on rhetorical reading to the exclusion of interpretive reading, given that literature is not usually assigned in such classes. I argue that in writing classrooms, prioritizing new readings allows for complex and interesting rhetorical analysis *and* meaning creating and interpretation—particularly when long-form news analysis pieces are the subject of study. Moreover, I contend that students learn to read with curiosity once they have written in the genres under consideration, having thus become aware of the challenges in producing them. The news report—a short, informative piece with well documented conventions—lends itself well to the first-year writing classroom. Teaching students to read news like reporters—a very specific type of writer—allows them both read rhetorically and create meaning.

What I offer here are four ways of teaching students to read like reporters in reading/writing assignments, and, using pseudonyms, four students' experiences attempting to do so in first-year writing courses at the College of the Holy Cross, as collected through student drafts, cover letters, and post-class surveys, all of which were included in an Institutional Review Board–approved study. The small liberal arts college at which I teach in Worcester, Massachusetts does not require a writing class beyond a first-year seminar program, which has writing goals but is not a first-year writing course. The students, then, opted to enroll in first-year writing voluntarily. They chose one general topic to follow in news sources of their choices throughout the semester, and their assignments asked them to pull from their independent reading. Each of the models I present combines reading and writing, and the students on whose work I rely to flesh out the methods were chosen because they presented challenges to my teaching and usefully explore the complications that can arise when students negotiate reading like reporters.

While I bring over a decade of experience to the table freelancing for newspapers and regional magazines, and did fact-checking work as a local television news and magazine intern with local television news, the models I propose do not require one to have worked as a journalist. But they do expect that instructors as well as students reflect on the way that they may, explicitly or implicitly, contribute to the flow of information online. This follows the call of Stephanie West-Puckett, Genoa Shepley, and Jessica Grey, who, in their chapter, develop the claim that educators ought to guide students to interpret the news (fake or otherwise) using heuristics that reflect a deep and complicated reading process, and not simply reverse false claims. After all, we may not all run out tomorrow and become reporters. But in an era where, as journalist and media analyst Brooke Gladstone writes "anyone with a cell phone can now presume to make, break, or fabricate the news" (2011, p. xiii), it is useful to offer students the opportunity to practice both consuming and producing news.

News as Narrative

Helping students read like reporters is, in many ways, asking them to become the sort of expert meta-readers who are aware of the reading/writing moves they make that Alice Horning describes in *Reading, Writing and Digitizing* (2012). More than that, however, it asks students to treat news as a form of narrative: as a text with an author who made rhetorical choices that create interpretive possibilities for readers. In the classroom, treating news as narrative allows deep analysis of texts, making the process of reading the news more than an exhausting exercise in trying to find, sort, and evaluate information amidst a deluge of sources. Students will ask more than: Who? What? When? Where? Why? They will ask: Who, according to this author? What, according to these sources? When, according to this date and time? Where, according to this perspective? Why, from this vantage point? Two news articles featuring the same information but framed differently might tell two competing stories. A news-as-text approach heightens students' awareness of subjectivity, fairness, and accuracy by analyzing narrative features rather than by simply fact-checking.

In many ways, this approach is far from new. Journalism and composition have a long symbiotic history, dating back to at least the 1970s, when Robert Bain (1975) wrote of the way that reporting assignments in first-year writing allowed students to approach core rhetorical concepts such as audience in useful ways. The 1980s and early 1990s saw a flurry of articles from journalism instructors who worked to integrate process pedagogy into their work (Zurek, 1986; Pitts, 1989). Sharon Logsdon Yoder (1992), in particular, applied composition revision practices—citing Nancy Sommers (1980)—in the journalism classroom, and Lyle D. Olson (1992) commented: "Many of us who have taught both news writing and English composition are convinced that news writing instruction is an excellent method of teaching writing" (p. 50). My four models of using news-as-text build on this work from the 1980s and 1990s to push students into what Elizabeth Wardle (2012), building on the work of David Perkins and Gavriel Salomon (1994), among others, calls a "problem-exploring disposition," whereby students would approach texts with curiosity, aware of different interpretive possibilities.

Yet interpreting news requires a facility with the conventions of story-building in the journalistic paradigm. In *Understanding News*, John Hartley offers a framework for thinking through the way that expert meta-news readers might work. He casts news literacy as a triad of activities: first, an ability to follow or understand information presented; then, an ability to recognize what he calls "a familiar cast of characters and events"; and finally, an ability to launch one's own interpretations of the world "in terms of the codes we have learnt from the news" (Hartley, 2013, p. 5). I understand the first of these moves to involve basic comprehension: understanding the words and ideas in a text such that the new information presented is identified. The second involves recognizing patterns—in the presentation of material (writing), in the organization publishing the material (source), or in the actors discussed in the material (experts, politicians, and others, alongside data and organizations, that frame the new information). Finally, the last step involves assessing the piece of news, slotting it into—or allowing it to change—one's world view. These align with three of the mental capacities for critical literacy that Horning outlines; they are forms of identification (recognizing or labeling), categorization (sorting into groups), and discrimination (distinguishing between or among things).

The assumption that students can, without training, successfully identify, categorize, or discriminate among sources is not one we should take for granted, as the Stanford History Education Group's *Evaluating information* study shows (2016). Further, the 2018 Project Information Literacy (PIL) study sponsored by the Knight Institute and Northeastern University revealed that students are simply not as familiar with traditional news sources as we might expect. Only 33% of the 6,000 students surveyed for PIL told researchers they regularly read print news (Head et al., 2018). And identifying news sources online, particularly on social media channels—the primary places PIL found that students accessed information, aside from conversations with peers—is challenging, especially when the top online source by far where college students reported finding their news was Facebook. Since Facebook announced its efforts in 2017 to stop the spread of what then vice president Adam Mosseri called "false news" by using third-party fact-checking organizations to first identify and flag inaccuracies and deceiving posts and advertisements so that readers could more critically engage with content, Patricia L. Moravec et al. (2019) have found that among undergraduates, fake news flags on Facebook pique students' interest but ultimately do not impact their views about what is true.

In some ways, students' reactions to the deluge of information they face daily is understandable. PIL found that students were overwhelmed by the sheer number of news sources with which they came into contact daily and preferred to read shorter digests like the Skimm (Head et al., 2018). Yet if we view news stories as narratives and ask core literary interpretive questions of the news we read (why this word, not another? what does this detail illuminate? displace?), analyzing the news has the potential to become a meaning-creating activity in ways that are in reach for first-year students, who are still in the process of developing digital literacies. Investigating what Stephen Colbert called the truthiness of a claim (Colbert qtd. in Zimmer, 2010)—that is, the emotional feeling that something is true even though it might not be—requires professors to model deep reading. Sitting with a story—even a manipulative one—teaches students to not just label stories in a binary way but rather to treat a story as a narrative to unravel, one whose narrators might be unreliable for particular reasons, intentional or unintentional.

The three main types of journalistic bias involving story-telling that I have found profitable to discuss with writing students include: visual bias, narrative bias, and fairness bias. Simply put, when there are photos, stories get more attention. And narrative bias reveals a penchant for telling a story with a beginning, middle, and end, though many stories are messy and do not, and perhaps should not, fit into such a neat narrative form.

Scientific discoveries, for example, never really end. Gladstone says such stories are "all middle" and some journalists "fix the problem by taking on a provisional ending, and reports appear more conclusive than they really are" (2011, p. 65). Finally, fairness bias involves giving equal pages space to all sides, even when it is not merited. Schiffer notes that it is easier to say, "Democrats say this, Republicans say that; now you decide" than it is to fact check both and report what is objectively happening (2018, p. 69). Teaching students to analyze the story of the news by looking at visuals (are they being exaggerated?), narrative (does this wrap up too neatly?), and fairness (what actually happened, and does everyone deserve to be quoted?) certainly involves more than simply performing a literary interpretation of the news. But reading critically can help students realize that more research is needed. Or, as one of my students put it, only "by reading multiple, different sources can I determine what is and what is not being said." Advocating a deep reading approach to news sources—including what we might consider bad ones—teaches students to embrace rather than run away from the deluge of news they face each day so that they might, by reading multiple sources, "refer to many different sources to get the best picture," as another student put it.

This is an idealistic vision of what students might do with their news reading. When I borrowed questions from PIL and surveyed my students after courses concluded, the students who replied (42% of my total enrollment in first-year writing in 2018), still defaulted to getting their news from social media and news feeds, and mostly chose to read about celebrities/entertainment, much like the wider group of students that PIL surveyed. Here is what changed. Before taking a news-focused first-year writing course, no students strongly agreed that they knew where to find credible news, nor did any student strongly agree they could determine the difference between a fact-based or opinion-based piece. Most disagreed that they knew how to evaluate a news article for bias. And my experience teaching drove this point home. For one homework assignment in fall 2018, students were asked to submit links to three hard news articles. Around 80% of the class submitted at least one editorial. Yet after the course, 100 percent of respondents agreed or strongly agreed they knew where to find credible news, could tell the difference between fact and opinion, and knew how to evaluate an article for bias. Of course, those most interested in the course and material likely responded to my survey. But not all who responded earned strong grades in the class. In other words, it was not just top students who seemed to derive benefits from a news-as-text approach.

Four Models for News-As-Text

The four models for using news-as-text involved students following the news on a topic throughout the semester. We talked through sources and where to find them, and at various points during the semester, students were called upon to critically analyze sources they found. The aim of allowing students to choose their own topics for the semester was to push them to authentically develop media literacy around an issue they would continue to follow after the course is over. Students chose to follow a range of topics, from school shootings, to the #metoo movement, to abuse allegations against priests in the Catholic Church, and many hit close to home for students or the campus community. The freedom of choice has also led to numerous students following the NFL in the fall semester and the NBA in the spring semester. The trick was to find a topic that was sufficiently broad, such that something would be written about it on a weekly basis, and not pushing students to choose topics that were so specific that coverage fizzled out within a week or two.

Students followed the news on a given topic so that they could complete their four assignments: writing their own news story; analyzing a news photograph; completing a bias evaluation essay, which asked students to critically analyze an entire news package (including headlines, text, and photos); and drafting recommendations about credible and useful sources for future students who might choose to follow their topic in the future. To help them understand how the media function in the United States, students were assigned Gladstone's *The Influencing Machine* (2011) and Schiffer's *Evaluating Media Bias* (2018). Reading strategies from *A Writer's Guide to Mindful Reading* (Carillo, 2017) and *Writing Analytically* (Rosenwasser et al., 2012) were presented, including previewing, the says/does approach, rhetorical reading, passage-based freewriting, and uncovering assumptions and tracking binaries, among others. These reading strategies helped students attend to critical details about news as narrative that moved class conversations forward. After reading Gladstone's description of the way the figure 50,000 was often thrown around as shorthand in the news, for example, one student, Jessica, wrote in her reading response: "I think that numbers have a big impact on the way people perceive the news because people have a tendency to accept data as facts and they don't think to look to the source. . . . When the author points out the fact that the number 50,000 is used a lot in the news, it made me realize that I shouldn't take numbers at face value." Hearing directly from Gladstone, a reporter, seemed to influence Jessica's view in a way that my caution to fact check numbers in class did not. Moreover, understanding how a reporter questioned the numbers other reporters cited stuck out to Jessica, and she began to think like a reporter when she began to write about why a reporter might be drawn to reporting a dramatic statistic even if it was difficult to verify: "When numbers like these are given, they catch the public's attention and make them listen." Jessica understood, in this moment, that it was all about story—that news was narrative.

Assigning the News Report

Once students understood that news is narrative, they were poised to engage with the news report assignment: to become reporters and to develop narratives of their own. The assignment involves having students attend a campus or community event, and then use tools and organizational structures of reporters to deliver a 500–600 word summary. The purpose of the assignment was to allow students to understand the writerly choices reporters made, and therefore hopefully help them become more attuned to those choices as they critically read later in the semester. We considered mentor texts from the student newspaper to prepare, reverse outlining stories, talking about what reporters call "ledes" (also known as hooks and leads) that made the audience want to keep reading and how to answer the key reporter's questions: Who? What? When? Where? Why? How? Students were instructed to reveal information in order of importance, not in chronological order.

Students drew unexpected lessons from the assignment. Jessica and David responded favorably to it in the post-class survey, agreeing that it helped them connect to campus, felt relevant to their other classes, and prepared them to write other essays in first-year writing. David spoke of the way the assignment helped him adjust to college writing, reflecting in his cover letter: "I changed my high school writing style to successfully write this new report by defeating or not using a 5-paragraph structure." Until David wrote this, I had not considered a positive writing implication of assigning the news report: it looks nothing like an academic essay. We shifted to academic prose soon after, but by assigning a non-academic form first, I signaled to my students that they would have to write differently than they did in high school. I received no five paragraph essays for any of the assignments I assigned in the semester that I began with the news report.

When we read Gladstone, it seemed that the class understood her points about objectivity and fairness in reporting. Interestingly, Jessica and David showed me that those ideas were either not fully absorbed after reading, or harder to apply than to talk about. For example, when Jessica wrote her first lead about her summer research fair visit, she focused on giving information: "Holy Cross undergraduate students seized experiential learning opportunities as they showcased their research discoveries; from limb regeneration to addiction, comparisons of veterans and athletes to overcoming traumatic childhoods." In her revision, she flipped the order of information, putting the list of details first, hoping they would capture the reader's attention more. She also relied on a number—though not 50,000—to capture the reader's attention. The second half of her revised sentence read: "Holy Cross undergraduate students showcased their research discoveries to hundreds of people inside the Hogan Ballroom." Jessica had internalized the message from Gladstone's book: numbers draw the reader's attention. But where did Jessica get that number? She had no source—she simply guessed, providing the same sort of Goldilocks Number Gladstone critiqued: a number that seemed reasonable, not too big, and not too small, but enough to signal importance. David, meanwhile, attended a college soccer game that ended in a 2–2 draw in double overtime. He wrote in his cover letter that he read and reread *Sports Illustrated* articles to get the tone right. Yet he was effusive about key moments in the game and his overall use of vague but positive adjectives distracted from its events revealing who he was cheering for. He changed his adjectives in the next draft. The "amazing bicycle kick" from the first draft became an "unexpected bicycle kick" in his second draft, and the "amazing" game became "hard fought." These subtle changes brought more specificity to the report, and the sort of difficulty he faced in rooting out demonstrative adjectives affected almost the whole class. Another student who wrote about a library fair noted in her cover letter: "One of my biggest revisions was eliminating phrases that invoked some kind of bias."

 I learned that students need coaching to learn to write news articles but that the experience is worthwhile because it pushes students to confront in their own writing the things they read about in texts, thereby deepening their reading experiences of both Gladstone and Schiffer. While Jessica's guesstimate of the hundreds of people in the ballroom might seem insignificant, the reason I delve into this particular detail of her story is to show that, though she provided an insightful reflection, in *writing* the news report she was able to confront Gladstone's words in practice and more fully understand them.

Analyzing News Photography

For this assignment, students were instructed to find a news article of their choice accompanied by an interesting image, and then to analyze the photos in context. I asked students specifically to answer the question: how does the photo earn its space on the page? What story does it tell? The goal of this assignment was to push students to read photos from the same critical stance with which they approach data and facts. Two main lessons stood out to me about my students' interaction with this assignment. First, choosing an image with enough detail or complexity is important. David chose a story about concussions in the NFL. It was accompanied by a computer-generated image of a helmet with a bullseye. He argued that the generic helmet signaled a sort of universality, and the angle of the helmet—though disembodied—suggested a charge. The bullseye was symbolic. But he ran out of steam after that; there was simply not enough to interpret.

Second, when they choose complex images, students need coaching to explain the meaning of what they see. Jessica's first draft included descriptions of her photo, which was of a protester holding a photo of Pope Francis with the universal "no" symbol over his face. She seemed overwhelmed with the amount of detail in the image, though she eventually explained that she saw a tension between protesters' anger and sadness in the photo. Jessica ended up citing the visual analysis essay as her favorite of the semester in the post-class survey, and she dedicated the majority of her end-of-semester portfolio reflection to talking about news photography. Her positive gains from this assignment seemed to stem from the fact that her image was more complex and gave her more to write about. Meanwhile, David left the visual analysis paper unranked in his post-semester survey. Ultimately, I saw this short exercise as useful because it helped students learn to read an image and not simply defer to a caption—a skill that came up in the next, most complex reading/writing assignment of the semester.

Evaluating Bias

This essay was the most difficult assignment in the writing sequence. It required students to evaluate bias in three articles that reported on the same recent event: one from a left-leaning source, one from a right-leaning source, and one from a more typically neutral source. The website Allsides.com was particularly useful in helping students find articles. We discussed publications typically regarded as left-leaning, right-leaning, and neutral and deferred to Ad Fontes Media's Interactive Bias Chart (Otero, 2019) in cases of doubt. It was important for this assignment that students find three articles on the exact same event, not just on similar topics. And if a student had access to unfiltered or unedited footage of the event—say, for example, a video of a press conference—then they could more fully understand what occurred and construct what Schiffer calls a baseline in *Evaluating Media Bias* (2018). Rather than compare and contrast stories to see which seemed most reasonable (a difficult prospect if one does not know what actually happened), students were to come up with a short description of what the objective baseline for the story was after finding the primary source from which all three stories drew. Then, they could contrast each story to the baseline. To define bias, we looked to Gladstone, Schiffer, and we read about the way that Ad Fontes Media used a veracity metric to rate how true a claim was, an expression metric to rate how the claim was presented to the reader, and a fairness metric to evaluate how relevant or fair the claim was to include in an article in the first place. The assignment involved a lot of moving pieces, but the ultimate goal was to read three articles in great depth and then to comment on the quality of each, explaining which was the fairest and why. This form of reading was the most rigorous and structured of all the news-as-text pedagogies I worked through.

I move now to two different students, Nora and Ana, whose bias analysis pieces were among the most complex and interesting I read over the two semesters I taught this method of reading the news—and who taught me to slow the pace of this assignment in future versions of the course. Nora chose to analyze the resignation of Senator Al Franken in the wake of eight women's accusations of sexual misconduct, and Ana chose to follow a debate in Congress about the legitimacy of the Deferred Action for Childhood Arrivals (DACA) policy. Nora, who worried about exceeding her word count for the assignment, wrote of how difficult the assignment was to complete. She ended up creating a table to compare and contrast each article to keep things straight. She wrote that she struggled with the "significance of objectivity" in her analysis. In other words, Nora—who had readily argued for objectivity as a core journalistic value after reading Gladstone in class—questioned its value when confronted with conflicting news reports.

Ana also found the topic difficult. She commented: "Each article had so much content to it that I wished that paper was longer so I could fully explore the articles thoroughly." The essay called for 1,500–2,000 words because I did not want to overwhelm students and I hoped they would narrow their focus to one or two things in each article that stood out. Reflecting on Nora and Ana's comments, I can see now that once students move into reading news as narrative and into interpreting articles, they have trouble knowing when to stop. Both Nora and Ana overdeveloped their ideas and showed me that I needed to model a form of narrative and interpretive reading that was deep but eventually had an end point. When I taught Jessica and David the next semester, I kept this in mind and slowed the pace of the essay, creating more pre-writing steps to help students work through complex metrics.

Like Jessica, who readily accepted Gladstone's ideas, Nora encountered cognitive dissonance when she confronted the words she read in Gladstone's text in action. Nora seemed troubled by the idea of objectivity in her cover letter, wondering if there were just different ways of seeing things. Ultimately, she found her way through the issue. She argued that getting stories factually right mattered because professional journalists can "reinforce the importance of women's voices." Nora's own views on the issue influenced her reading of the pieces; she believed that women's voices deserved to be heard, so she tended to credit sources that gave accusers more page space. Her analysis was nuanced and acknowledged her own views, and as a result her essay provided a sophisticated look at the complexities of reporting on #metoo. Ana was also worried about representation in the news but moved forward with her own views trickling into her prose more substantially. She argued: "[DACA] needs the best coverage from the media because the lives of many are depending on this situation very hopefully, so the media should not be taken lightly as well as the rest of the nation."

Throughout the piece, Ana moved between identifying problematic language or stances in each article and developing this larger claim about what constituted the "best coverage." In her enthusiasm for writing about her topic, Ana emphasized how different legitimate perspectives needed to be cited but forgot to develop a baseline against which to compare each article. The claims in her final draft felt more compelling once she was able to clearly and specifically identify whose voices were being emphasized and whose voices were being left out—that is, when she defined the "best coverage." Nora and Ana taught me that in evaluating sources' potential biases, it is important to remind students to acknowledge their own so that we can see how and where our views impact our assessment of fairness. Both Nora and Ana developed a sense that journalism could be a force for social change, a specific way of viewing the media that was not pervasive in other students' essays. Ultimately, they and other students came to discover concluded what Schiffer (2018) observes: that hard news reports from professional media sources do not often reveal much partisan bias. Many news sites typically regarded as right or left leaning often run the same content. Both classes of students came to see that headlines and photos often seemed less objective than reporters' prose.

Recommending Sources

Finally, I asked students—after a semester of following the news—to develop recommendations about where best to find information on their topic. The specific question was: "Where should consumers turn for accurate and unbiased information on your topic?" The goal of this assignment was to put students' reading skills to the test. Nora struggled, she wrote, because #metoo was still so new in early 2018. Ultimately, she leaned into the challenge, recommending that consumers turn first to Twitter—a space she viewed as democratic and open to all, and the space where the #metoo conversation was happening. Then she suggested readers turn to reports by investigative journalists at *The New York Times*, a publication she thought was committed to #metoo. Consulting just the *Times* would not allow a reader to understand the full picture, she argued. Meanwhile, Ana seemingly gave up on the news. She wrote that "there are various places that offer information about DACA but not one place will give the reader everything they need to know about DACA." She ultimately suggested readers go "straight to the source"—in this case, the U.S. Citizen and Immigration Services, which she understood to be up-to-date at the time. But to understand the way people felt about DACA, and how it was being debated politically, she recommended going to both right and left-leaning sources to glean opinions. In other words, after coming to terms with news as narrative, Nora and Ana came to believe that if students wanted a full, comprehensive view of a subject, reading neutral or balanced articles did not suffice. Students need to read credible news sources and catch up on what people *thought* about them. Part of understanding the news, they implicitly argued, was understanding the way that different groups of people read and reacted to it.

Final Thoughts

Adopting a news-as-text model involves heightening students' awareness of interpretive possibilities of news narratives, as Koupf and West-Puckett et al. also argue, by teaching them to read and write as reporters. Such an approach helps students come to terms with the so-called truthiness of what they read in their daily newsfeeds by identifying and questioning the rhetorical framing of the news—an approach which I argue becomes far less arduous and therefore far more practical in a quick-reading situation than fact checking each and every detail of a news story. And after analyzing the work of students in my classes who both wrote news stories and analyzed professional journalists' work, I posit opening up an optimistic view of young news consumers. I found that once students could identify slanted phrasing in their own work, I had meaningful reference points moving forward when we discussed expression and fairness. Students became increasingly critical of exaggerated headlines and suspiciously manipulated statistics and actively made suggestions that others interrogate sources and seek out additional information to understand an issue. I am reminded that students are producers and sharers as well as consumers. A news-as-text pedagogy takes one step forward in preparing students to curiously and ethically contribute to the 21st-century 24-hour social media news cycle.

References

Bain, R. (1975). Journalism and composition. *Freshman English News*, 4(1), 1–3.

Bergstrom, C. T., & West, J. (2019). Calling bullshit: Data reasoning in a digital world. Retrieved from: https://callingbullshit.org/syllabus.html#Fake

Bunn, M. (2013). Motivation and connection: Teaching reading (and writing) in the college classroom. *College Composition and Communication*, 64(3), 496–516.

Carillo, E. (2017). *A writer's guide to mindful reading*. The WAC Clearinghouse.

Evaluating information: The cornerstone of civic online reasoning. (2016). Retrieved from: https://stacks.stanford.edu/file/druid:fv751yt5934/SHEG%20Evaluating%20Information%20Online.pdf

Gioia, D. (2007). To read or not to read: A question of national consequence. Retrieved from: https://www.arts.gov/sites/default/files/ToRead_ExecSum.pdf

Gladstone, B. (2011). *The influencing machine*. Norton.

Hartley, J. (2013). *Understanding news*. Taylor & Francis.

Head, A. J., Wihbey, J., Metaxas, P. T., MacMillan, M., & Cohen, D. (2018). How students engage with news: Five takeaways for educators, journalists, and librarians. Retrieved from: http://www.projectinfolit.org/news_study.html.

Horning, A. S. (2012). *Reading, writing, digitizing: Understanding literacy in the electronic age*. Cambridge Scholars Publishing.

Logsdon Yoder, S. (1992). Teaching writing revision: Attitudes and copy changes. *Journalism and Mass Communication Educator*, 47(4), 41–47.

Moravec, P. L., Minas, R. K., & Dennis, A. R. (2019). Fake news on social media: People believe what they want to believe when it makes no sense at all. *MIS Quarterly*, 43(4), 1343–1360.

Olson, L. D. (1992). Effect of news writing instruction in English composition classes. *The Journalism & Mass Communication Educator*, 47(2), 50–56.

Otero, V. (2019). Media Bias Chart. Retrieved from: https://www.adfontesmedia.com/

Perkins, D., & Salomon, G. (1994). Transfer of learning. In *International encyclopedia of education* (pp. 6452–6457). Oxford: Elsevier/Pergamon.

Pitts, B. (1989). Model provides description of news writing process. *Journalism & Mass Communication Educator*, 44(1), 12–59.

Rossenwasser, D., & Stephen, J. (2012). *Writing analytically* (6th ed.). Wadsworth.

Schiffer, A. J. (2018). *Evaluating media bias*. Rowman & Littlefield.

Sommers, N. (1980). Revision strategies of student writers and experienced adult writers. *College Composition and Communication*, 31(4), 378–388.

Sullivan, P., Tinberg, H., & Sheridan, B. (2017). Introduction. In *Deep reading: Teaching reading in the writing classroom* (pp. xiii–xxvii). NCTE.

Wardle, E. (2012). Creative repurposing for expansive learning: Considering 'problem-exploring' and 'answer-getting' in dispositions in individuals and fields. *Composition Forum, 26*. Retrieved from: https://compositionforum.com/issue/26/creative-repurposing.php

Zimmer, B. (2010, October 13). Truthiness. *The New York Times*. Retrieved from: https://www.nytimes.com/2010/10/17/magazine/17FOB-onlanguage-t.html

Zurek, J. (1986). Research on writing process can aid newswriting teachers. *The Journalism & Mass Communication Educator, 41*(1), 19–23.

Part III. Teaching Visual and Digital Media Literacy in the Era of Fake News

12. *How Information Finds Us: Hyper-Targeting and Digital Advertising in the Writing Classroom*

Dan Lawrence

Hyper-Targeted Digital Content Distribution

The purpose of this chapter is to emphasize the importance of taking time with our students to explore *how information finds us*. Yes, we want to show our students our library resource portals and how to identify credible, peer-reviewed information. Composition instructors have been doing this for decades and it remains incredibly significant (Connors, 1997). But with the relatively new, emergent phenomenon of highly-targeted digital advertisements, there is another side of these issues, one that involves ethos and credibility. A person may see thousands of advertisements a day. Many are well disguised as content marketing or native advertising. Some are commercial, some are political, and some are ideological. Most are delivered through advanced targeting using troves of user data, demographic information, and geographical parameters. We can help our students explore how they have been targeted and for what purposes.

We can encourage our students to think about procedural rhetoric and actually experiment with these targeting tools in the classroom, such as the Facebook Advertising Manager, to help students better understand how they are targeted by companies, organizations, political parties, foreign governments, and individuals. The Facebook Advertising Manager is a web-based tool that allows organizations, companies, and individuals to design, schedule, and target advertisements. Advertisements are targeted at other Facebook users, Instagram users, or across Facebook's third-party advertising network. Anyone can run an advertisement on Facebook or its subsidiary company

Instagram, and the companies do little to regulate their advertisements, if only because the sheer volume of ads which are processed through these platforms daily is too much to manage. Social media advertising is no longer a niche field or purely experimental space; the total, global digital advertising spend has surpassed the total, global television advertising spend, and the trend seems to be that more and more resources will be put into hyper-targeted advertisements in the near future.

Engaging students in this work is important, particularly in light of recent studies that indicate students' challenges discerning the different kinds of information online, as well as the credibility of this information (Breakstone et al., 2017, 2019). As noted in the Introduction to this volume, a 2017 study of more than 7000 student responses conducted by the Stanford History Education Group found that more than 50% of the students could not perform the required tasks, which included distinguishing between a news story and a paid advertisement.

In a follow-up study, which took place between June 2018 to May 2019, The Stanford History Education Group administered a similar assessment to 3,446 high school students across the country. Reporting their findings in "Students' Civic Online Reasoning: A National Portrait," the researchers describe that their assessment of U.S. high school students' digital literacy skills uncovered "troubling" results (3). In short, U.S. high school students are failing to recognize paid content and even more are failing to recognize flagrant conflicts of interest: "Two-thirds of students couldn't tell the difference between news stories and ads (set off by the words "Sponsored Content") on Slate's homepage" and "Ninety-six percent of students did not consider why ties between a climate change website and the fossil fuel industry might lessen the website's credibility"(3). My focus in this chapter will be to explore this space within the lateral distribution of paid information as it is published and targeted at users on Facebook.

To illustrate the type of intricate, highly targeted advertisements I am discussing, I want to share an anecdote about the time I spent designing advertisements for a hospital system. While managing digital strategies for a regional healthcare company, I was presented with some new data about vasectomies and basketball. Sizable populations of men who were electing to undergo this sterilizing procedure were choosing to schedule their surgeries during March Madness. This way, patients could take a few sick days off from work and enjoy some televised sports at the same time. All in all, it's not a bad deal, if you like basketball and don't want children (or have enough kids already). And it turns out there's a large population where those two interests overlap.

I naturally began getting the ethical jitters once we started discussing the creative content and "drilling down" on the demographics. I'll intentionally blend up some of the details, here, though this is not an uncommon, general digital marketing scenario for 2019–2020 in many industries. Let's say our target audience would be men in their 30s–50s with incomes above $40,000 and a college degree. We would consider creative content for our demographic sub-sets: married men and single men. The Facebook Advertising Manager allows us to create multiple audience sets based on education, marital status, children, income, spending habits, likes and interests, and behaviors.

Our two demographic groups require different creative content to appeal to them, of course. Stock photos of messy houses and poopy diapers might be suggested to persuade against procreating for the single guy group. Durex has used similar strategies in their condom advertisements. Smiling, white-teethed, heterosexual, fit, "normative," nuclear family photos of husbands and wives with two kids are suggested for the married sub-set. In other words, we make a visual rhetorical argument: are you sure you want to mess this up with another kid? There's the power of the enthymeme.

Our small marketing team ended up having a few conversations within the organization and the ads never ran while I was there. But undoubtedly other health care systems went forward with these strategies. Having laid out, here, just a glimpse into the bizarre and complex considerations which go into the delivery of targeted digital content, I will move to explore ways in which we can help students analyze these delivery systems using procedural rhetoric, and introduce suggestions for exercises within the classroom.

Procedural Rhetoric for Digital Advertisement Analysis

Procedural rhetoric offers us a useful tool to analyze complex distribution systems, such as those that are used by advertisers to run targeted advertisements within Facebook. Ian Bogost, in his *Persuasive Games: The Expressive Power of Videogames*, uses the term "procedural rhetoric" to explain how arguments are made through "rule-based representations and interactions" (Bogost, 2007, p. ix). An example that works well in the classroom involves thinking about a character creation screen in a contemporary role-playing video game. An instructor or professor can even pull up an example to show in class (as I recently discovered I could use the HDMI out on a Nintendo Switch console to connect to the projector in my classroom): Start a new game in Bethesda's Elder Scrolls V: Skyrim, and have the class note the options within the character creation menu. Bear with me here to see the connection to digital advertising.

It becomes evident rather quickly when using one of these character creation modelers that not every single skin color, nose shape, body shape, height, weight and so on is available for the player to select. Thus, the designers and publishers of this game are making an argument about, we might say, what is normative, by creating rules around the available dimensions of the creation of an in-game character. Here is procedural rhetoric. The rules of the game—its structure, its processes, what it permits or does not permit—create an argument. This is a common theme that the video game industry continues to try to address—allowing players to even select a female character was not as widely available as it is in the current year. This is a fine problematic to consider in its own right.

But we should move beyond video games with procedural rhetoric. It's important to note that these games are a serious subject matter—the global video game industry now consistently earns more revenue than the global movie and music industries combined, and has been doing so for nearly a decade. Games make a useful cultural touchpoint across age gaps between instructors and students, and games are useful for demonstrating the fundamental concepts of procedural rhetoric before applying them to digital advertising. Not all instructors have this interest in digital games and not all classrooms are suited for a gaming activity. The applications for procedural rhetoric are far-reaching: in the design of our software (what does your smartphone operating system allow you to do, or not do?) to the design of our machines to the design of cities (say, considerations of proxemics and civil engineering in terms of transportation and access to critical locations like hospitals and grocery stores), and in the organization of businesses and communities (how do laws influence behavior and how do policies and protocols shape an institution?).

From this understanding of procedural rhetoric, we can begin to draw an important connection to our writing classrooms, in thinking about the creation, distribution, and analysis of digital advertisements. Here is where we can help students begin to answer the question: how do these advertisements find me? Why do videos about Donald Trump or Bernie Sanders constantly show up in my news feed on social media sites? What data have I uploaded to Facebook or what behaviors do I commit online that have made me a target? We already conduct visual and textual rhetorical analyses on political speeches, videos, articles, and content. We can consider, too, these mechanisms of how this information pops onto our screens.

There are two immediately expedient layers to think about in the procedural rhetoric of digital advertisement development and creation. Career professionals like social media managers and digital marketing specialists, both in-house and at marketing agencies, use the sets of rules and parameters within the Facebook Advertising Manager to define hyper-targeted demographics to which they deliver their creative content. Further, government employees and agents across the world are often tasked with creating "disinformation" campaigns, and can just as easily use Twitter or Facebook's advertising platforms to create and deliver content. This was the case when surprised American Twitter users started seeing recruitment advertisements for ISIS on Twitter in 2012. Yes, anyone can create a social media advertisement, including ISIS members.

Of course, companies have marketing budgets which further set parameters around the number of ads they can run and how many people they might reach. And an explicit purpose, or in marketing terminology "call to action," is in mind with every advertisement. Do we want people who see this ad to buy a product, sign up for a newsletter, register for classes, donate to a cause, vote a particular way, think about a topic differently?

The types of questions we can ask to analyze a digital advertisement and its distribution are questions of *purpose/call-to-action, funding, medium/form, origin, and distribution*. To this analysis procedural rhetoric adds the considerations of distribution: how was I targeted and what were the algorithmic rules used to discover my digital identity and match me with this content or advertisement?

While we may not be able to perfectly discern the answers, we can still ask and explore, which leads us to better understand why and how an advertisement was produced and how it reached us, allowing us to see past its construction and define its intent. We can teach students to use rhetorical toolkits to conduct rhetorical analyses of digital ads, and apply concepts of procedural rhetoric to think about how we were targeted and identified in receiving the advertisement:

- Who were the real people who imagined, planned, researched, designed, and scheduled this advertisement?
- Who is the intended audience? What age, income level, education, interests? What features or characteristics or information have I entered online which allowed my digital profile to be identified by an advertiser? Who else did it reach, in addition to you?
- What is the medium of the advertisement? Is it a video, a linked article, a lead form, an event, an external link to a website, a gallery of images?
- What does the ad want you to do (call to action)? What does it want you to think? What is its argument?

- What would the creator of this ad consider as a successful "conversion"? Would it be ordering their product, signing up for their newsletter, entering your e-mail address in an online form?
- Who paid for this advertisement? What is the page or account associated with the advertisement? What linked information can you find—a Facebook business page, a personal page, a website you are directed to?

Then, the second layer, beyond the rhetorical analysis, are all the "black box," behind-the-scenes algorithms and development that the Facebook company has created as its Advertising Manager software: why can we target individuals based on age, income, and education level but not whether or not they are homeowners? This is the balance of the data that Facebook collects and how it is used.

These are the rules and procedures that are defined by the company through the engineering of its software, specifically its web-based Advertising Manager. Facebook defines the means by which advertisers can target us. Advertisers then play with their data, demographics, geographical radius to attempt to generate more sales, urge voters to the polls, or plant a tree.

Within this space, I encourage writing instructors to experiment and explore with their students. An instructor might create a Facebook Business Page for the class and begin playing around with the "sandbox" of the web-based software of the Facebook Advertising Manager in class. Because anyone can create a Facebook advertisement, so can you, and so can your students. Show students how you can select a geographical radius in the Advertising Manager. Demonstrate the demographic targeting mechanisms: income level, education, interests. Drill down into the highly granular categories and sub-categories: ask students to come up with seemingly unlikely scenarios and see if you can find populations of people who fit the criteria: for example, identify the audience who likes both artisanal cupcakes and wakeboarding who is also married and between the ages of 30–35 and potentially has two or more cats and a Master's degree and a problem with excessive credit card spending. You'll find more than one person, in the U.S., who fits the bill. Also show students the relationship between the targeting you are conducting and the populations: you will see while using the Facebook Ad Manager that about 50% of the population of any given geographic area in the U.S. has a registered Facebook account, making it the largest medium of any style for connecting with the highest percentage of a population.

Like West-Puckett, Shepley, and Gray in their chapter in this collection, I am arguing for encouraging our students to learn the technologies through which they are being targeted. West-Puckett, Shepley, and Gray explain how heuristics such as the CRAAP test reveal themselves to be inadequate in the complex, "networked media landscape" of digital and social media. The authors encourage students to use an open-source HTML extension to "overwrite" on top of fake news articles, and stress that their program "encourages independent technology learning as a key outcome" vital to a student's information literacy in the era of fake news. By encouraging our students to use these digital tools, they will better understand the rhetorical and economic circumstances that lead to their creation and to their targeting.

As Reynolds and Jarrett also write in their chapter in this volume, "Students are more likely to get their news and help with homework from social media sites and Google." Yet, as they rightly recognize, our "digital native" students represent a wide range of digital literacy skills, and the type of fluency with digital tools that we expect of a digital native does not equate to high information literacy. The ability to operate a graphical user interface designed for a Facebook user is not the same as digging into its Advertising Manager. And herein is why I continue to emphasize the significance of the economic and advertising elements involved in the distribution of information. Paid placements in search engines, marketing teams composed of digital gurus and SEO experts, and native advertising are pushed across the web, globally, with billions of dollars. As I often joke with my students, "wouldn't it be so convenient that the study funded by Pepsi Co. discovered that diet sodas with aspartame are healthy?" But these types of corruptions of information happen on all scales. And showing students how content is paid and distributed is a key factor in the development of a 21st-century digital and information literacy.

Why do I focus, here, so much on Facebook? Facebook remains the market leader in processing digital advertising volume, by an enormous margin, at the time of writing this chapter. Students may mention that they use Instagram more than Facebook. Instagram, with around a billion monthly active users, is more popular with younger audiences, certainly. Still, Instagram is owned by Facebook and advertisements for Instagram are typically designed and ordered through Facebook's Advertising Manager. There are many targeting technologies and many social media platforms, and Facebook will not always be the most widely used or the most relevant. Yet, the framework of procedural rhetorical analyses that I have demonstrated within this chapter may be applied beyond Facebook. Distribution channels that use targeting methods rely on complex procedures, and we should be diligent in attempting to understand the new ways in which organizations and companies attempt to deliver information to us.

Cambridge Analytica and Moving Beyond Commercial Applications of Hyper-Targeting

A 2019 documentary film, *The Great Hack*, does a fair job of demonstrating the role that UK data and marketing firm Cambridge Analytica played in the 2016 U.S. presidential election by using scraped Facebook profile data to identify "persuadable" voters in key states and develop highly-targeted creative content pushed through social media (primarily Facebook) to convince those on-the-fence voters to formulate political positions and then vote (Amer & Noujaim, 2019). Data scraping is the process of harvesting information from one web source to another, or from the web to a local drive. In this case, the Cambridge Analytica firm developed a quiz that, when installed within Facebook, the user would (unknowingly) give permission to the application to collect data from the user and the user's connections. Through this process, several thousand data points were collected on each of millions of U.S. citizens who use Facebook, and Cambridge Analytica used this data and an understanding of the relationship between Big-5 Personality Traits and political ideology to target users they deemed as "persuadable" in the 2016 U.S. presidential election.

In an opening scene, Professor David Carrol tells a group of students that our smart phones aren't actually using audio data to listen to us and send us advertisements based on this information. Rather, we use the web so much more than we realize, and input so much data into search engines, complex cross-platform accounts with Google, and third-party applications within applications, that there is just an enormous chunk of data that can be used to target a person, and these advertisements and content that are delivered to us are based on so much data, that we are given the sense that we are being listened to. This is part of the picture. These large technology companies collect tons of data and then allow advertisers to use this data to create and deliver targeted advertisements based on selectable criteria, such as education level, income, marital status, likes and dislikes, hobbies, interests, spending habits, and much more.

Yet, this isn't the whole picture. Speech-recognition technology has made extraordinary leaps in the last few years. See YouTube's automated caption option, which can nearly-instantaneously convert human voice to text in a number of languages. And, YouTube is owned by Google. If you don't think that your voice can be converted to text and that data can be swung back around at you with a targeted advertisement or stored on a server for 1,000 years, then you may not be living in the same 2020 as I am.

Nonetheless, we have to start somewhere with our students, and discussing Facebook CEO Mark Zuckerberg's testimony to the U.S. Congress in 2019 and the serious implications of digital advertising for democracy help to ground these discussions in the classroom beyond commercial advertisements. Our lawmakers hardly understand how Facebook works, even asking Zuckerberg what Facebook's business model is. Zuckerberg replied, of course, "We sell ads." How can we expect lawmakers to keep an eye on what they fundamentally misunderstand?

Digital content is being used to attempt to change the way we think and how we might vote. The stakes are high. It matters what types of content is allowed, disallowed, paid for, supported, and how it is treated or sorted by algorithms. Most of our students will already have been exposed to thousands of ideologically charged digital advertisements, in the form of articles, memes, videos, and graphics, before they even begin college. There's a lot to sift through.

Inspiration for Classroom Activities and Assignments on Procedural Rhetoric, Digital Distribution, and Hyper-Targeting

Where are these conversations and activities which deal with the analysis of digital distribution systems situated in the field of rhetoric and composition? We can look to the sub-field of digital rhetoric. Building on ideas from James Zappen, Douglas Eyman, early in his *Digital Rhetoric: Theory, Method, Practice,* suggests that the "primary activities within the field of digital rhetoric" include "the use of rhetorical strategies in production and analysis of digital text," as well as the "examination of the rhetorical function of networks" and "the use of rhetorical methods for uncovering and interrogating ideologies and cultural formation in digital work" (2015, p. 44). Eyman also draws from Bogost to demonstrate that emergent technologies, like games or complex social media advertisement distribution systems, may require new forms of rhetorical analysis to thoroughly dissect. Within this space of digital rhetoric, we see new pedagogical opportunities emerge. How better to identify the "characteristics, affordances, and constraints of new media" than to actually use these new media forms in our classrooms?

A number of activities that allow students and instructors to explore, discuss, analyze, and use these targeting and distribution technologies can be easily conducted in a college classroom. I suggest taking these ideas and modifying them for your own classroom, your students, university or class goals, or preferred pedagogical approach. I suggest to writing instructors, as well, that they take time to research and experiment with these technologies. There are countless, free, video tutorials widely available that show how tools like the Facebook Advertising Manager are used. We can learn with our students, as well, and learn from them. These activities all explore several layers of rhetorical considerations within the distribution of digital advertisements. Here are some considerations for activities and assignments:

- Ask students to record every digital advertisement they see, for an entire day. This should include banner ads, pop-up ads, native advertisements, search result ads such as Google paid search result placements, social media ads, sponsored products, e-mails, geo-targeted ads, video ads, and re-targeted ads. Ask students to record *where* the ad was seen with a high degree of detail and describe its content. This quickly becomes a daunting task as students may see thousands of advertisements a day. You might begin by showing students a number of advertisements in a typical casual Internet usage flow path by logging into a Facebook account and noting the sponsored posts. Or, search for a term in Google and show students how to identify paid placements in Google search results.
- Ask students to select an advertisement that they have seen recently that was "eerily accurate" or particularly invasive or uncomfortable. Ask students to consider how they were targeted or what information they left behind in which sites on the Internet that may have given away their interest in this particular domain.
- Ask students to write a narrative about their experience with using social media, a time they were targeted by an advertisement, or a sort of digital literacy self-assessment. What platforms do they use? How often do they use these platforms? What type of information do they share, between profile data, e-mails, photos, video uploads, searches, your network?
- Ask students to review their privacy settings in social media accounts, whether applications have access to their microphone, and ask them to do a "deep dive" into their digital footprint. What can they find out about themselves on the Internet? What can others find?
- Ask students to create a demographic profile of themselves: age, income, education, likes/dislikes, geographic locations most visited, and consumer habits. They can use criteria from the Facebook Advertising Manager to do so.
- Go beyond the commercial element of targeted advertising. Ask students to reflect on the type of *editorial* or *political* or *ideological content*

that has been advertised to them. Conduct a rhetorical analysis in class of one of these social ads, which often take the form of creative content and video.
- Give students a demographic profile and a product, and have them select a stock photo and write advertising copy with a CTA (call to action) for the Facebook Advertising Manager. Make sure to have them pay attention to the rules and regulations: pixel dimensions, image to text ratio, and so on. Then, design creative content that appeals to this specific audience.
- Give your students a $20 marketing budget to design an advertisement that targets themselves and will show up in their own news feed on Facebook or Instagram. This exercise works better in rural or semi-rural universities/colleges or areas with lower population density. Results may vary, depending on if students have updated their location in Facebook from their previous city/state. But when it works, students should be able to target themselves with an advertisement and see how effective these platforms can be.
- Invite the social media manager, digital marketer, web manager, or another member from your university's marketing team to come talk to your class about how your university's digital marketing strategy works, and how digital tools are used to target individuals.

Further Research and Looking Ahead

The game of highly-targeted advertising is just beginning, and the landscape is constantly shifting. Twitter CEO Jack Dorsey announced in October/November 2019 that Twitter will no longer run paid political advertisements on its platform (Dorsey, 2019). Yet, Facebook continues to do so. It is partially an issue of volume. Humans cannot possibly check the content of hundreds of millions of advertisements. And the algorithmic rules for content regulation, set by Facebook, seem to do very little: for example, an advertisement might be automatically rejected by breaking a rule such as using too much text within the advertisement's image, or including a sensitive or inflammatory word. We cannot yet expect automated processes to do the hard work of judging the trustworthiness of our information for us, and we cannot always expect our large technology companies or lawmakers to make the right decisions.

What *The Great Hack* film gets wrong and what many technologists and thinkers are now concerned about is the rapid advancement of speech language recognition technologies, and the "always on" problem of smart phone microphones. It is not difficult to imagine a company easily converting speech to text from a smartphone microphone and then using this data to deliver advertisements based on keyword matching or even non-speech audio recognition. You sneeze near your phone, you get an advertisement for Kleenex in your Instagram mobile app. These technologies are already developed, and I suspect many companies are making significant progress in their implementation and now piloting some of these listening-based advertisement delivery mechanisms. We give our microphones more permission than we realize. And this is just what's on the nearest horizon.

With further developments in artificial intelligence, social credit systems, Neuralink-type devices integrating technology into the body, augmented reality, virtual reality technologies, we need to help students understand how they are targeted and *how information finds them*. It's no longer enough to solely incorporate lessons on how to find and evaluate credible information. So much of what our students watch and read has been *delivered* to them. Some quick but thoughtful lessons on procedural rhetoric and using the Facebook Advertising Manager can provide a useful glimpse into this world. Additionally, bringing the Facebook Advertising Manager into the classroom shows potential careers in marketing, social media, and digital media to students who may be interested in the more ethical usage of these types of targeted advertisements, which may exist. These types of explorations fit nicely into curricula for college composition, professional/business writing classrooms, technical writing, rhetoric, multimodal composition, academic writing, and communication.

What does understanding the distribution of paid digital information solve? Not everything. But it can show students how carefully crafted messaging is designed and funneled to them. Information that finds us is not necessarily flawed, but we should be especially careful with it. When we receive a digital advertisement, we were almost always targeted with a purpose in mind. To buy something, to try something, to think something, to believe something, to feel something. Discussions can grow from these starting points. Look at examples of "native advertising" in class, or content that is disguised to look like editorial content but is a paid advertisement. Start a discussion with big questions that are relevant to the technology: What is truth? There are great connections here to can make between the fields of Philosophy and Technology. We can look to media theory, digital media studies, psychology, and political economy for more interdisciplinary assistance with understanding how these technologies work and are working on our students (and the rest of us). These questions and problems are not limited to one piece of software or one program. Composition instructors might continue to look to the discipline of Technical Communication for more explorations of the study of ethics in writing and the ethical considerations surrounding computer technologies. Writing and language programs should continue to consider offering Technical Writing courses that give time and consideration to ethics in writing. We can also innovate in these emergent spaces with developing new curricula that address the gaps between technology and the humanities. Meanwhile, students continue to graduate from accredited universities lacking the advanced technological skills needed for the job market. We can do better to dig into the back-end of technology in our work in the humanities, and those who use these technologies can look to the humanities for some measure or compass in terms of the ethical and purposeful usage of these types of technologies.

References

Amer, K. (Director, Producer) & Noujaim, J. (Director, Producer) (2019). *The great hack* [Motion picture]. United States: Netflix.

Bogost, I. (2007). *Persuasive games: The expressive power of videogames.* MIT Press.

Breakstone, J., et al. (2017). The challenge that's bigger than fake news: Civic reasoning in a social media environment. *American Educator, 14*(3). Retrieved from https://www.aft.org/ae/fall2017/mcgrew_ortega_breakstone_wineburg

Breakstone, J., et al. (2019). *Students' civic online reasoning: A national portrait.* Stanford History Education Group. Retrieved from https://sheg.stanford.edu/students-civic-online-reasoning

Connors, R. J. (1997). *Composition-rhetoric: Backgrounds, theory, and pedagogy.* Cornell University Press Services.

Dorsey, J. (2019). *We've made the decision to stop all political advertising on Twitter. . .* [Tweet]. Twitter. Retrieved from https://twitter.com/jack/status/1189634360472829952

Eyman, D. (2015). *Digital rhetoric: Theory, method, practice.* University of Michigan Press.

Stanford History Education Group. (2016). *Evaluating information: The cornerstone of civic online reasoning.* Stanford History Education Group. Retrieved from https://sheg.stanford.edu/upload/V3LessonPlans/Executive%20Summary%2011.21.16.pdf

13. Preparing Students to Read and Compose Data Stories in the Fake News Era

Angela Laflen

As instructors consider ways to help students become more critical readers of the texts they encounter online and elsewhere in the fake news era, we must be sure to consider the unique difficulty associated with reading and composing data stories. Data stories are multimodal texts that combine words, iconography, and data displays to make numeric data comprehensible for the public, decision makers, and other audiences. They have always been recognized as powerfully persuasive texts. Today, though, as technology has resulted in an information explosion, data storytelling has become an essential strategy for managing data. Infographics guru Cairo (2013) explains the purpose of visualizing data as "giv[ing] shape to data, so that relevant patterns become visible" (p. 16). The point of making these patterns visible is, as Knaflic (2015) explains, to turn data "into information that can be used to drive better decision making" (p. 2). Writing instructors are well-equipped to help students understand how data stories are composed to appeal to specific audiences and achieve persuasive goals, and a growing body of scholarship focuses on how data function rhetorically (Beveridge, 2015; Wolfe, 2010). This chapter contributes to that work by considering specific classroom strategies useful for helping students to practice reading and producing data stories. I share a unit-long project I have used in composition courses at different levels to introduce data storytelling to students.

The ability to read data stories critically is important for students as an academic skill and in order for them to participate as fully literate members of democratic society. In 2016, the Stanford History Education Group (SHEG) sounded an alarm about the state of U.S. students' "civic online reasoning," which they define as "the ability to judge the credibility of information that floods young people's smartphones, tablets, and computers" (p. 3).

The results of their large national study of elementary through college-level students revealed that, "Overall, young people's ability to reason about the information on the Internet can be summed up in one word: *bleak*" (p. 4). Based on the exercises used in the study (which are available online at the SHEG website), SHEG clearly considers the ability to read data stories critically an important part of civic online reasoning. For example, one exercise for college-level students presents them with a tweet from MoveOn.org that shares a surprising statistic about NRA members' beliefs about background checks and asks them to explain (1) why this tweet might be a useful source about NRA members' beliefs about background checks and (2) why this tweet might not be a useful source about NRA members' beliefs about background checks. Few students were able to evaluate the usefulness of the tweet:

> Only a few students noted that the tweet was based on a poll conducted by a professional polling firm and explained why this would make the tweet a stronger source of information. Similarly, less than a third of students fully explained how the political agendas of MoveOn.org and the Center for American Progress might influence the content of the tweet. (p. 23)

The authors of the SHEG study conclude that "when it comes to evaluating information that flows through social media channels, ['digital natives'] are easily duped" (p. 4), and as a result, "we worry that democracy is threatened by the ease at which disinformation about civic issues is allowed to spread and flourish" (p. 5). Certainly, data stories can be effective vehicles for spreading mis- or disinformation quickly online. Increasingly, fake news creators include misleading or false data displays to imbue their stories with an aura of credibility and increase online engagement. As Chun (2017) explains, the appeal of data stories is their accessibility: "A tweet with an embedded image gets 150 percent more retweets .... Sharing an eye-catching data visualization that has an air of credibility (because it's scientific!) is hard to resist, especially with the low-friction tap of a retweet." The appeal of data stories makes them particularly effective at injecting false and misleading information into decision making and public discourse. SHEG's response is to argue for the development of curricula designed to support instructors' teaching of civic online literacy.

As we develop curricula to combat the spread and influence of fake news, it is important to make data literacy a priority since there are at least three distinct challenges to helping students improve their abilities to read data stories. First, earlier studies of readers asked to evaluate arguments presented with and without data displays have observed that readers are more willing to accept data visualizations as accurate than they would be other types of information, particularly if the visualization is used to confirm a bias they already have (Tal & Wansink, 2014). In Tal & Wansink's (2014) study, for example, readers were asked to evaluate two articles on a scientific claim, both identical except in one regard. One included a graph and the other did not. While only 68% of readers believed the claim in the article without a graph, nearly all—97%—of readers believed the same claim with the graph included—despite the fact that, as Tal & Wansink explain—"no additional information is supplied or even implied by the graphs" (p. 23). The effects were especially pronounced for readers who already had a greater belief in science and were more likely to be affected by the graph in the study (p. 117). Similarly, the SHEG study found that students were more likely to judge claims as credible when accompanied by graphs and images, even when these lacked a data source or cited a non-credible source. Whether the students were awed by the "prestige of science" as Tal & Wansick (2014) suggest (p. 24) or simply because a graph or visual helps support comprehension, students need more training in reading and evaluating data visualizations.

Second, the difficulty of composing accurate data stories means that, as Chun (2017) explains, "There is a long trail that leads from the raw data to the final visualization, with many opportunities along the way to introduce bogus information, making the accuracy of graphs more difficult to assess." Beveridge (2015) describes this "long trail" to argue that compositionists should attend to how quantitative visuals are invented for persuasive purposes:

> Techne and data visualization are contingent upon the accessibility of: (1) The underlying data, how it is collected, and how it is archived and accessed; (2) How the data is processed, cleaned, and organized to prepare for analysis; (3) How the data is analyzed and visualized; (4) How the analyses and visualizations are delivered to an audience.

Both Beveridge (2015) and Wolfe (2010) insist that more awareness of how quantitative arguments are invented is necessary to avoid treating quantitative data as " 'extrinsic' or 'inartistic' proof" (Wolfe, 2010, p. 439) or as "impenetrable and unquestionable forms of evidence" (Beveridge, 2015). Wolfe argues that students need opportunities to practice creating data-based arguments so it will be easier for them to recognize the ways in which data they encounter are always invented to achieve specific purposes. Lack of familiarity with the data storytelling process seems to have been at the heart of the problems students faced in evaluating data stories in the SHEG study. Though the SHEG researchers were looking for evidence that students recognized that data stories are invented and rhetorical in nature, students' responses instead showed them taking the data stories at face value rather than considering the larger contexts in which the stories were created, including who gathered the data and for what purpose, and how they were cleaned and analyzed.

A third, and more recent, challenge to reading data stories critically involves the way these texts reach the public and circulate online. Today, misinformation spreads more quickly than ever before. Miller & Leon (2017) explain that "Fake news circulates through botnet networks that use algorithms to profile users and feed them stories that fit their individual biases" (p. 10). Consequently, Laquintano & Vee (2017) point out that the widespread dissemination of fake news stories online indicates the limitations of "many of the tenuous ways we've learned to discern what's true online" (p. 46). Fake data stories, like fake news stories in general, "often emulate the look and titles of professional news sources," so that "even if a story has been shared a million times on social media, and if it is found on a website that looks and sounds newsy, and if it is repeatedly linked from a popular hashtag, there's no guarantee that it's a credible story" (Laquintano & Vee, 2017, p. 46). In the context of online information ecosystems, it is not enough to migrate criteria for evaluating print sources to networked information. As Lawrence discusses in this volume, "with the relatively new, emergent phenomenon of highly-targeted digital advertisements, there is another side of these issues of ethos and credibility." In this environment, distinctions between primary and secondary sources and between sources subject or not subject to peer review remain useful but are not sufficient for helping students assess the credibility of networked information.

In light of the difficulties students have reading data stories and the growing importance of these texts in online and professional discourses, they deserve special attention in our composition courses. In particular, instructors who include multimodal assignments in their courses need to recognize the centrality of data storytelling to multimodal genres such as infographics, white papers, and social media posts. Reading and producing effective multimodal texts increasingly requires students to possess a basic understanding of strategies for representing numeric data. The need to analyze and produce arguments that are at once multimodal and quantitative adds complexity to the incorporation of these new genres in composition courses. Elsewhere in this volume, Canfield recommends that teachers encourage the rhetorical practices of listening, considering, and responding as a way to "slow down the communication process and allow for thoughtful consideration and deliberation." Slowing down runs contrary to "the technique characterized by a sensationalized, attention-grabbing heading that provides a link to another article or website …. There is no time for careful listening nor considering because link-clicking moves the consumer from place to place rapidly."

Helping students to build habits of slowing down and engaging with texts is especially important in the case of easily shareable and digestible data stories.

Data Storytelling in the Composition Classroom

My approach to data storytelling draws on my background teaching data visualization in professional and technical writing courses and is informed by the work of quantitative reasoning (QR) across the curriculum advocates along with rhetoric and composition scholars. QR-across-the-curriculum advocates such as Steen (2004) and Rutz & Grawe (2009) stress that quantitative reasoning focuses more on the study of logic than of advanced mathematics, while rhetoric and composition scholars provide frameworks for considering how data function rhetorically in multimodal texts. My goal for data storytelling assignments is not to make students experts at data storytelling, which requires more time and practice than is possible during a single-semester course focused more broadly on writing. Rather, it is to equip students with strategies they can use to engage data stories more critically—as readers and users of data in their own writing.

Introducing data storytelling principles and giving students opportunities to work with data helps students to appreciate the extent to which data are shaped through the composing process and to read other data stories critically. Data stories are ubiquitous both on and offline in social media posts, slideshows, infographics, interactive data visualizations, white papers, and fact sheets, among others; curated examples of good and bad data stories are available at Cairo's website (http://albertocairo.com/) and Knaflic's website (http://www.storytellingwithdata.com/). Nevertheless, despite how pervasive data storytelling is, undergraduate students rarely have opportunities to create or visualize data. These skills are typically reserved for upper-level disciplinary research methods courses, or, even more commonly, graduate courses. What Daniels (2019) argues about students learning to read digital texts by producing their own digital texts is also true of data stories: "as students write digitally they gain a better understanding of the ways in which they can approach digital reading: the production of the text, and gaining that literacy, is equally as important as the consumption of it" (p. 134). In order to become data literate, students need to experience the data story composition process, and though we cannot expect them to master this process, they can cultivate data literacy skills to engage critically the data stories they encounter. The unit-long project that I describe moves from reverse engineering others' data stories to composing a data story, and it asks students to explore how data stories are invented throughout the entire composing process.

Data Storytelling Project

My data storytelling project asks students to work with public data related to an important issue on campus or in the community and to create data displays (tables and charts) accompanied by text and other visuals in order to make interesting or significant patterns clear to a relevant audience. Students are not required to recommend solutions or even research solutions to the issues they write about, though adding such a requirement would be a way to extend the assignment. Instead, I ask them to help an audience which needs to understand the issue visualize the scope of the issue (by focusing on questions such as how many people does it effect? What are its costs—financial, psychological, etc.? Is the issue increasing or decreasing over time? What offices or groups on campus or in the community handle this issue?). Students complete several process activities in preparation for composing their own data story and reflective analysis.

This project fulfills a number of goals related to research writing in both professional writing and first-year composition courses. It provides an opportunity for students to practice identifying relevant data, using them as evidence to support larger claims, organizing and developing an argument clearly for a specific audience, and citing sources correctly. The purpose of using public data is to give students practice finding this information and also to facilitate instructor access to the same data in order to check for accuracy. There are numerous sources of public data related to specific schools and communities. As one example, colleges and universities are required to publish annual reports with statistics on specific campus safety issues in compliance with the Clery Act. The assignment also provides opportunities to cultivate visual and digital literacies as students design their own data stories and determine the appropriate delivery mechanism for them.

Introducing Data Storytelling Principles

To teach data storytelling to undergraduates, I have adapted terms and concepts provided by Beveridge (2015), Knaflic (2017), Wolfe (2010), and others in their discussions of data storytelling. I begin by introducing data storytelling principles (see Appendix A). To help students understand these principles, it has proven useful to reverse engineer a set of data stories, such as in Figures 13.1-A and 13.1-B, that use a common data set to ensure that students understand how data stories are invented during each step of the composing process.

Both of the data stories in Figure 13.1 use the same open data set published by YouGov (2018), a British international Internet-based market

Preparing Students to Read and Compose Data Stories　　199

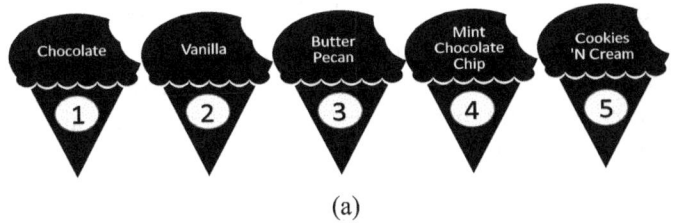

(a)

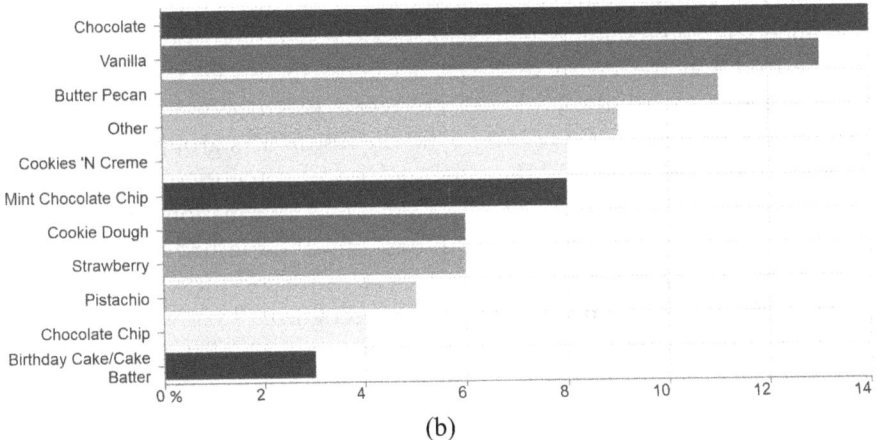

(b)

Figure 13.1: A and B: Two Data Stories Based on the Same Data Set. Source: Author

research and data analytics firm that specializes in market research through online methods, to tell a different story about Americans' ice cream preferences. While Figure 13.1-A emphasizes how popular ice cream is among Americans (consumed by 96% of Americans), Figure 13.1-B illustrates the popularity of all 11 flavors included in the study in addition to the category of "other," which came in fourth in the survey. The stories also take different approaches to depicting flavors that tied in the rankings (such as mint chocolate chip and cookies 'n cream). Figure 13.1-A places mint chocolate chip ahead of cookies 'n cream, while Figure 13.1-B reverses the order. These data stories combine textual, statistical, and visual information to create appealing stories that are easy for students to read and understand, but because each one included different data and visualized that data differently, they do tell slightly different stories.

Though the differences between the data stories are obvious simply by comparing them, less obvious is how the data were invented in the first place through the process of being gathered and prepared for analysis. In the case of the YouGov (2018) study, the data set is available online. By examining the data set used to create these stories, we can ask questions about who conducted this study and why it was designed as it was. Some of the questions that are important to consider include: Who/what is YouGov? Why did the group conduct this survey about Americans' ice cream preferences? Who was surveyed and how were these people chosen? In the case of YouGov, answers to these questions are available online, and enough details are provided about the process of creating and conducting the survey that students accept the credibility of YouGov and the survey results.

Once students establish who gathered the data and for what purpose, we question how the survey itself was designed. Questions that students ask about the survey include: How did the researchers decide which ice cream flavors to include in the survey? Why did the researchers group ages together the ways they did? How did they choose income categories? For the study, what counted as "Northeast," "South," etc.? This information is not available online, nor is it typically included with data sets or published in the methods sections of research studies, so we cannot get answers to these questions. The purpose of this exercise is to help students recognize (1) how the data were gathered in this study and prepared for analysis and (2) that different survey questions and choices could have led to different results and consequently different data stories based on those results. Optionally, to extend this lesson, students can be asked to design their own survey questions related to ice cream preferences: What flavors would they include? How would they delimit different groups included in the survey?

Comparing data stories based on the same data set leads to questions about which of the data stories represents the "real" answer about Americans' ice cream preferences. The answer is that neither of them do. They both depict partial results of a single study. In this way, this discussion can help students to "dwell in uncertainty," which Koupf recommends in this volume as a strategy for "promoting more integrative thinking." As Koupf explains, "Complicating reading, truth and fiction, fact-checking and fact-bending is important in alleviating binary thinking and recognizing the rhetorical construction of all writing, even facts." Though in the case of the ice cream study, some will argue that by omitting the "other" category, Figure 13.1-A is less accurate—perhaps even less ethical—than Figure 13.1-B, the most important takeaway is that no data story—or data visualization—can represent the Truth. Nevertheless, accurate and ethical data stories can be useful in helping readers to understand data better.

After the class has examined how data were gathered in the case of the sample data set, students are asked to think about their own data storytelling projects. They have time to brainstorm a topic about which they want to learn more and raise awareness. Once they choose their topic, they locate public data to use for the project. Additionally, they identify traditional scholarly sources to use for background, such as articles and books. Next, we talk about how data are cleaned or prepared for analysis and visualization. For example, the data stories in Figures 13.1-A and 13.1-B differ from one another because of the flavors they chose to include and how many flavors they included in their stories. Figure 13.1-A does not provide any numeric information about how popular the 5 most popular flavors are that it depicts—and it also omits the "other" category that was included in the YouGov (2018) survey and ranked in the top 5 of responses. Figure 13.1-B includes all 11 flavors included in the survey along with the information that 9% of participants chose "other" as their favorite and that 7% of respondents said they did not eat ice cream. Every data story is the result of these kinds of choices.

At this stage, students are encouraged to think about how they want to define the parameters of data to include in their study. As they begin to identify data to use, it is useful for them to think about the multiple stories their data might be capable of telling. Time permitting, they can be encouraged to look for disconfirming or contradictory evidence that might complicate their story or help them to provide a fuller picture of the topic.

Visualizing Data

Once students understand how data are invented in the process of being gathered and prepared for analysis and visualization, they are ready to learn more about the process of data visualization. Data visualization can be overwhelmingly complex, however. The key is to focus on a few basic principles that students can use to create simple visualizations that will allow them to see for themselves how visualization shapes data stories.

I provide students with specific vocabulary to discuss the visual mode and in particular the visual aspects of written text, using language such as that recommended by the authors of *Writer/Designer: A Guide to Making Multimodal Projects*, who explain the visual mode in terms of color, layout, style, size, and perspective (Arola, Sheppard, & Ball, 2014, p. 6). Following this introduction and discussion, I ask students to analyze the visual elements of sample data stories we have read for class and to discuss how these elements contribute to the persuasiveness of the story.

Students also need an introduction to the most common types of graphs and charts to understand what each is best at communicating. This introduction helps them better understand how to approach reading data displays as well. Wolfe (2009), in a survey of industry/government technical reports and academic journal articles, found that tables, line graphs, and bar graphs are by far the most commonly used chart types (p. 363), so I focus on these in my class and show students how to use Excel to create these basic charts. Each one is good at communicating different kinds of information. Tables are effective at displaying a lot of information in a small space, presenting data with different units, and conveying exact values. Bar charts allow writers to convey highs and lows and make spotting "winners" and "losers" easy, but they are effective at conveying only a limited amount of information. Line graphs are best at depicting change over time. We talk about how the type of graph we use will help us see different patterns in the data and contribute to the reader's understanding or misunderstanding the data we gathered, and we practice working with a sample data set to create visualizations. It quickly becomes clear that while creating charts is not difficult, it takes some work to create charts that make patterns easily visible for readers.

For example, Figure 13.2-A is an accurate rendering of the six most popular ice cream flavors broken down by age range using the YouGov (2018) data set, but the chart does not make any particular pattern easy to see. It includes too much information for a bar chart to make identifying the highs and lows easy. In contrast, Figure 13.2-B, which includes only the top ice cream flavors for the groups 18–34 year olds and 55+, makes the contrast in preferences between these groups easy to see.

Equally important is when a chart or graph is not really needed at all, such as when a writer only needs to share one key statistic or finding in a data story. For example, if someone just wants to explain that 14% of adults 18–34 chose cookies 'n cream as their favorite flavor, then a chart is likely not necessary. A writer could use other visual strategies, such as color, font size, or a shape such as a callout box, to draw attention to the statistic without creating a chart.

Once students have experienced creating a variety of visualizations from a sample data set, they are ready to produce data visualizations related to their own projects using different types of charts and graphs. It is important that students have the opportunity to test their visualizations with classmates and the instructor at this point to get feedback on where their visualizations are unclear or could be improved.

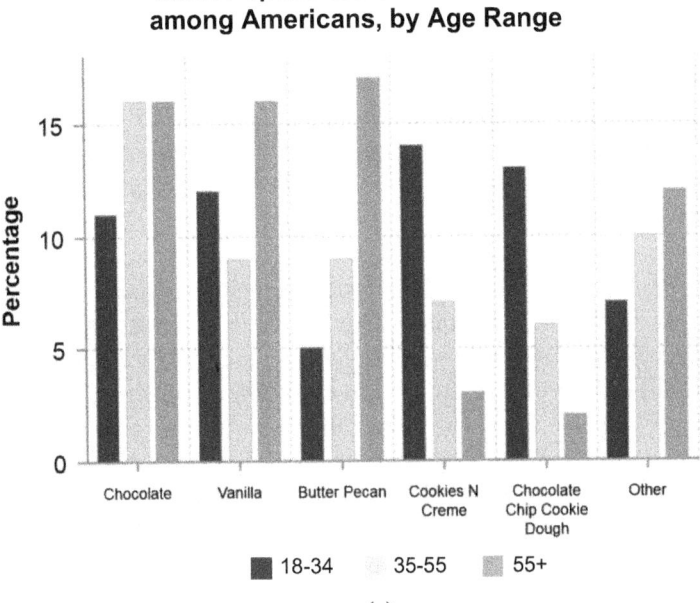

(a)

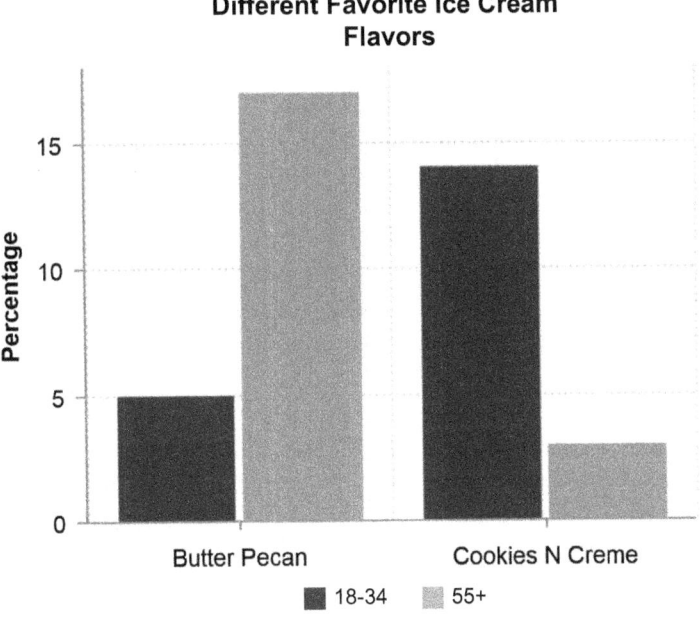

(b)

Figure 13.2: A and B: Comparison of Two Bar Charts. Source: Author

Delivering Data Stories

As we discuss how to deliver our data, we talk about various genres that frequently include data displays, focused especially on online genres such as tweets, Facebook posts, infographics, fact sheets, profiles, and online articles. We begin to read different examples from these genres to see how writers tailor their stories to reach specific audiences through particular genres. For example, infographics are designed to be shared online and are often intended to drive traffic to a website for more information. As Malhotra (2017) explains, they only need to "make one good point," but they need to do that clearly. The most widely shared infographics vary in the number of words from 200 to 500, depending on how much text is required to make the one point clearly (Malhotra, 2017). In contrast, while online articles are also intended to be shared, they serve another purpose of retaining the reader's attention—since engaging the reader for a longer period of time increases opportunities for advertising. Since online articles are created to capture and hold readers' attention, it is not surprising that the most widely shared online articles average 1600–1700 words of text (Lee, 2018).

We create rhetorical strategies for examples of data stories online so we can determine how and why the creators made the composition choices they did based on their audience, purpose, and context. We also identify any areas of weakness or misalignment between the story's purpose and audience and its actual construction. Students practice critically reading actual data stories as they also gain additional insight into the composition process.

Through this process, students recognize that ethical data stories help readers understand what data mean in order to drive better decision making and are characterized by providing context, including who, what, when, where, and why data was created, so readers can understand how and for what purpose the data were invented. In contrast, misleading or unethical data stories distort data and either obscure or falsify information about the context in order to support the writer's argument. What matters in these stories is not helping readers make better decisions but supporting an argument even if that means distorting data to do so.

At this stage, students write a rhetorical strategy for their own data story, which helps them think through the many decisions they must make in composing their data stories. The data stories that students have read become mentor texts that help guide their decision-making at this stage, and students' rhetorical strategies also provide insight into their critical reading skills. For example, if students struggle to articulate how they will visualize data for a specific audience, this difficulty may indicate the need for additional practice closely reading sample data stories. Drawing on their experience of reading multiple data stories, students identify their audience and purpose, think about what kind of data will be most persuasive in the context of their project, and make initial plans regarding the visualization of data and design of their data story. Students also consider what form their data story should take to reach their audience most effectively, whether an infographic, fact sheet, or online news article. The rhetorical strategy is a working document, so it is subject to change as they proceed, but it gives them a starting point for drafting their data story.

Data Story and Project Reflection

The data story and project reflection are the culmination of the student's work on data stories. The data story itself should conform to the conventions of whatever genre students have chosen to work with: these usually take the form of fact sheets, online articles, or infographics. Whatever form their data story takes, students include textual, numeric, and visual elements to tell a story with data, and the data should not be extraneous to the argument but should shape that argument. I do not specify a size or length for the data story since being able to adjust the size to accommodate the information included is a feature of data stories. And I don't require students to submit hard copies unless they are creating fact sheets that are intended for printing. Students receive peer and instructor feedback on their data stories-in-progress.

I also require students to submit a reflective analysis of their data story along with their final data story. The reflective analysis is arguably the single most important component of the project because it asks students to reflect on their own learning about data storytelling and data literacy more generally. In this analysis, they reflect on their experience creating the data story, outline goals for their story, and self-assess the success of their story. It is in these reflections that students also think through the meaning of the challenges and successes that they experienced and what they learned about reading and composing data stories. I ask them to describe the critical reading strategies they used in detail and to consider which of these were most useful to helping them understand data stories. Finally, they discuss how their experience with the project will impact their future reading and composing of data stories.

Despite the challenges of juggling several different kinds of skills and information for the data storytelling project, my students have responded to it enthusiastically and report enjoying the process of creating the data story. They describe it as an assignment that is "relevant" to them, that they feel gives them valuable practice working with data and creating effective graphics, and that helps them think about making arguments in a new way. Figure 13.3 represents a sample data story—an infographic that uses public data provided in the annual campus Clery Report to tell a story about campus safety—a topic that students are frequently drawn to for this assignment. This sample is intended to illustrate what is reasonable to expect from students in this assignment. Successful student data stories will inevitably be simple, focused on making one or two key pieces of information easy for readers to understand and providing context.

Conclusion

The data storytelling assignment represents my response to calls by SHEG (2016) and others to develop curricula to foster students' critical literacies and combat the spread and influence of fake news. Data stories can be effective vehicles for spreading mis—or disinformation, particularly online, because they possess an aura of credibility and increase reader engagement. Because data stories are both increasingly pervasive and also notoriously difficult to read, I believe they warrant special attention as we prepare students to participate in 21st-century information environments. Students need strategies to help them read these texts critically and discern when data stories provide greater understanding of an issue and when they are instead designed to mislead. The approach I advocate is based on introducing the data storytelling composing process to students and then working with them to reverse engineer sample data stories and to create their own data stories. Having experienced the data storytelling composition process for themselves, students are better situated to read critically the data stories they encounter in the future.

Composition instructors are well situated to help students practice reading and composing data stories. In fact, assigning students reading or writing assignments in today's information landscape increasingly means dealing with multimodal texts that include data stories. As Edwards-Grove (2010) explains when arguing for the importance of multimodal writing in composition courses, "the view here is that multimodality does not replace important foundational writing skills but that the elements of the writing process are extended to account for the shift in textual practices that technology demands" (p. 62). Similarly, the challenge of incorporating data storytelling assignments in composition courses is keeping the focus on developing students' rhetorical knowledge, abilities to compose in multiple environments, and knowledge of conventions for data stories, rather than emphasizing advanced mathematical skills or sophisticated computer programs for analyzing and visualizing data.

Preparing Students to Read and Compose Data Stories

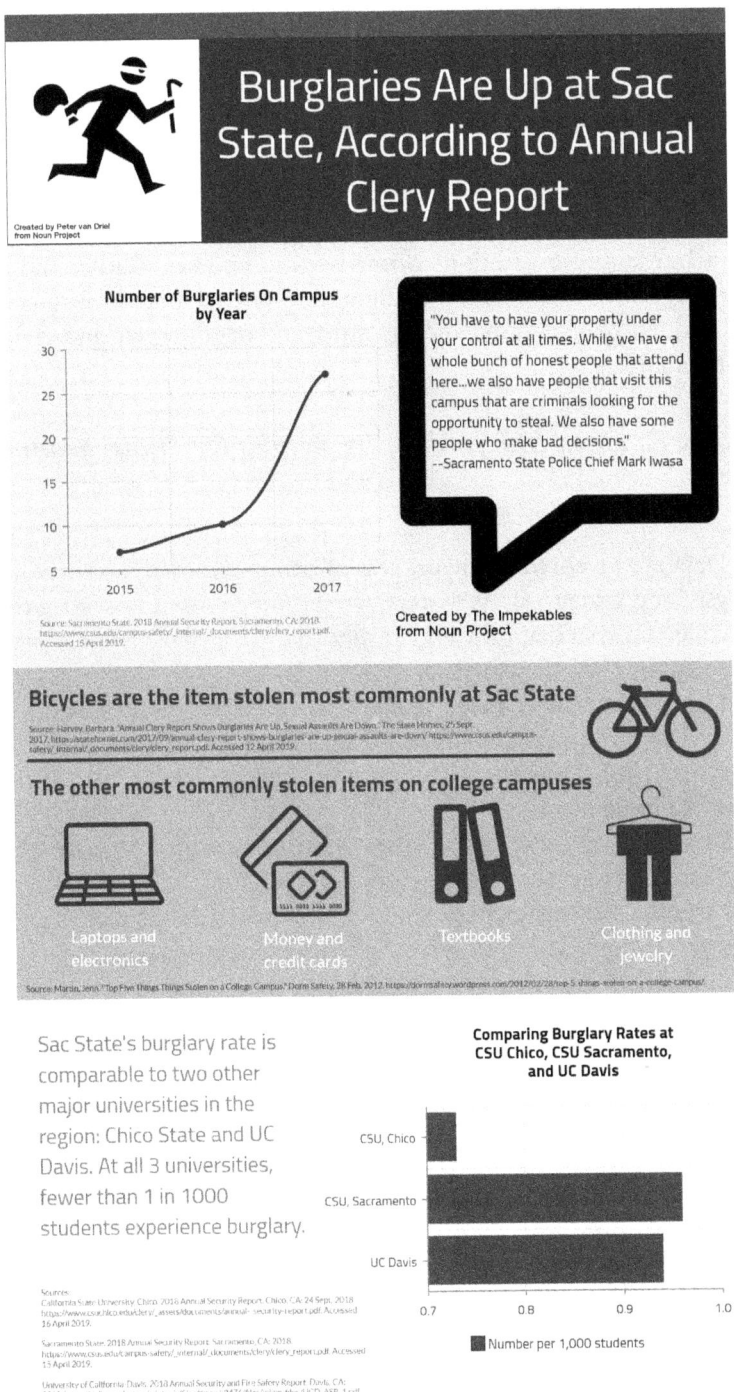

Figure 13.3: Sample Data Story. Source: Author

As Steen (2004) has argued, quantitative reasoning "is sophisticated reasoning with elementary mathematics more than elementary reasoning with sophisticated mathematics" (p. 9). Introducing the data storytelling process to students allows even introductory students to appreciate how these texts present carefully crafted arguments and to determine when they are reading a data story that is using data in ethical or unethical ways. If data storytelling assignments are clearly tied to course learning outcomes and goals, these need not be a burdensome addition to our writing courses. Rather they can be another way to include writing, reading, and critical analysis in our courses, with the added benefit of promoting students' data literacy and civic online reasoning abilities.

Appendix A: Data Storytelling Principles for Undergraduate Writers

1. Data are invented in the process of being gathered, prepared for analysis, and visualized. As writers, we should choose to use data that were collected systematically and ensure that we analyze and visualize them accurately.
2. Data visualization helps readers see patterns in data. Choosing an appropriate type of visualization makes seeing and understanding patterns easier. Using basic design principles makes the visualization easier to understand.
3. The form or genre of the story and the medium through which it is distributed help set reader expectations for it.
4. Ethical data stories help readers understand what data mean. They provide context (who, what, when, where, and why) so readers can understand how and for what purpose the data were invented. They do not distort data for persuasive purposes.

References

Arola, K. L., Sheppard, J., & Ball, C. E. (2014). *Writer/Designer: A guide to making multimodal projects.* Bedford/St. Martin's.

Beveridge, A. (2015, Fall). Looking in the dustbin: Data janitorial work, statistical reasoning, and information rhetorics. *Computers and Writing Online.* http://cconlinejournal.org fall15/beveridge/

Cairo, A. (2013). *The functional art: An introduction to information graphics and visualization*. New Riders.

Chun, R. (2017, February 23). The dangers of fake news spread to data visualization. *MediaShift*, Feb. 23, http://mediashift.org/2017/02/the-dangers-of-fake-news-spread-to-data-visualization/

Daniels, M. E. (2019). Situating design: Cultivating digital readers and writers in the composition classroom. In M. R. Lamb, & J. Parrott (Eds.), *Digital reading and writing in composition studies* (pp. 130–143). Routledge.

Edwards-Grove, C. J. (2010). The multimodal writing process: Changing practices in contemporary classrooms. *Language and Education*, 25(1), 49–64.

Knaflic, C. N. (2015). *Storytelling with data: A data visualization guide for business professionals*. John Wiley & Sons.

Laquintano, T., & Vee, A. (2017). How automated writing systems affect the circulation of political information online. *Literacy in Composition Studies*, 5(2), 43–62. doi:10.21623%2F1.5.2.4.

Lee, K. (2018). *Infographic: The optimal length for every social media update and more*. Buffer, https://buffer.com/library/optimal-length-social-media

Malhotra, N. (2017, July 24). Best infographics: What I learned analyzing 1,000 infographics. *Growista*. https://growista.com/best-infographics/

Miller, T. P., & Leon, A. (2017). Introduction to special issue on literacy, democracy, and fake news: Making it right in the era of fast and slow literacies. *Literacy in Composition Studies*, 5(2), 10–23. doi:10.21623%2F1.5.2.2.

Rutz, C., & Grawe, N. D. (2009, December 3). Pairing WAC and quantitative reasoning through portfolio assessment and faculty development. *Across the Disciplines: A Journal of Language, Learning, and Academic Writing*, Article 6. https://wac.colostate.edu/atd/assessment/rutz_grawe.cfm

Stanford History Education Group. (2016, November 22). *Evaluating information: The cornerstone of civic online reasoning*. https://stacks.stanford.edu/file/druid:fv751yt5934/SHEG%20Evaluating%20Information%20Online.pdf

Steen, L. A. (2004). *Achieving quantitative literacy: An urgent challenge for higher education*. Mathematical Association of America.

Tal, A., & Wansink, B. (2014). Blinded with science: Trivial graphs and formulas increase ad persuasiveness and belief in product efficacy. *Public Understanding of Science*, 25(1), 117–125. doi:10.1177/0963662514549688.

Wolfe, J. (2009). How technical communication textbooks fail engineering students. *Technical Communication Quarterly*, 18(4), 351–375. doi:10.1080/10572250903149662.

—. (2010). Rhetorical numbers: A case for quantitative writing in the composition classroom. *CCC*, 61(3), 434–457. https://www.jstor.org/stable/40593335

YouGov. (2018). *Ice cream* [Data set]. https://d25d2506sfb94s.cloudfront.net/cumulus_uploads/document/np6jy2g6j4/7.9.18%20-%20Ice%20Cream%20Results.pdf

14. Sleuthing for the Truth: A Reading and Writing Pedagogy for a New Age of Lies

Chris M. Anson and Kendra L. Andrews

Ubiquitous Falsehoods

The image in Fig. 14.1, showing a large pack of timber wolves, has been posted many times on social media sites such as Facebook, LinkedIn, Reddit, and Inc, as well as on the websites of business and entrepreneurial consultants, and is accompanied by the following (verbatim) description:

> **A little food for thought ... The three wolves in front are old & sick**; they walk in front to set the pace of the whole pack so they will never be left behind. The next five are the strongest and best; their task is to protect the front side if there is an attack. The five wolves at the tail of the group are also among the strongest; they are in charge of protecting the back side from any possible threat. The group in the middle is always protected from any attack. **The very last wolf is the LEADER.** He ensures that no one is ever left behind and he keeps the pack united on the same path. So if anyone wants to know what it really means to be a leader here is your answer. **A true leader never leaves anyone behind but cares for each and every member of the "pack," laying the foundations of a society built upon humanity, care and respect.**

On the surface, the photo's explanation might inspire people as they scroll through their social media sites. After all, there is nothing troubling about the idea that leaders should protect others, a principle said to be "the foundation of a society built upon humanity, care and respect."

But there is one problem: the description of the image is false.

This photograph was taken by Chadden Hunter and is featured in *Frozen Planet*, a 2011 BBC documentary. The BBC script describes a "massive pack of 25 timber wolves hunting bison on the Arctic circle in northern Canada ...

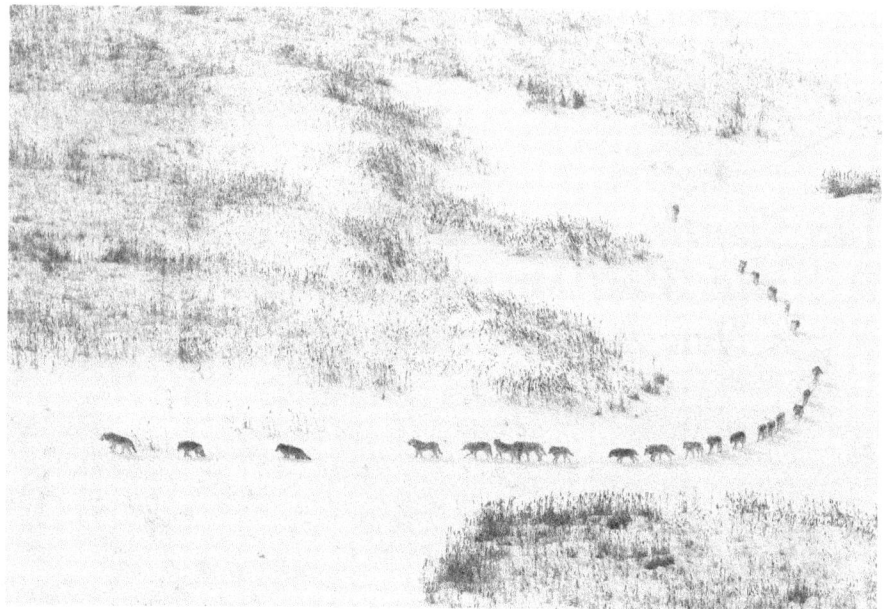

Figure 14.1: Wolf Pack. Source: Nature Picture Library

The wolf pack, led by the alpha female, travel single-file through deep snow to save energy." Yet in spite of the original and more authoritative account, the photo and its false caption populate sites across the Internet, misleading the public into believing something about wolf behavior that isn't true.

Consider another case. The claim that a language's lexicon reflects its speakers' preoccupations was first proposed in 1911 by the anthropologist Franz Boas. Asian languages, for example, have many words that describe connections to family members and blood relatives (Ferrante, 2006), suggesting the cultural importance of relationships. Boaz was fascinated with the Inuit of Baffin Island. He recorded that the Inuit had four distinct words for the singular phenomenon of snow: *snow on the ground, falling snow, drifting snow, and snow drift*. This observation was later picked up by Benjamin Lee Whorf, originator of the Sapir-Whorf Hypothesis—that a culture's language reflects its perception of reality. In his famous article "Science and Linguistics" (1940), Whorf's reference to multiple Eskimo words for "snow" forms the foundation, with other examples, of his theory.

These historical antecedents are described in a 1986 article by Laura Martin published in the *American Anthropologist*. Martin shows how the claim that the Inuit have many words for snow was expanded and extended in anthropological textbooks from the 1950s through the 1970s by authors

Edward Hall, Roger Brown, and others. "Textbook references to the example," Martin writes, "have reached such proliferation that no complete inventory seems possible." Subsequent "years of carelessness" spread the falsehood to the point when a 1986 *New York Times* editorial cited Whorf in reference to a "tribe" that distinguishes "one hundred types of snow" (Martin, 1986, p. 420).

The several groups of Inuit, Martin explains, speak agglutinative languages that readily create compounds:

> Eskimo words ... are the products of an extremely synthetic morphology in which all word building is accomplished by multiple suffixation .... The structure of Eskimo grammar means that the number of "words" for snow is literally incalculable, a conclusion that is inescapable for any other root as well. (Martin, 1986, p. 419)

And so it is for many languages (consider *wind* and its derivatives in English: *windy, wind-swept, wind-blown, wind storm, whirlwind, windmill,* etc.).

The two untruths represented in the wolf pack and the snow cases should not be surprising. Misunderstood phenomena, misleading information, information borne of ignorance, deceitful information, rumor and hearsay, and myth are an irrevocable part of human knowledge production and dissemination. But the examples differ in one important way. The Inuit case realized its falsehood over decades of slow replication and exaggeration and recontextualization, gradually embedding itself into the collective consciousness of everyday people, making it, as Martin puts it, "immune to challenge" (1986, p. 421). In contrast, the more recent wolf pack case spread virally and instantly over the Internet, misleading tens of thousands of people in just a short time, shared with exponentially larger cohorts through simple upvotes, reposts, and digital replications.

Admittedly, both cases seem relatively harmless. Beyond Martin's concerns about insensitivity to the cultural and linguistic complexity of the Inuit, neither case exerts major social, political, or actionable consequences. But when we consider that the aim of education is for students to learn what is most true about any subject at the time—and to recognize that the search for truth drives every conceivable branch of knowledge—the growing amount of falsehood in our daily lives becomes more alarming and calls for intervention. Students today are swimming in a sea of information, but its currents threaten, like a rip tide, to suck them into the dangerous waters of untruth and falsely motivated action. Helping them to distinguish between what is factual and not, what can be supported and what can't, has become a matter of growing urgency and is increasingly a part of our need to stem the tide of lies, fabrications, and deceptions that now characterizes the flow of information.

This largely pedagogical chapter will describe a method of teaching first-year composition courses that turns "research" into a trail of fact-finding on topics generated by potential falsehoods. The method borrows from several inquiry-based curricula, but it consciously and deliberately focuses on the subject of truth and falsehood and methods for distinguishing between the two. Before describing these pedagogies, however, we will more fully contextualize our claim that the explicit search for truth should be the next and most urgent reform of first-year composition courses.

Post-truth in the Age of the Viral

Before the advent of digital technology, information still came from many sources, including radio and TV, the newspaper and magazines, books and library materials, encyclopedias peddled by door-to-door salesmen, and social gossip and hearsay. But few methods (besides leaflets dropped from planes) existed to spread large amounts of inaccurate or deliberately misleading material to millions of people—instantly. Journalists staked their reputations on reporting the news factually, and when a newspaper or TV news program made a mistake, it recanted and published retractions so that it could maintain the trust of its readers or viewers. But we have now entered an era when the sheer amount of misinformation, the sheer number of lies spread both innocently and deceitfully, and with political purpose, overwhelms us to the point where it's exhausting to keep up with the truth, and we let it flow into and around us, sometimes ignoring it, sometimes pledging to interrogate its accuracy (and then not taking the time), sometimes hoping that someone else will step up later and correct the record if necessary. In the midst of so much untruth, new generations of students appear to lack the healthy skepticism and skills necessary to separate fact from falsehood. A recent study at Stanford University of 7,800 middle school, high school, and college students in 12 states found a "stunning consistency" in their inability to evaluate the credibility of information (Wineburg et al., 2016).

Social media and the internet are clearly major culprits in this growing problem. But the digital may be only a symptom of the conceptual or philosophical—a conduit for broader changes in the way we think about knowledge and truth. Some scholars have recently blamed the intellectual movement of postmodernism for contributing to the proliferation of false information—broadly, that all truth is relative and socially constructed (Edsall, 2018; in the field of composition alone, scholars have documented a distrust of empirical research; see Anson, 2008; Durst, 2006; Fulkerson, 2005; Haswell, 2005). But in "The New Subjectivism," Carlos Prado (2018) calls our current condition not the condition of postmodernism, which was never entirely antithetical to objective truth, but "'Post-truth'—the final step in the misguided move away from objective truth to relativization of truth. If truth is objective, assertions or propositions are true depending on how things are. If truth is relative, assertions or propositions are true depending on how people take things to be" (2018, p. 2).

Of course, it would be spurious to claim that a movement toward postmodernism has contributed to a national disregard of facts, evidence, and truth. But if technology has the power both to deceive and to correctly inform, the way it is used might be seen to mirror trends in the way the public thinks about and pursues truth or propagates falsehood. As the technology continues to develop, it offers ever more robust and attractive ways to deceive. Today, for example, photo and video manipulation programs have become so sophisticated that social critics predict a near future in which "perfect" (untraceable) alterations of audiovisual information, such as the speeches of politicians, can be created on home computers (see Ovadya, 2018; Warzel, 2018).

Pessimists claim that these dystopian scenarios cannot be stopped. Ovadya (2018), for example, predicts the onset of "reality apathy": beset by a torrent of constant misinformation, people simply "stop paying attention to news and that fundamental level of informedness required for functional democracy becomes unstable" (n.p.). But of all the contexts in which we might find hope for forestalling such a future, the strongest is education, whose lifeblood is the pursuit of truth. It has ever been so: at the institutional level most colleges and universities inscribe their dedication to truth in their mission statements and even in their mottos and seals, which commonly feature the word "veritas." But this belief in the pursuit of truth more strongly characterizes the university research mission than its instruction, which continues to convey to students a static view of the current state of knowledge. The centrality of truth-finding in the broad context of higher learning needs to be pulled out of the shadows of its historical traditions, dusted off, and placed boldly into the light. Although we have always occupied a truth-seeking context, educators need to do far more to counter the trend toward post-truth, and it starts with a more deliberate, intentional focus on exposing misinformation and giving students strategies for discerning the difference between truth and falsehood by developing critical reading skills and engaging inquiry-based research. That focus, we believe, should begin in the most common course requirement for entering students: first-year composition.

In the following sections, we describe a first-year composition pedagogy built primarily on the search for truth in contexts where it may be mixed with falsehood or where there is nothing but falsehood. We begin at the meta-level, offering a curricular structure modeled in part on David Jolliffe's *Inquiry and Genre* (1998) approach to composition as well as Bruce Ballenger's work in *The Curious Researcher* (2018) and Ken Macrorie's "I-Search" (1988) research model. At the core of these approaches lies a question that the student wants answered and the agency to choose how to best answer it. With our particular research focus on the pursuit of truth, students develop research topics with an emphasis on critical reading and information literacy. Students work on both long-term projects designed to follow a series of ever more accurate iterations of inquiry, and shorter-term assignments designed to correct falsehoods in contexts that do not require such extensive research.

Students can be asked to render their research in a number of genres designed for a range of audiences, including broad sectors of the public, general academic audiences, and more specialized audiences within specific fields. At the core of their explorations is a continuous attempt to read critically (in our context, "read for truth"), investigate claims, reflect on the broader implications of their work, and develop a mindset of productive skepticism. Instructors and administrators can adopt or adapt this model to structure a first-year or advanced composition course that requires sustained investigation of an area, topic, or question about which there is lore, misunderstanding, and falsehood. We then provide ideas for more specific assignments and classroom strategies within this structure. There are many opportunities to supplement these curricular and pedagogical ideas with material about the nature of truth—for example, from philosophy, psychology, or political science.

The Path Forward: A Reading and Writing Course Based on the Pursuit of Truth

A classroom framed by a curriculum of curiosity or inquiry-based pedagogy necessarily resists uniformity in design and implementation. However, the spirit of inquiry and curiosity can be channeled through a range of pedagogical possibilities in media, genre, and level. Since inquiry-based pedagogy can transpire in multiple ways, we suggest an inquiry heuristic that builds from Jolliffe's Inquiry Contract Model (1998) and includes five main stages: *laying the groundwork, starting to wonder, exploring the research, analyzing toward synthesis,* and *adding to the conversation*. Although these stages could be accomplished over the course of a semester, they are also recursive and elastic in that one part informs (and is informed by) the others. We have found the exploratory, collaborative, iterative, and connected nature of inquiry aligns well with digital and multimodal composition that can be similarly characterized.

The general design of the course assumes a constructivist approach to learning (Biggs, 2003; Steffe & Gale, 2009) that emphasizes active engagement. Students choose topics they are interested in and render their explorations in multiple genres (see Larson, 1982; Davis and Shadle, 2007). Collaboration and experimentation are encouraged, and there is an emphasis on authentic feedback provided from the perspective of readers who bring many prior beliefs, attitudes, and knowledge to their reading (Beaufort, 2008; McCormick & Waller, 1987; Melzer, 2014). In the following sections, we describe each component of the approach in detail, along with a range of activities and strategies that can be adopted, adapted, or replaced with others.

Laying the Groundwork

Before students begin to individualize their inquiry interests and topics, it is important to develop a shared vocabulary and framework for how this type of intellectual detective work is conducted. Through individual, small-group collaborative, and full-class activities both inside and outside the classroom, students sharpen their intellectual detective skills through inquiry-based models and shared learning experiences.

Student Media Self-Analysis

As writing teachers, we know that one way to ease more "reluctant" writers into academic writing is to have them start with a topic that they know about: themselves. By embarking on an extensive inquiry into fake news, the media, or rhetoric with students' own media usage, students start with something that they know about and/or are comfortable with, and also find incentive for their work by seeing themselves as stakeholders. This media self-analysis could vary from individual definitions of relevant terms to mini-ethnographies in which students document their media usage for 24 hours, analyze the types of news they receive, or spend a full-day of media blackout and reflect on the experience. Throughout, there is a strong emphasis on reading: what they notice, how they think about it, where else it sends them, and what they learn about the context and authorship of the material. In Lilian Mina's "Critical Digital Reading between the Role of the Professor and Students' Responses" (this volume), her student reflects on a similar assignment, the media autoethnography, and describes the realization that "the problem of misinformation was not only outside of myself." By performing a self-analysis of their media habits, students gain not only more authority on understanding the widespread and easy consumption of media, but they also gain more agency in doing something about it.

Fact vs. Opinion

The *New York Times* (see Appendix for direct hyperlink) has a trove of lesson plans and assignment ideas on information and news literacy, including Student Opinion Questions archived at the website for retrieval. With questions such as "how often do you check to make sure what you are sharing or commenting on is real?" and "what responsibility do you think journalists have when sharing or linking stories?", the formative assessment can take place at any time or at the beginning and the end of the unit for students to reflect on what they have learned. Students can take weekly news quizzes, including a question asking them to decide whether four news titles came from the *New York Times* or *The Onion*.

Working with Memes

Whether it's clickbait asserting the immortality of lobsters or altered images of inauguration crowds, one of the hallmark texts of fake news is the internet meme, which Davison (2012) defines as "a piece of culture, typically a joke, which gains influence through online transmission." Davison's meme components include the *manifestation* ("its observable, external phenomena"); the *behavior* ("the action taken by an individual in service of the meme"); and the *ideal* ("the concept or idea conveyed"). Students can use these guidelines to analyze popular memes or compare contemporary memes with analog counterparts. They can also conduct a rhetorical analysis of a meme (Serio, 2018), create a timeline of a meme's evolution, or trace its influence and movement online. Following a set of criteria agreed on by the class, students can collaboratively create an original meme on different news topics.

Starting to Wonder

Inquiry-driven research begins with a question that interests the researcher in a meaningful way. Although the topic may be directed (for example, "inquire into a topic within your discipline"), student researchers should not only have agency in their inquiry question but also a personal stake in the process of uncovering the information.

Mini Investigations

Performing smaller investigations into fake news stories is necessary scaffolding for students before conducting their larger inquiry research projects. Any of the investigations below could be conducted at the individual or collaborative levels, inside or outside the classroom, and singularly or as part of a series of mini investigations.

- Crowdsource students to locate and analyze fake news websites or stories
- Define terms such as "fake news," "satire," "parody," or "mockumentary"
- Select a news story hashtag and analyze its connection to virality
- Choose one news topic, statistic, or fact, and analyze how it is treated on various news sites
- Develop a concept map that connects the research on the fake news story
- Evaluate online images or videos for alteration (ex., Nuclear Flowers at Fukushima)
- Make "Fake News" spotting a daily game with brief de-bunking activities
- Deconstruct a Viral Video or a Viral News Story (Genre Conventions Analysis)

Exploring the Research

When the topic and inquiry question have been established, the student researcher begins to become familiar with the conversation (both academic and popular) surrounding the topic. The exploration of the research should represent a wide swath of resources and allow for flexibility through deductive reasoning in which the research leads the direction of the researcher rather than the converse.

Tracing Truth and Knowledge

In the initial stages of their research process, students can develop their "working knowledge" of a topic (the ability to talk about the topic for one minute without repeating yourself)—essentially the general online conversation about their topic (more pop culture than formal academic). They cast a wide net of informal online research, look for articles, copy links, find videos, insert pictures, and make notes of things that they personally find interesting and might want to go back to later when they get deeper into their topic. This working knowledge, or "living bibliography," can be demonstrated by an annotated source map that shows connections between sources (drawn by hand or through Prezi). Typically, our students use a page on their writer's website as a "Research Page" to link and include the sources with a quick summary and evaluation.

Individual Inquiry Blog on a Topic

In a similar fashion as the Inquiry-Based Research Project, the Individual Inquiry Blog provides students with the opportunity to locate and contribute to the conversation surrounding a particular research topic. Using a blogging platform such as Wordpress, Wix, Tumblr, or Blogger, students write posts not only about their research topic but also about their research process. The interactive nature of blog platforms offers myriad opportunities for peer feedback during the research process as well as the ability to incorporate multimedia for fake news topics that are often inherently multimodal.

Analysis toward Synthesis

After students outline the conversation and map the research, they must draw connections among the different sources and synthesize those findings. By delineating the primary conversation and demonstrating where connections can be made, they can identify where they can contribute a new voice to the conversation.

Digital (Visual) Annotated Bibliography

The annotated bibliography is often a staple of traditional research projects as it teaches students to select, analyze, and summarize academic scholarship. Building on those important learning objectives, the digital annotated bibliography gives students practice synthesizing their sources by creating connections among their annotated entries. Using a visual or digital platform such as Prezi, Canva, or Pages, students can draw connections (or disconnections) they find between different sources and demonstrate where the "truths" about a topic diverge. By visualizing these connections, they can synthesize the sources and gain a greater understanding of the research conversation about their topic before deciding what they want to contribute to it.

Sounding Boards and Discussion

To maintain the participatory nature of composition and the inquiry process, providing opportunities for peer feedback on the inquiry research should happen early and often. Students can serve as sounding boards for each other when they are working through the invention level of choosing a topic before moving on to deeper research. These sounding boards can take place in class in small groups or with the whole class through post-its to the "board," which provides substantive feedback without the wait time of full class response. Sounding boards occur online through page comments, which work effectively for web-based assignments, and are important not only to provide feedback to the researchers, but also to demonstrate how constructing knowledge is often a social endeavor.

Adding to the Conversation

With a clear representation of what the conversation, narrative, or truth has been, the researcher creates a space in the conversation by taking a stance or making an argument within the research context. This unique contribution is not necessarily an "answer" to the original inquiry question, but becomes a new, knowledgeable voice to add to the conversation. As with all instructional practices, implementation varies depending on the classroom context; however, several major assignments help students to perform the intellectual detective work that we have described. The following major writing projects with general descriptions are offered as a starting point for instructors who are designing an inquiry-based curriculum.

Inquiry-Based Research Project

With a traditional research paper, students tend to come up with a thesis first and then hunt down all facts and people supporting that thesis. However, inquiry-based research is predicated on the idea that somewhere "out there" is something to discover that isn't already known. As described by Adler-Kassner and Estrem (2003), "the core of the researched essay is the belief that research should begin with genuine interest and inquiry, and the shape of the essay should grow out of the development of that inquiry" (pp. 123–124). Students should think about themselves as discoverers, readers, learners, and writers after they leave the writing classroom; writing shouldn't be some stagnant piece that doesn't contribute anything new. Therefore, students use the research project as an opportunity not simply to practice researching, planning, and writing a research paper, but to learn how research can be a way of thinking in complex ways. Students move beyond reporting on something that is already known and move toward contributing something new to an ongoing conversation. Students can conduct inquiry-based research on common misconceptions or falsehoods, established cultural narratives, producers of fake news or viral falsehoods, and cultural comparisons of truth in journalism, among a range of other possibilities. The Inquiry-Based Research Project lends itself not only to a traditional paper format, but it works well as an original website, digital portfolio, or individual blog with varying posts on the inquiry topic.

Classwide Fake News Website

Based on extensively scaffolded coursework on the rhetorical aspects of fake news, which are described in more detail below, students can apply their knowledge of the genre connections by collaboratively building a class website that models the news stories that they have studied. Using a collaborative and performative model for completion, students can serve in team-based or individual roles as reporters/writers, editors, publishers, and graphic designers. Although the majority of fake news is disseminated online, the news publication could take the form of a journal or 'zine. Stephanie West-Puckett, Genoa Shepley, and Jessica Gray offer another direction for a news writing project in their chapter on "Hacking Fake News" (this volume) by highlighting more ethical practices in news writing.

Resources for Building It Out

At the end of this chapter, we provide an appendix that offers inquiry-driven textbooks, supplemental resources, and online media that are relevant to the suggested curriculum. When selecting a primary text for the course, we have found it helpful to choose one that offers frameworks and/or strategies that are open and flexible enough to allow for student discovery and varied processes, such as Ballenger's *The Curious Researcher* (2018). The textbooks suggested in the appendix are inquiry-driven texts that focus on questions rather than answers, embrace the messiness of discovery, recognize the nuances of conversation on a topic, and locate a space to enter that conversation and contribute something new.

Aside from primary textbooks, the appendix provides a variety of supplemental resources varying from video clips to academic articles to popular readings to conceptual texts. Providing multiple and varied readings on fake news and post-truth from a variety of disciplines and multiple media is essential for grounding the course theme and as a model for students' own exploratory research. For specific examples of fake news, the appendix includes a host of popular media outlets that have capitalized on the ludic nature of many traditional news programs and print journalism. As early as 2004, Jon Stewart described *The Daily Show* as a "fake news" program that relied on the "absurdity of the system" of media and politics, and that show along with a cadre of new series, continues to interrogate the concept of truth in media. These shows can be incorporated into the inquiry classroom; students can watch and discuss specific programs, using them as models when creating fake news websites or broadcasts. (Many clips from the show are available on YouTube, which does not disadvantage students who do not have access to cable TV.)

In describing these components of an inquiry-based course, we have avoided providing many current examples from the media because they have a short lifespan and rapidly become dated. However, their effect on the (inter) national consciousness lasts much longer and may affect entire generations' approach to information and truth. The best source of material, therefore, is what is happening at the moment students are enrolled. Our strategic suggestions must be populated with the rich, messy, and often uncomfortable material flowing around us at any point in time.

Epilogue: The Search Is Never Over

Even well-educated people are satisfied to stop at the first correction of an erroneous fact, in part because corrections come in the guise of truthful inquiry. But truth and fact lie on a continuum, with ever more granular and complex information that often leads to a conclusion of uncertainty and the need for more research. In many respects, the idea ingrained in all academic experts that disciplines never "finalize" their truths is a significant threshold concept for students, many of whom come into higher education as dualists, believing that their instructors hold the answers to all disciplinary questions and that they must learn and demonstrate those answers to show competence.

Dissatisfaction with reaching "the truth" of a matter would reveal that even the BBC account of the timber wolves is flawed. According to David Mech, a senior scientist with the Biological Research Division of the US Geological Survey, the term "alpha" is not accurate when describing most of the leaders of wolf packs; "in natural wolf packs, the alpha male and female are merely the breeding animals, the parents of the pack, and dominance contests with other wolves are rare, if they exist at all" (Mech, 1999, p. 1198). The wolf at the front of the pack in the photo happens to be a strong wolf, not an alpha wolf, and definitely not its weakest member—and may not be a female (see also Mech & Boitani, 2007).

Can a persistent search for truth undermine the spread of falsehood? In many cases, yes. The truth about the Inuit words for snow appears finally to be weakening. Nunberg (1996) reported on a database search of 60 American newspapers for passages containing the closely adjacent words "Eskimo(s)," "word(s)," and "snow" following the publication of Martin's article. His research generated 190 citations that, with the exception of one entry, all debunked the myth of the Eskimo snow words. "It's clear," he concluded, "that the myth is showing signs of melting under the light of Martin's scholarship . . . "(p. 205).

Like Martin, students can also be enlisted to debunk myth, falsehood, conspiracy theories, and other material too eagerly spread and consumed in our culture. In her chapter on "News-as-Text" in this volume, Kristina Reardon suggests a journalistic context for engaging students in an active, critical reading process that "involves negotiating one's understanding of the world with one's understanding of the way new developments in the world are represented in writing" (p. 8). Providing them with critical reading and inquiry strategies, and the thoughtful disposition that never takes anything too quickly at face value, can take us a long way toward restoring faith in our ability to find truths and make visible our institutions' commitment to doing so. In this chapter, we have argued that we are increasingly experiencing unprecedented amounts of false information, often perpetrated deliberately for political and other purposes but then spread virally by virtue of digital technologies and social media. The sheer amount of misinformation threatens many aspects of our current societies and democracies but has a particularly insidious effect on the construction of young people's ideologies of knowledge and truth.

While skeptics believe that nothing can stem the tide of falsehood, we believe that education should be the first and most important context in which to combat it, and that the first and most important place within higher education to begin that struggle is in the almost universally required first-year writing course. The curricular designs, strategies, and activities we have sketched in this chapter are just a starting point. At the core of such a course, however, is a conscious, deliberate, overarching goal of helping students not only to recognize the extent to which they are being deceived, but to take on a mindset of skepticism and to acquire a robust set of tools for ferreting out the truth about any piece of information, any Tweet or virally-spread story on social media, or any broader and more academic claims they might encounter. With a widespread adoption of such a course, we may be able to shape a future in which we can once again have faith that much of what we read, see, and hear has a basis in fact.

References

Adler-Kassner, L., & Estrem, H. (2003). Rethinking research writing: Public literacy in the composition classroom. *WPA: Writing Program Administration, 26*(3), 119–131.

Anson, C. M. (2008). The intelligent design of writing programs: Reliance on belief or a future of evidence. *WPA: Writing Program Administration, 32*(1), 11–36.

Ballenger, B. (1999). *Beyond notecards: Rethinking the freshman research paper.* Boynton/Cook.

Beaufort, A. (2008). *College writing and beyond: A new framework for university writing instruction.* University Press of Colorado.

Biggs, J. B. (2003). *Teaching for quality learning at university* (2nd ed.). Open University Press.

Davis, R. L., & Shadle, M. F. (2007). *Teaching multiwriting: Researching and composing with multiple genres, media, disciplines, and cultures.* Southern Illinois University Press.

Davison, P. (2012). The language of internet memes. In M. Mandiberg (ed.), *The social media reader* (pp. 120–134). New York University Press.

Durst, R. (2006). Research in writing, postsecondary education, 1984–2003. *L1 Educational Studies in Language and Literature, 6*(2), 51–73.

Erdsall, T. B. (2018, Jan. 27). Is President Trump a stealth postmodernist or just a liar? *New York Times*, 1–11. www.nytimes.com/2018/01/25/opinion/trump-postmodernism-lies.html

Ferrante, J. (2006). *Sociology: A global perspective.* Thompson Learning.

Fulkerson, R. (2005). Composition at the turn of the twenty-first century. *College Composition and Communication, 56*(4), 654–687.

Haswell, R. H. (2005). NCTE/CCCC's recent war on scholarship. *Written Communication, 22*(2), 198–223.

Lakoff, G., & Johnson, M. (1980). *Metaphors we live by.* University of Chicago Press.

Larson, R. L. (1982). The "research paper" in the writing course: A non-form of writing. *College English, 44*, 811–816.

Macrorie, K. (1988). *I search.* Boynton/Cook.

Martin, L. (1986). "Eskimo words for snow": A case study in the genesis and decay of an anthropological example. *American Anthropologist, 88*(2), 418–423.

Mech, L. D. (1999). Alpha status, dominance, and division of labor in wolf packs. *Canadian Journal of Zoology, 77*(8), 1196–1203.

Mech, L. D., & Boytani, L. (Eds.). (2007). *Wolves: Behavior, ecology, and conservation.* University of Chicago Press.

Melzer, D. (2014). The connected curriculum: Designing a vertical transfer writing curriculum. *The WAC Journal, 25*(1), 78–91.

McCormick, K., & Waller, G. F. (1987). Text, reader, ideology: The interactive nature of the reading situation. *Poetics, 16*(2), 193–208.

Nunberg, G. (1996). Snowblind. *Natural Language & Linguistic Theory, 14*(1), 205–213.

Ovadja, A. (2018, 2 Feb.). What's worse than fake news? The distortion of reality itself. *Washington Post.* https://www.washingtonpost.com/news/theworldpost/wp/2018/02/22/digital-reality/

Prado, C. G. (2018). The new subjectivism. In C. D. Prado (Ed.), *America's post-truth phenomenon: When feelings and opinions trump facts and evidence* (pp. 1–14). Praeger.

Serio, J. (2018, March). Meme analysis assignment prompt. Paper given at the Conference on College Composition and Communication, Kansas City, MO.

Steffe, L. P., & Gale, J. (Eds.). (2009). *Constructivism in education.* Routledge.

Warzel, C. (2018, 11 Feb.). He predicted the 2016 fake news crisis. Now he's worried about an information apocalypse. *BuzzFeed.* https://www.buzzfeednews.com/article/charliewarzel/the-terrifying-future-of-fake-news#.oteMeA4BdY

Whorf, B. L. (1940). Science and linguistics. *Technology Review, 42*(6), 229–231, 247–248.

Wineburg, S., et al. (2016). Evaluating information: The cornerstone of civic online reasoning. Stanford Digital Repository. http://purl.stanford.edu/fv751yt5934

Appendix: Resources for Assignment and Course Design

Textbooks

Ballenger, B. A. (2016) *The curious writer* (5th ed.). Pearson.

Ballenger, B. A. (2018). *The curious researcher: A guide to writing research papers* (9th ed.). Pearson.

Bloom, L. Z., White, E. M., & Borrowman, S. (2003). *Inquiry: Questioning, reading, writing.* (2nd ed.). Pearson.

Browne, M. N., & Keeley, S. M. (2014). *Asking the right questions: A guide to critical thinking* (11th ed.). Pearson.

Greene, S. A., & Lidinsky, A. (2017). *From inquiry to academic writing: A text and reader* (4th ed.). Bedford/St. Martin's.

Jolliffe, D. A. (1998). *Inquiry and genre: Writing to learn in college.* Allyn & Bacon.

Marshall, M. J. (2009). *Composing inquiry: Methods and readings for investigation and writing.* Pearson.

McComiskey, B. (2017). *Post-truth rhetoric and composition.* Utah State University Press.

Rallis, S. F., & Rossman, G. B. (2012). *The research journey: Introduction to inquiry.* The Guildford Press.

Online Resources

Adichie, C. N. (2009). *The danger of a single story.* [Video]. TED Conferences. https://www.ted.com/talks/chimamanda_ngozi_adichie_the_danger_of_a_single_story?language=en

Amanpour, C. (2017). *How to seek truth in the era of fake news*. [Video]. TED Conferences. https://www.ted.com/talks/christiane_amanpour_how_to_seek_truth_in_the_era_of_fake_news?language=en

American Press Institute. (2016). A new understanding: What makes people trust and rely on news. *Media Insight Project Report*. https://www.americanpressinstitute.org/publications/reports/survey-research/trust-news/single-page/

Boyd, D. (2017, January 5). Did media literacy backfire? *Data & Society: Points Blog*. https://datasociety.net/output/did-media-literacy-backfire/

Center for News Literacy. (n.d.). Stonybrook University. https://www.centerfornewsliteracy.org/

Domonoske, C. (2016, November 23). Students have 'dismaying' inability to tell fake news from real, study finds. *The Two Way*. https://www.npr.org/sections/thetwo-way/2016/11/23/503129818/study-finds-students-have-dismaying-inability-to-tell-fake-news-from-real

Graham, D. A. (2019, June 7). Some real news about fake news. *The Atlantic: Ideas Blog*. https://www.theatlantic.com/ideas/archive/2019/06/fake-news-republicans-democrats/591211/

Kiely, E., & Robertson, L. (2016, November 18). How to spot fake news. *FactCheck.org: A Project of the Annenberg Public Policy Center*. https://www.factcheck.org/2016/11/how-to-spot-fake-news/

Maheshwari, S. (n.d.). *How fake news goes viral: A case study*. New York Times. https://www.nytimes.com/2016/11/20/business/media/how-fake-news-spreads.html

Matthews, J. (2019, April 17). A cognitive scientist explains why humans are so susceptible to fake news and misinformation. Neiman Lab: Neiman Foundation at Harvard University. https://www.niemanlab.org/2019/04/a-cognitive-scientist-explains-why-humans-are-so-susceptible-to-fake-news-and-misinformation/

McCaughey, J. (2018). Authenticity and the rhetoric of 'selling' on social media: A role-writing assignment set. *Prompt, 2*(2), 15–28.

Miner, H. (1956). Body ritual among the Nacirema. *American Anthropologist, 58*(3), 503–507. https://www.sfu.ca/~palys/Miner-1956-BodyRitualAmongTheNacirema.pdf

New York Times. (n.d.). *The Learning Network*. https://www.nytimes.com/section/learning

Postman, N. (1969, November 28). Bullshit and the art of crap detection. Paper delivered at the National Council of Teachers of English, Washington, D.C. https://criticalsnips.wordpress.com/2007/07/22/neil-postman-bullshit-and-the-art-of-crap-detection/

Rosenbaum, S. (2017). *The end of fake news*. [Video]. TED Residency. https://www.ted.com/talks/steve_rosenbaum_the_end_of_fake_news

Yurkova, O. (2018). *Inside the fight against Russia's fake news empire*. [Video]. TED Conferences. https://www.ted.com/talks/olga_yurkova_inside_the_fight_against_russia_s_fake_news_empire?language=en

Models of Fake News Media

The Daily Show
The Colbert Report
The Onion
Last Week Tonight
Full Frontal with Samantha Bee
Daily Buzz Live
Empire News
NewsBuzzDaily
InfoWars
World Truth TV

15. Hacking Fake News: Tools and Technologies for Ethical Praxis

STEPHANIE WEST-PUCKETT, GENOA SHEPLEY, AND JESSICA GRAY

Introduction

According to the Pew Research Center, nearly two-thirds of Americans report that fake news is a significant problem that threatens democracy (Barthel et al., 2016). But what do we mean by the term "fake news?" Who uses it? When? Where? To what end? While President Trump's definition of fake news grew in late 2018, it continues to center on news headlines that portray his administration negatively, conflating truth with flattery (Keith, 2018). In contrast, rhetoric and composition scholars define fake news as an "insidious form of post-truth rhetoric" and argue that fake news is made dangerous by its virility as each share spreads mis—or disinformation and its breadth of circulation is inversely proportional to the constrained thinking and reasoning that it engenders (McComiskey, 2017, p. 19).

At all levels, faculty and students are negotiating this complicated media landscape, chasing truth across genres, media, modes, and distributed fora; however, our evaluative tools, while more necessary than ever, are falling short in the pursuit. For example, the general education outcome for information literacy at the University of Rhode Island (URI), the state's flagship land-grant, sea-grant, and urban graduate research university (URI, 2016), specifically names the CRAAP test (Blakeslee, 2004) as the preferred tool for evaluating sources. This checklist, designed to evaluate peer-reviewed academic sources, is adequate for that task. However, when ported into a fast-paced, dynamic, networked media landscape where currency is measured by the minute, the CRAAP test reveals itself as a crude tool. It is insufficient for navigating truth in an ecosystem where messages can be generated, shared, and amplified digitally by anyone, anywhere—including automated news bots—for a variety of personal or political reasons. In what some are calling the "dark age" of news (Simons, 2017; Gable, 2019), checklists like the CRAAP test are insufficient in helping students claim agency and enfranchise themselves as informed and confident news consumers. The CRAAP test encourages a linear, close reading strategy, which research has shown is inefficient and ineffective when working in dynamic media landscapes where understanding context is a central way that readers orient toward accuracy and reliability (Wineburg & McGrew, 2018).

To address this insufficiency and better equip students to both pursue and generate fact-based news, educators can move beyond reading and analysis to production by engaging students in overwriting fake news with ethical, evidence-based materials. Similar to the evidence-based web design project that Anson and Andrews outline in their chapter in this collection, the First Year Writing program (FYW) at URI developed an assignment titled "Hacker" that asks students to combat fake news by producing ethical news stories and publishing them using digital tools. Hacker is one of a host of optional project assignments that students can complete in the FYW course and is part of a larger ecosystem of digital badging that allows students to pursue their interests in the course and earn badges that signify their project-based learning experiences (West-Puckett & Shepley, 2020).

A popular badge option, Hacker employs scaffolded self-directed inquiry that uses heuristics as opposed to checklists. The project culminates by challenging students to use an open-source application to remix or *hack* existing fake news web texts. Through this project, students are prompted to develop more sophisticated tools to discriminate between reliable information and fabrication; to become empowered to reject the texts, people, and organizations wishing to manipulate their thinking; and to engage in the participatory practice of writing fair, accurate, and verifiable news. In this chapter, we will discuss the features of this flexible curriculum to address the problem of fake news as well as present and analyze student work produced in response to the curriculum. Before we outline our pedagogical approach, however, we briefly examine historical perspectives on news and neutrality, examine the complicated contemporary fake news landscape, and argue for a paradigm shift from information literacy to media ethics, outlining the rationale for the Hacker Badge.

Historical Perspectives on News and Neutrality

"Oh no, these facts and opinions look so similar," opines the character Joy in the Disney film *Inside Out* when she inadvertently mixes the facts and opinions "boxes" inside the head of the story's protagonist (Docter et al., 2015). Tossing the now jumbled collection into one box, Bing Bong, her companion, responds, "Ah, don't worry about it. Happens all the time." This scene, fancifully constructed as an extended metaphor to illustrate the mind of an adolescent, represents a condition shared by people of all ages and through all time periods. Indeed, the notion of objective news is a relatively new phenomenon in a long history of news that simultaneously conveyed (mis)information, opinion, and/or prescription that dates to the first news conveyances. Scholars have chronicled this phenomenon from Roman times through the present (Stephens, 1988).

Going back not millennia but to the nineteenth and even into the early 20th century, newspapers were variously rife with opinion and polemic, especially as concerned partisan politics, coupled with highly sensationalized stories, frequently under the aegis of news (Rogers, 2019; Shepley, 2015; Mindich, 1998; Schudson, 2001; Stephens, 1988). Their audiences would have been unfamiliar with the kind of allegedly objective, uninflected news coverage that audiences came to expect later in the 20th century. The first step in understanding how any individual—not just college students—might register and respond to fake news is to understand its long historical trajectory. While much of the historic admixture of "truth" and "falsehood" served hegemonic rhetorical purposes, scholars have argued that the news/historical record-keeping traditions of disenfranchised cultures also blend sensationalized accounts, aspirations, fears, firmly held unsubstantiated beliefs, predictions, and pronouncements that served a variety of ends, among them, creating through narrative a central position for marginalized groups (Addison, 1992).

Before attempting to teach students to discern, and, moreover, to produce truthful, evidence-based news writing, it is worth contemplating what has been a historical human tendency to conflate fact and fiction, evidence and assertion, what purpose these behaviors serve, and why these stories resonate with so many people. The fact that students, when asked to address and revise fake news—even when presented in the objective news form—their tendency is often not to counter inaccuracies with accurate objective accounts. They respond initially with some combination of conjecture, opinion, and even fantasy. Some of these responses parrot ambient hegemonic (or counter-hegemonic) discourses. Like their historical antecedents, they also seem to reflect a strong impulse to assert agency and reposition their ideas within a larger public narrative, particularly for individuals who feel unempowered.

The Contemporary Fake News Landscape

Fake news has become an increasingly dangerous influence which helps to sustain out-of-touch ideological echo chambers on the internet. While the news itself might be fake, the emotions it stirs up are anything but. Whether the motivations behind its creation are propagandist, monetary, satirical, or some combination thereof, fake and distorted news stories proliferate through websites, blogs, podcasts, YouTube videos, memes, and message boards. Automated bots and social media algorithms are designed to make content "go viral," allowing a fake story from an obscure corner of the internet to reach millions of users. Algorithms used by platforms like Facebook and Twitter "recommend" content similar to what the user already engages with, or that users with similar "likes" have clicked or followed, unintentionally creating filter bubbles. The very nature of a social media news "feed," where content from legitimate journalistic sources, overtly biased sources, clickbait, partisan memes, and random personal "takes" on news are all displayed equally without distinction, hierarchy, or, in some cases, even an easily identifiable URL, has an overall flattening or equalizing effect on the users' perception of the content they scroll through. Given the fast-moving nature of things online, by the time something false gets debunked, people have already moved on, but not before internalizing what they've seen as confirmatory of their fears and frustrations.

The algorithmic balkanization of political discourse results in fragmented and insular online communities watching the same narratives play out on their screens over and over, encouraging audiences to disregard information that challenges their viewpoints. An article in *The Washington Post* explored how content designed for satirical trolling purposes ends up amplified in earnest by audiences who are not in on the joke (Saslow, 2018). Saslow chronicles the online news consumption of Shirley Chapian, a self-identified mainstream-media skeptic following more than 2,500 far-right Facebook pages and who "trust[s] most her own ability to think critically and discern the truth" (2018). One of Chapian's trusted news sources is "America's Last Line of Defense," and despite it identifying itself as a political satire site, disclaiming that "nothing on this page is real," Chapian regularly shares content from the page in earnest, including one headlined "BREAKING: Chelsea Clinton and Michelle Obama Give President Trump 'the Finger' During National Anthem." Accompanying the post was a photo of a White House ceremony, with two women behind Trump circled in red—not Clinton or Obama, but actually former White House staffers Hope Hicks and Omarosa Newman—and neither woman is making the obscene hand gesture. Despite numerous comments on the post identifying it as a fake story, letting readers in on the joke, Chapian resists: "Of course Michelle Obama and Chelsea Clinton had flipped off the president. It was true to what she knew of their character. That was what mattered" (Saslow, 2018).

From Media Literacy to Ethics of News-Making

Critical media theorist danah boyd (2017) argues that, in the U.S, media literacy has backfired. While well-meaning, the instructional invective to "question more" has eroded trust in the media and created a void of alienation, distrust, and disenfranchisement, particularly among adolescents and young adults. This void is filled by those who wield information as a weapon of mass destruction. Propaganda outlets like *Russia Today* (RT) coach consumers to cultivate reading practices guided by unrelenting skepticism. As Koupf demonstrates in her chapter in this collection, skepticism can be part of a critical reading strategy that moves audiences away from binary thinking toward more capacious understandings of rhetorical construction; however, boyd argues that skepticism can also prompt audiences to rely on self-interpretation and leave them vulnerable to conspiratorial thinking and cognitive errors. boyd wants educators to help students recognize these appeals to skepticism and to analyze their corresponding psychological responses. Similarly, boyd calls attention to how different groups of people construct knowledge. By educating people to become aware of common errors in human thinking such as confirmation bias and selective attention and to understand and interrogate different ways of knowing through different processes (i.e., logic and reasoning or metaphors and narratives), boyd believes we might better equip students to recognize and resist the perversions of fake news and reestablish trust in the media.

Building on boyd's argument, as well as more recent practitioner-focused curricular interventions in the humanities (Carillo, 2019), we argue that writing teachers can take up this call to engage systematic errors in thinking and promote epistemological transparency in two ways. First, we suggest that teachers move beyond using simple checklists created for academic source evaluation and introduce more refined tools that assist students in recognizing the hallmarks of fake news: appeals to skepticism, clickbait headlines, ease of sharing across media, deep-faking photographic or videographic evidence, and heightened emotional responses. The News Literacy Project (2019) has developed robust teaching resources that have helped us (and, by proxy, our students) to identify the conventions of fake news. From their materials, we created a heuristic that students use to evaluate the veracity of articles

Title of Article Once you've answered all questions, highlight FAKE NEWS titles in red.	What is your emotional response to this article?	Headline: Is there excessive punctuation or the promise of "secret knowledge" or conspiratorial thinking? Explain.	Are you prompted to share on social media? Why or why not?	Source: Is it well-known? Is the author credentialed? Are there editorial standards? Is there an about page & contact info? Does a Google search of the source return questionable results?	Is there a date? What is it? Is it current?	Evidence: Are there official & expert sources? Is the story verified by other news outlets? Which ones? Are there hyperlinks to other unaltered sources?	Do a Reverse Image Search. Are the photos original? If not, are they credited? Are they used in the appropriate context? Do you have reason to believe they've been doctored?	What do you find from checking Snopes.com, FactCheck.org, and PolitiFact.com?
"Middle Schoolers"								
"Police Find""								
"Georgia Duo"								
"Kentucky Law"								
"American College"								

Figure 15.1 Evaluation Heuristic. Source: Author

purposefully selected to challenge their interpretive skills (see Figure 15.1). To avoid creating a binary between "fake" and "real" news, we encourage students to develop their own definition of what counts as "fake" as they work with this heuristic.

In addition to introducing more sophisticated interpretive tools built for networked contexts, we propose a more radical intervention for writing classrooms which engages all students, not just those who are majoring in journalism, in the professional rhetorics of the press. In other words, we are calling for an interdisciplinary renaissance of expertise in news-making—one that honors the professionalism of journalism and its public commitments in the form of ethical codes. By making plain how professional journalists construct and justify knowledge as well as how those beliefs rationalize their conduct, students can understand a grounded, well-articulated, ethical approach to news-making.

Ethics of Journalism

Scholars in writing studies hold that rhetorical ethics is a mode of inquiry (Fontaine and Hunter, 1998; Micciche, 2005; Porter et al., 2000; Henning, 2011). Rhetoricians "recognize ethics as a contingent set of practices that are always in process, localized, and based on principles of difference" (Micciche, 2005, p. 161). Thus, when we turn to professional ethics, we must remember that these are not absolute rules about right and wrong, good and bad;

instead, these are ways of asking questions about specific beliefs and actions by specific people in specific times and places. Rhetorical ethics concerns itself with the contextual evaluation as moral obligation, the process by which groups decide what is worth doing, and how that doing improves life for individuals and their community.

The Society of Professional Journalists (SPJ), founded in 1909, is the nation's flagship professional organization for journalists and "is dedicated to encouraging the free practice of journalism and stimulating high standards of ethical behavior" (SPJ, 2014.) To promote those high standards, the SPJ has developed a detailed code of ethics that revolves around four principles: seeking truth and reporting it, minimizing harm, acting independently, and being accountable and transparent. Congruent with writing studies scholars' understanding of rhetorical ethics, the SPJ states that the code, "... is not a set of rules, rather a guide that encourages all who engage in journalism to take responsibility for the information they provide, regardless of medium." Each principle is further expanded upon with specific links to action, which we've paraphrased in the following subsections.

Seeking Truth

Seeking truth includes ensuring accuracy, verifying information, and using original sources; providing context and avoiding oversimplification; stewarding the story, even after publication; making informed decisions about source anonymity and explaining to audiences why anonymity is granted; providing opportunities for persons named in a story to respond; prompting civil and respectful dialogue across differences by representing multiple points of view; amplifying marginal voices and holding those in power accountable; avoiding pandering to stereotypes and clearly labeling advocacy and opinion commentary; using unadulterated visual materials with clear labels; attributing sources and avoiding plagiarism.

Minimizing Harm

This guideline includes weighing public good against individual harm; acting in compassionate and culturally-appropriate ways to people who may be affected by the news, particularly special populations; recognizing the difference between legal and ethical action; providing greater privacy to private individuals have than public figures; considering the implications of naming suspects before trial in light of public good; understanding the permanency of publication and taking action to keep stories up-to-date.

Acting Independently

Acting independently involves avoiding or clearly articulating conflicts of interest; refusing gifts or services that could create obligations to other parties; never compensating sources and disclosing identities when possible; resisting pressure from advertisers or influencers; making clear distinctions between paid content or advertising and news reporting.

Being Accountable and Transparent

This principle includes sharing ethical decision-making and editorial processes with audiences and being accountable to them; quickly addressing accusations of inaccuracy, unfair reporting, and lack of clarity; owning mistakes, correcting them, and explaining the corrections; bringing to light unethical reporting behaviors in your own institution and beyond; holding yourself to the same professional standards to which you hold others.

These principles have both historical and professional gravitas as they were first adapted in 1926 from the American Society of Newspaper Editors and developed by experts in the field who sought to formalize professional conduct around honesty and integrity. Ethical codes that govern the behavior of members of the SPJ are quite different from partisan initiatives such as the "Ethics in Journalism Act," (Georgia HB 734, 2019–2020) which many journalists and academics believe is being wielded as a weapon to restrict the rights of a free press, thus infringing on U.S. constitutional rights.

The Hacker Badge Project

The Hacker Badge is one of seven projects students can choose to complete in FYW at URI (West-Puckett & Shepley, 2019). As mentioned in the introduction, it is one of the most popular project badges, and students report that they choose it because they doubt their abilities to separate fact from fiction in our hyper-mediated culture. In this section, we detail the levels of the badge that increase in difficulty, moving students from uncertain news consumers to well-appointed news contributors.

Hacker Badge, Level One

Students use Ted Talks and other videos to explore the landscape of fake news, who creates it, for what reasons, and its devastating real-life effects. Students choose to watch two of the following three talks: "How Fake News Does Real Harm" by CNN editor and journalist Stephanie Busari (2017); "We

The Voters—Mediaocracy" by Gunpowder & Sky, an independent film media organization (Gunpowder & Sky, 2016); and "Here's How Fake News Works and How the Internet Can Stop It" (WIRED, 2017). Students summarize the videos and respond to how the videos broaden, confirm, or challenge their personal theories of fake news. Many students understand fake news as a political weapon; however, they are surprised to learn that the creation and circulation of fake news is a profitable venture and casualties result when real situations like the Boko Haram kidnapping of 276 female students in Chibok, Nigeria are dismissed as fake news.

Hacker Badge, Level Two

Students engage in lateral reading across the web and the evaluation of false, misrepresentative, and sensationalized stories as well as unlikely stories that are accurate and substantiated. While we change the articles regularly to preserve the integrity of the exercise, the current articles include, among others: "Police Find 12 White Female Bodies in Garage Freezer Tagged with 'Black Lives Matter'" (Wayback Machine, 2019), "Georgia Duo Sentenced to Years in Prison for Terrorizing Birthday Party With Confederate Flag" (Reuters, 2017), "Student Pours Bleach and Water on Men's Crotches to Stop Them Manspreading" (Hartley-Parkinson, 2018). Students use the heuristic FYW program leaders adapted from the News Literacy Project (see Figure 15.1), to consider their own affective responses to news, to analyze headlines, to consider ease of circulation, to pay attention to source credentials and editorial standards, to consider manipulation or staging of videos and photos, and to fact-check the article using sites like Politi-fact and Snopes. In addition to vetting these articles, students read and analyze prior FYW students' fake news hacks as mentor texts. At the conclusion of level two, students select a fake news article—either from the articles we've selected or from their own experiences—and gather and interpret sources that will help them write an honest, fair, and balanced report.

Hacker Badge, Level Three

To overwrite the fake news article, students use an open-source hypertext mark-up language (HTML) desktop extension offered by Mouse Incorporated. Once the student activates the Mouse browser extension, the software makes a copy of the original website. The visual and spatial layout of the original website are left intact, and with a rudimentary knowledge of HTML, students remix the article's photos, videos, hyperlinks, and text. While some students are taxed by the competing demands of using unfamiliar technologies for functional, critical, and rhetorical purposes (Selber, 2004), our program encourages independent technology learning as a key outcome. Students must consider both genre and audience and use rhetorical strategies without sacrificing accuracy of information to reach and convince the article's original audience. This process finds students not just writing a research essay, but visually embedding their researched writing within the digital medium itself. After reviews and revisions, students conclude by creating a screencast video in which they describe their process of hacking fake news and share their commentary on the definition of fake news and its impact on democracy.

Student Examples and Analysis

The call for proposals for this collection sent us into our nascent FYW archive, investigating six student examples of the news hacks published in our student anthology *Rhody Writes*. We had a felt sense that some examples were more sophisticated than others, but we hadn't developed an assessment instrument that guided us in evaluating these projects. Thus, we used qualitative coding to collaboratively understand the general patterns of student writing produced in response to this badge, patterns we detail in the following section. To identify these patterns, the authors independently coded the student texts using a priori codes developed from the SPJ's code of professional ethics to mark the presence or absence of the four ethical news-making behaviors. After discussion of the initial coding process and collaborative resolution of discrepancies, we identified specific trends, such as "error correction" or what we refer to in the example as "just confirming the facts" which enabled us to conceptualize patterns of student response to fake news. This pattern analysis has helped us to name and understand a continuum of approaches that moves from less to more sophisticated engagement with fake news guided by the SPJ's code of professional ethics.

Using the SPJ's four guiding principles, we categorized student examples using a superlative structure—successful, more successful, and most successful. Successful examples of student fake news hacks move beyond opinion, invective, and the polemic to engage a singular tenant of journalistic ethics. More successful examples engage two tenants of journalistic ethics. The most successful examples, then, engage three or four SPJ ethical principles: seeking truth, minimizing harm, acting independently, and being accountable and transparent. We recognize that students in our FYW have varying levels of experience in their abilities to critically approach this project; thus, increasing levels of sophistication provide opportunities for diverse groups of students to engage fake news from a low-barrier, high-ceiling, wide-walls approach (Resnick, 2016).

Single Ethical Criterion Example

Once students have made the distinction between fact and opinion, their next inclination is often to "correct" the factual inaccuracies, though in some cases students struggle to move beyond simple negation of the false story, that is, this claims X happened, but actually X didn't happen. This can be seen in the following example by a student, who found an article falsely claiming that URI's president had shot down an initial agreement to hire Rick Pitino as the men's basketball coach.

The original article "Dooley Kills Hiring of Pitino at URI" appeared on GoLocalProv.com (2018), a digital local news platform, and stated that "multiple sources" claimed that URI's athletic director had initiated a deal to hire Pitino as a replacement to the departing Men's Basketball coach, but that the university president vetoed the hiring due to concerns over Pitino's involvement in various controversies. The rewritten article demonstrates the SPJ principle of seeking truth by ensuring accuracy, verifying information, and including original sources. The student confirms that this, in fact, never happened: he replaces the unnamed "multiple sources" from the original article with a quote from Pitino denying he was ever in talks at URI and identifies the actual front-runner for the position (Karabots, 2018). However, simply reversing a false claim doesn't leave much room for development, and once this single falsehood has been corrected, the rewritten article loses its sense of rhetorical purpose. While this single-principle approach does qualify as successfully rewriting a fake news article, the *just confirming the facts* strategy leads to a limited, less sophisticated rewrite than those which engage multiple principles of ethical journalism.

Double Ethical Criteria Example

Faced with a complex problem of restoring an inaccurate "news" story to an accurate, ethical account, students are often flummoxed. What if the author has made the story up from whole cloth, and there is no authentic correlative? In these cases, we guide students to select an angle with the goal of correcting one aspect of a story. In other cases, the student will find an article that posits a single premise that just sounds wrong to them, and in fact, does not hold up to scrutiny. While this may seem like taking the easy route, hacking this kind of article often still raises a number of nuanced questions in terms of rhetorical choices and ethical behaviors. Such was the case when a student decided to take on an article touting the benefits of coffee enemas.

The original article, published by Honey Colony, claims to help "empower you to be your own best health advocate while putting honesty back into the food supply" (Young, 2016). With a little help from leading health experts and what are referred to as "top-notch journalists in the field," Young lists ten benefits of coffee enemas, among them pain and anxiety reduction, improved digestion, skin health, and mental acuity. The piece adduces evidence of these claims by citing what seem like reasonably reliable sources—practitioners in the fields of nutritional therapy and chiropractic medicine.

In the service of seeking truth, one student, Connelli (2019) questioned the evidence presented in the article and the credentials of the practitioners. In the hacked article, he acknowledges the original claims, as well as some of its evidence, without casting aspersions on its sources. In this way, he is modeling a civil debate. He then cites several experts with more extensive clinical experience who contradict the article's assertions. He uses, for instance, respected news sources and a well-established medical journal. An article in the latter, accompanied by extensive citations, chronicles the experiences of three doctors from Georgetown University School of Medicine whose patients who have suffered the deleterious effects of coffee enemas, including the specific health consequences endured by one (unnamed) subject. These tactics lend credibility to his discussion. The student attributes his sources properly and includes the links to the original articles for the purpose of providing further information and offering transparency.

Connelli demonstrates a second principle of ethical journalism, working toward the public good, by elucidating the dangers of what is becoming an increasingly popular practice. Young omits one key piece of information that might shed light on this trend, while Connelli reveals in his hacked revision that one of the driving forces behind the upswing in coffee enema use is the promulgation of a kit offered by celebrity entrepreneur Gwyneth Paltrow. He might have chosen to preserve her anonymity, but when weighing the potential influence—and damage—of celebrity endorsement on the readers of this article, he opted for the greater good. He does not launch a critique of Paltrow; he merely states a connection between the celebrity and the increased use of coffee enema.

Connelli's article shows a student grappling with the problem of fake news, using means that illustrate the power of ethically driven rhetorical choices. If even in small subtle ways, these student-driven efforts help to reinforce our faith in the power of civil discourse.

Multiple Ethical Criteria Example

An article titled "Maine: House Democrats Vote to Allow Female Genital Mutilation" by Robert Spencer (2018) was published by the website *Jihad Watch* on April 3, 2018. *Jihad Watch* is a forum for a fringe anti-Muslim group which has become mainstream in America by peddling its conspiracy theories about Islam and its alleged tyrannical political rule (Bail, 2019, p. 19). The original article covers the Maine House of Representatives debate over LC 745, "An Act to Prohibit Female Genital Mutilation (FGM)" (Maine Legislature, 2018). Spencer's article accuses Democrats of "flagrant Islamopandering," and states that Democrats voted to allow FGM, when in fact the Republican-sponsored bill was originally tabled for discussion.

In his hack of the original article, a student takes on fallacies and misrepresentation apparent in the Spencer article (Duvally, 2019). Duvally changed both the headline and the article lead, citing that Democrats, "... killed a bill that targeted religious and ethnic communities" (p. 72). Duvally goes on to discuss why Democrats killed the Republican-backed bill noting that it is important to understand the cultural context of such practices and work in collaboration with community health experts "in favor of gaining a better perspective on who this law will impact before making any final decisions" (p. 72). Duvally provides a global picture of FMG and its devastating impact on women world-wide, noting that the World Health Organization states that one-quarter of Muslim women worldwide have been altered. This statistic responds to Spencer's erroneous claim that all Muslim women are circumcised as mandated by Muhammad. To allow different viewpoints to be heard, Duvally provides space for Rep. Sirocki who introduced the bill to comment on her frustration with the Democrats lack of action as well as space for the ACLU to clarify that Democrats do not support the practice, but were troubled by the prospect of a bill "... crafted without the input of policy experts or affected communities" (p. 73). In his screencast video, Duvally outlines many of these choices and shares his commentary on why fake news is a threat to U.S. democracy.

Our analysis of Duvally's news hack demonstrates three out of four of the SPJ ethical principles: seeking truth, minimizing harm, being accountable and transparent. As is evidenced in his attributions, he gathered several sources to "seek truth" as well as provide context that helped readers to understand the Maine Democrats' decision to table the original bill. He included multiple points of view in the story by integrating quotations from both Rep. Sirocki and the Maine ACLU. Unlike Spencer, Duvally did not reify harmful stereotypes about the Muslim community and alleged tyrannical rule. Duvally minimized harm by working to understand the world-wide practice of female mutilation and its impact on women, and reiterated the need to work with Muslim communities to find solutions to this pressing problem. Finally, Duvally pointed out the inaccurate and unfair reporting from the Spencer organization, illuminating the unethical behaviors of Spencer and his associates, and holding himself to higher professional standards. We were unable to find evidence of "acting independently" which is admittedly difficult given the context in which we are applying the SPJ code of ethics. We did, however, notice that Duvally did not change the advertisement on the article which hawks Spencer's controversial book. By making that change, Duvally could have demonstrated that he was resisting pressure from influencers and removing paid content which clearly attempts to persuade readers of an Islamic teleology from its origins to contemporary terrorism. As Lawrence argues in his chapter in this collection, teaching students about algorithmic rules of advertising and engaging them in manipulating those rules and procedures can lead students to better understand the imbrication of news and paid content in online forums.

Conclusion

To help students become critical consumers and producers in today's media landscape, educators have the challenging task of guiding students in the interpretation and response to the information with which they are constantly bombarded. The history of journalism and a critical analysis of the current Internet-driven media environment provide insight into the precedents and cultural forces that so often lead students toward unproductive interpretation and response. Current evaluative tools and media literacy attempts have proven inadequate—and even deleterious—in this effort. Educators need a new set of approaches and tools that take all of these complexities into account while giving students a strong sense of agency in their investigations and compositions. We advocate for more sophisticated heuristics that allow students to identify inaccuracies in news reporting and encourage the systematic application of well-established ethical codes used by professional journalists.

Through this project we've discovered how the SPJ's code of ethics can provide concrete and tangible outcomes for our students who choose the Hacker Badge as an opportunity to examine fake news and take a proactive stance against it. In line with action research paradigms that make curricular intervention a key outcome of inquiry, we made the following revisions to the Hacker Badge:

- Level One: Engage students in reading about, understanding, and naming ethics of news-making and news-sharing
- Level Two: Provide categorized student models that meet the one, two, and three-or-more criteria examples
- Level Three: Prompt students to name the ethical principles they've engaged and describe how they engaged them in their screencast videos

We are now prompting instructors to use the SPJ ethical principles as they provide feedback to student drafts to help students better understand audience and promote more culturally responsive writing behaviors.

Contemporary understandings of fake news revolve around our expectations that news should be fair, accurate, and balanced—expectations that are quite new in the history of sharing remarkable information about recent, significant events. In a complicated media landscape where most anyone—including our students—can create or share news, writing teachers must rethink traditional approaches to information literacy. The interdisciplinary move to engage the profession of journalism makes apparent the ethics and ethical behaviors of news-making and, ironically, allows us to return to our wheelhouse, teaching rhetorical ethics that guide the production and spread of information.

References

Addison, E. H. (1992). *When history fails: Apocalypticism in the ancient Mediterranean.* PhD Diss. University of California, Santa Barbara.

Bail, C. (2019). *Terrified: How anti-Muslim fringe organizations became mainstream.* Princeton University Press.

Barthel, M., Mitchell, A., & Holcomb, J. (2016). Many Americans believe fake news is sowing confusion. Pew Research Center. http://www.journalism.org/2016/12/15/many-americans-believe-fake-news-is-sowing-confusion/

Blakeslee, S. (2004). The CRAAP test. *LOEX Quarterly, 31*(3). https://commons.emich.edu/loexquarterly/vol31/iss3/4

boyd, d. (2017). Did media literacy backfire? *Journal of Applied Youth Studies, 1*(4), 83–89.

Busari, S. (2017, February). *How fake news does real harm.* TED. https://www.ted.com/talks/stephanie_busari_how_fake_news_does_real_harm?language=en

Connelli, W. (2019). Coffee enemas are still unproven and harmful, according to medical professionals: Hacked news article. In S. West-Puckett & G. Shepley (Eds.), *Rhody writes: A student anthology* (pp. 66–68). Hayden-McNeil.

Docter, P., Del, C. R., LeFauve, M., Cooley, J., Rivera, J., Poehler, A., . . . Smith, P. (2015). *Inside Out* [Motion picture]. Walt Disney Studios Motion Pictures.

Duvally, T. (2019). Maine House Democrats vote to discuss the specifics on female genital mutilation before banning it. In S. West-Puckett & G. Shepley (Eds.), *Rhody writes: A student anthology* (pp. 72–74). Hayden-McNeil.

Fontaine, S. I., & Hunter, S. M. (1998). *Foregrounding ethical awareness in composition and English studies.* Boynton/Cook.

Gable. J. (2019). The dark age of the internet or a digital enlightenment: Is democracy in danger in the information age? The Forum Network. https://www.oecd-forum.org/users/327909-john-gable/posts/55509-the-dark-age-of-the-internet-or-a-digital-enlightenment-is-democracy-in-danger-in-the-information-age

Georgia House Bill 734. (2019–2020). Ethics in Journalism Act. http://www.legis.ga.gov/legislation/en-US/Display/20192020/HB/734

GoLocalProv Sports Team. (2018, April 2). President Dooley kills hiring of Pitino at URI. https://www.golocalprov.com/sports/uri-president-dooley-kills-hiring-of-pitino

Gunpowder & Sky. (2016, August 30). *We the voters: Mediaocracy* [Video]. Vimeo. https://vimeo.com/180771524

Hartley-Parkinson, R. (2018, Sep. 26). Student pours bleach and water on men's crotches to stop them manspreading. MetroUK. https://metro.co.uk/2018/09/26/Student-pours-bleach-and-water-on-mens-crotches-to-stop-them-manspreading-7979562ito=cbshare?ito=cbshe

Henning, T. (2011, July). Ethics as a form of critical and rhetorical inquiry in the writing classroom. *English Journal, 100*(6), 34–40.

Karabots, W. (2018). Confirmed! URI is in no talks with Rick Pitino: A revised news article for the Hacker project. In S. West-Puckett & G. Shepley (Eds.), *Rhody writes: A student anthology* (pp. 109–111). Hayden-McNeil.

Keith, T. (2018, Sep. 2). President Trump's description of what's 'fake' is expanding. National Public Radio. https://www.npr.org/2018/09/02/643761979/president-trumps-description-of-whats-fake-is-expanding

Maine Legislature. (2018, April 18). Roll call details for house roll-call #633.

Micciche, L. R. (2005). Emotion, ethics, and rhetorical action. *Journal of Advanced Composition, 25*(1), 161–184.

Mindich, D. (1998). *Just the facts: How "objectivity" came to define American journalism.* NYU Press.

McComiskey, B. (2017). *Post-truth rhetoric and composition.* University Press of Colorado.

News Literacy Project. (2019). Ten questions for fake news detection. http://www.thenewsliteracyproject.org/sites/default/files/GO-TenQuestionsForFakeNewsFINAL.pdf

Porter, J., Sullivan, P., Blythe, S., Grabill, J. T., & Miles, L. (2000). Institutional critique: A rhetorical methodology for change. *College Composition and Communication, 51*(4), 610–642. https://www.jstor.org/stable/358914

Resnick, M. (2016). Designing for wide walls. *Design Blog.* https://design.blog/2016/08/25/mitchel-resnick-designing-for-wide-walls/

Reuters. (2017, Feb. 27). Georgia duo sentenced to years in prison for terrorizing birthday party with confederate flag. *Huffington Post.* https://www.huffpost.com/entry/georgia-duo-sentenced-confederate-flag_n_58b4b65be4b060480e0b36e6

Rogers, T. (2019, Aug. 22). Is sensationalism in the news bad? https://www.thoughtco.com/is-sensationalism-in-the-news-media-bad-2074048

Saslow, E. (2018, Nov. 17). 'Nothing on this page is real': How lies become truth in online America. *The Washington Post.* https://www.washingtonpost.com/national/nothing-on-this-page-is-real-how-lies-become-truth-in-online-america/2018/11/17/edd44cc8-e85a-11e8-bbdb-72fdbf9d4fed_story.html?noredirect=on

Schudson, M. (2001). The objectivity norm in American journalism. *Journalism, 2*(2), 149–170.

Selber, S. A. (2004). *Multiliteracies for a digital age.* Southern Illinois University Press.

Shepley, G. (2015). By which melancholy occurrence: The disaster prints of Nathaniel Currier, 1835–1840. *Panorama, 1*(2). https://editions.lib.umn.edu/panorama/article/by-which-melancholy-occurrence-the-disaster-prints-of-nathaniel-currier-1835-1840/

Simons, Margaret. (2017). Journalism faces a crisis worldwide—we might be entering a new dark age. *The Guardian.* https://www.theguardian.com/media/2017/apr/15/journalism-faces-a-crisis-worldwide-we-might-be-entering-a-new-dark-age

Society of Professional Journalists. (2014, Sep. 6). SPJ Code of Ethics. https://www.spj.org/ethicscode.asp

Spencer, R. (2018, Apr. 23). Maine: House Democrats vote to allow female genital mutilation. *Jihad Watch.* https://www.jihadwatch.org/2018/04/Maine-house-democrats-vote-to-allow-female-genital-mutilation

Stephens, M. (1988). *A history of news: From the drum to the satellite.* Viking.

University of Rhode Island. (2016). Learning outcomes. https://web.uri.edu/general-education/students/learning-outcomes/

Wayback Machine. (2019, Aug. 27). Police find 12 white female bodies in garage freezer tagged with "black lives matter." https://web.archive.org/web/20160926183216/, http://now8news.com/garage-freezer-black-lives-matter/

West-Puckett, S. J., & Shepley, G. (2019). *Hacker Badge.* URI First Year Writing Website. https://makercomp.wordpress.com/portfolio/badge-4/

West-Puckett, S. J., & Shepley, G. (2020). Radical museology/radical pedagogy: Curating beyond boundaries. *Journal of Multimodal Rhetorics, 4*(1). http://journalofmultimodalrhetorics.com/4-1-issue-west-puckett-shepley

Wineburg, S., & McGrew, S. (2018, July 28). Lateral reading and the nature of expertise: Reading less and learning more when evaluating digital information. *Teachers College Record 121,* 1–40.

WIRED. (2017, February 14). *Here's how fake news works (and how the internet can stop it)* [Video]. YouTube. https://www.youtube.com/watch?v=frjITitjisY

Young, K. (2016, July 14). Coffee enemas & weight loss, plus incredible healing benefits. *Honey Colony.* https://www.honeycolony.com/article/coffee-enemas-weight-loss/

List of Contributors

Dr. Kendra L. Andrews is a Professor of the Practice in Core Writing and a WAC Consultant for the faculty at Fairfield University in Fairfield, Connecticut. She earned her Ph.D. in the Communication, Rhetoric, and Digital Media Program at North Carolina State University, and she worked in North Carolina classrooms for twenty years while highly invested in critical pedagogy, teacher development, and 21st-century literacies. Kendra teaches courses in Rhetoric and Composition, Writing Processes in the 21st Century, STEM Communication, and Composition Research Methodologies. In addition to her teaching and scholarship at Fairfield University, Kendra has served as the Graduate Assistant Director of the First-Year Writing Program and as a Graduate WAC Consultant for the Campus Writing and Speaking Program at North Carolina State University. Her full c.v. and teaching portfolio are available on her professional website, www.kendralandrews.com.

Chris M. Anson is Distinguished University Professor, Alumni Association Distinguished Graduate Professor, and Director of the Campus Writing and Speaking Program at North Carolina State University, where he teaches graduate and undergraduate courses in language, composition, and literacy and works with faculty across the disciplines to enhance writing and speaking instruction. He has published 19 books and 130 articles and book chapters relating to writing and has spoken widely across the U.S. and in 31 other countries. He is Past Chair of the Conference on College Composition and Communication and Past President of the Council of Writing Program Administrators. His full c.v. is at www.ansonica.net

Courtney Bradford is a graduate research assistant in the Master of Professional Writing Program at Kennesaw State University and a technical writing intern in Atlanta. She has served as an editorial assistant for three Green Card Voices collections of immigrant essays. Her areas of interest include technical writing and editing as well as community writing and engagement.

Jeaneen Canfield is a Ph.D. Candidate in English: Rhetoric & Writing Studies at Oklahoma State University. She has participated in the Bedford New Scholars Advisory Board, is published in *Praxis: A Writing Center Journal*, and has presented her work at various conferences. Research interests include pedagogical approaches to forms of resistance in the classroom space, visual rhetoric, multimodal composition, digital literacies, and critical pedagogy. Her current work explores ways merging cartographic techniques with composition pedagogy impacts productive instructional strategies. To rejuvenate, she enjoys textile hobbies, as well as almost all things outdoors.

Paul T. Corrigan is currently a Visiting Assistant Professor of English and Writing at the University of Tampa. His essays on teaching have appeared in *Pedagogy, Profession, Reader, Teaching English in the Two-Year College, Teaching & Learning Inquiry*, and other venues. He recently wrote a book on teaching literary reading and has begun one on teaching creative writing.

William FitzGerald directs the Writing Program and the Teaching Matters and Assessment Center at Rutgers University-Camden. He has published widely on the pedagogy of style, science writing, and literacy in addition to his work as co-author/co-editor of the *The Craft of Research, A Manual for Writers of Research Papers, Theses and Dissertations* (aka Turabian), and *The Student's Guide to Writing College Papers* (all U. of Chicago Press). He is also author of the monograph, *Spiritual Modalities: Prayer as Rhetoric and Performance* (Penn State Press, 2012).

Joseph Forte is a third-year Ph.D. student in the Purdue University English Department's Rhetoric and Composition Program. His research interests include educational assessment (especially writing assessment), professional and technical writing (especially as it pertains to educational applications in digital spaces) and the intersection of rhetorical theory and politics. When he is not doing research or completing coursework, he enjoys the duties that accompany his role as Content Coordinator for the Purdue Online Writing Lab (OWL).

Jessica Gray is an instructor of Writing and Rhetoric at the University of Rhode Island. Her research interests include digital rhetoric and culture, particularly how the spread and exchange of information on the internet challenges traditional notions of credibility, authority, and expertise. She has presented at conferences on topics ranging from memes and 18th-century pamphleteering to the merging of the personal and the public sphere in Walt Whitman's journalism, and her writing has appeared in several blogs, wikis, and reference books.

Stephanie Jarrett is a doctoral student in Developmental Education at Texas State University with a specialization in literacy. Stephanie currently works as a doctoral research assistant, but has been a developmental reading instructor, special education instructor, and teaching assistant in the past. Her research is currently focused on bridging the gap between developmental literacy research and pedagogy to ensure all students are receiving an equitable education.

Daniel Kenzie is an Assistant Professor of Practice in the Department of Pharmacy Practice at North Dakota State University, where he teaches writing courses for pre-professional, professional, and graduate students. His scholarship has appeared in *Technical Communication Quarterly* and *The WAC Journal*, and his current research investigates discourses of clinical trial failure for traumatic brain injury.

Danielle Koupf is an Assistant Teaching Professor in the Writing Program and English Department at Wake Forest University. Her research interests include composition pedagogy, invention, textual reuse, and rhetorics of making and crafting. Her scholarship has appeared in *Composition Forum* and *enculturation*.

Angela Laflen, Ph.D., is an Assistant Professor of English at California State University, Sacramento. She teaches in the areas of digital writing and professional writing. Her published work focuses on digital and multimodal literacies and writing response practices, and her work has appeared in *Computers and Composition*, *Assessing Writing*, and the *Journal of Response to Writing*, among others.

Dan Lawrence is an Assistant Professor of Writing at the University of Wisconsin—Superior, where he teaches courses on Digital Writing, Technical Writing, Professional/Business Writing, Introduction to Academic Writing, and Advanced Rhetoric. His interdisciplinary research examines issues in the digital distribution of information and emergent media and has appeared in peer-reviewed journals such as *Harlot: A Revealing Look at the Arts of Persuasion*. His teaching focuses on blending theory and practice while integrating contemporary digital technologies into the writing classroom. His textbook, *Digital Writing*, will be published by Broadview Press in 2021.

Lilian Mina is an Associate Professor and the Director of Composition at Auburn University at Montgomery. She researches digital rhetoric with focus on multimodal composing and writing teachers' use of digital technologies. Her research also focuses on the intersection between multimodality and transfer of writing knowledge and practice. She is interested in WPA scholarship, especially (technology) professional development of writing teachers, program assessment, and curriculum development. Her work has appeared in journals like *Computers & Composition, Composition Forum*, and *Kairos: Rhetoric, Technology, Pedagogy*, and in multiple edited collections.

Kristina Reardon is Associate Director of the Center for Writing and Director of the Writer's Workshop at the College of the Holy Cross, where she also teaches composition. She actively freelances for news publications such as *Worcester Magazine* and *Rhode Island Monthly* and wrote a column for a dozen New England newspapers for almost a decade.

Genoa Shepley serves as senior lecturer and assistant director of first-year writing at the University of Rhode Island. Her area of specialization is visual rhetoric and the relationship between text and images in a historical context, frequently with a focus on the analysis of news media. Her work has appeared in a wide variety of publications from newspapers to scholarly journals.

Ellery Sills is an Assistant Professor of English at Minnesota State University Moorhead, where he teaches multimodal composition, technical writing, English education, and first-year composition. His previous research has appeared in College Composition and Communication and the Journal of Writing Assessment.

Jessica Slentz Reynolds is a First-Year Seminar Lecturer at Texas A&M University-San Antonio. She is also a doctoral student in Developmental Education at Texas State University. Her dissertation examines writing center training and tutors' self-efficacy for providing feedback. Her other research interests include exploring critical literacy in developmental reading and

List of Contributors

writing contexts, and understanding the role writing centers play within colleges and universities.

Lara Smith-Sitton, Ph.D. is the Director of Community Engagement and Assistant Professor of English at Kennesaw State University. She teaches writing and rhetoric courses as well as oversees the graduate and undergraduate internship program and community engagement initiatives. She is the co-editor of Green Card Youth Voices: Stories from an Atlanta High School. Her publications and research areas include community writing, engaged scholarship, internship program design, and 18th- and 19th-century rhetoric.

Stephanie West-Puckett is an assistant professor of Writing and Rhetoric and director of first-year writing at the University of Rhode Island. Her research focuses on equity, access, and diversity in writing curriculum and assessment, and she specializes in digital, queer, and maker-centered composition practices. In 2018, her dissertation won the College Composition and Communication Lavender Rhetorics award for queer interventions in writing studies theory and practice, and her scholarship has been published in *College English, Journal of Multimodal Rhetorics, Journal of Adolescent and Adult Literacy, Contemporary Issues in Technology and Teacher Education*, as well as in several edited collections.

Index

academic identities 133
academic research skills 104–107
academic writing 52, 190, 217
ACT reading test 2–3
advertisements 41, 165, 242
   digital content 179–180, 182–186, 188–190
Amnesty International 103
analysis of science accommodation (ASA) 117
Aristotle's *Nichomachean Ethics* 148, 150
assignment
   community-based learning 69–71
   critical interrogation 149–151, 154–156
   data story and project reflection 197–198, 205–206
   digital advertising 187–188
   empathy in writing 52–54, 56–57
   instructional context 137–38, 140
   reporting news 167–172
authorial agency 51–53

bias 36, 38, 58–59, 96, 98, 101, 107–8, 118
   critical empathy 58–59
   digital reading 98, 101
   reporting news 161, 166, 169–171
Bush administration 50

Cambridge Analytica 2016
   U.S. presidential election 186–187
circulation 7, 12, 41, 47, 99, 114–115, 117, 119, 121, 123–125, 229
Citizen Evidence Lab 103
civic online reasoning 16, 46, 174, 193–194, 209
Civil Rights Movement 135, 138
classroom
   critical reading and writing 12–15
   digital advertising 181–182, 187, 190
   hyper-targeting activities 187–189
   inquiry-based pedagogy 216–217
   news as text 161–163
   reporting technique 146–147
   science literacy 114–116
commentary 11, 37, 41, 101, 238, 241
Common Core State Standards 126
communication 34–35, 129, 152, 225–26, 244, 247, 250
community-based projects 63–76
   social activism 75–76
   US immigration practices and policies. 67–71
   value and impacts 71–75
corequisite model 134, 140–141
CRAAP (Currency, Relevance, Authority, Accuracy, and Purpose) 104–106, 108, 185, 229–230
creative content 181, 183, 189

credibility 20, 85, 87, 96, 99, 104–5, 108, 119–21, 124, 179–80, 193–94, 196
critical pedagogy
 ethical framework 147–149
 interrogation assignment 149–157
 propaganda *versus* persuasion 148
 rhetorical practice 147–148
 21st-century implications 145–146

DACA (Deferred Action for Childhood Arrivals) 68, 70, 171–73
data stories
 classroom composition 197
 composing difficulties 195–196
 definition 193
 delivering 204–205
 online circulation 196–197
 project implementation and reflection 198, 205–206
 sample 207
 SHEG study 194
 teaching principles 198–201
 undergrauate writers 208
 visualization 201–203
developmental reading 130–132, 134, 140–141
digital advertisement 181–182, 187, 190
 procedural rhetoric 181–185
digital content 97, 100, 102, 105
 hyper-targeted distribution 179–181
digital reading 9–10, 64
 academic skills 104–105
 critical skills 98–104, 109–10
digital technology 7, 33, 214

ecological models 10, 34–35, 39, 42, 44–45
educators 10, 15, 33–34, 41, 43, 113, 125, 131, 163, 230, 233, 242
emails 19–23, 25, 28, 30–31
English composition classes 96, 164, 174
essay draft 81–82, 86, 92

Facebook 13, 103, 165, 179–86, 189, 211, 232

fact-checking 4, 12, 43–44, 81–89, 92–93, 163–165, 200, 237
fake news
 2016 presidential election 132
 alternative facts 7, 49
 audiences 41, 44
 bias, skepticism and research 107–108 (*See also* Niha, Shifat)
 community-based learning 64
 ecological metaphor 33–34, 41–44
 data stories 193–208
 digital-media texts 95–110
 fighting 95–97
 hacking 229–243
 historical foundation 66–67
 immigration debates 63–76
 instructional context 128–130, 139–141
 mini investigation 219
 negative ramifications 106–107 (*See also* Mills, Dakota)
 real-world controversy 33–45
 student media self-analysis 217–218
 teaching students on 7–11, 43–45
 tracing the truth 217–219, 222–223
 Trump's definition 229
 See also untruths
false information 42, 67, 139–40, 214, 224
falsehood 14, 33, 41, 44, 75, 211, 213–16, 222, 224, 231
feedback 202, 221, 250
first-year writing (FYW) course 121–122, 125, 230, 236–238
 Hacker Badge 236–238
 Latour's excerpts 122
 student examples 238–239

Google 129, 185–86, 188
Great Hack, The (film) 186, 189–190
Green Card Voices 69–70, 73

Hacker Badge 230, 236–37, 242
headlines 36, 42, 167, 172–73, 237, 241
heuristics 55, 150–51, 155–56, 163, 185, 230, 233–34, 242

Index

hyper-targeting
   classroom activities 187–189
   commercial application 186–187
   digital content 179–181

information literacy 4, 10, 61, 93, 144, 185, 216, 229–30
inquiry 44, 56, 64, 85, 141, 150, 216–17, 221, 234, 242
   critical 153
   extensive 217
   mutual 60
   self-directed 230
   truthful 223
inquiry-based pedagogy
   annotated bibliography 220
   classroom activities 216–217
   class websites 222
   frameworks and strategies 222–223
   general descriptions 221
   individual inquiry blog on a topic 220
   information processing 218
   journalistic context 223–224
   memes components 218
   mini investigations 219
   peer feedback 221
   research project 221–222
   working knowledge 219–220
Inside Out (film) 230
Integrated Reading and Writing (IRW) 130
   argumentative unit 136–137
   epistemological components 131
   expository unit 135–136
   instructional context 130–131
   project implementation 134–135
   in the 2010s 132
   student's reflections 137–140
   See also developmental reading
internet 105, 108, 129, 132, 136, 188, 194, 212–14, 232, 237
interrogation 122, 154, 156
   critical 145, 148, 150–51
   productive 157
interviews 3, 67, 72–73, 75, 86, 91
   fabricating 91
   individual 71, 73
   personal 121
   recorded 70

journalism 14, 85–86, 91, 136, 164, 172, 174–175, 222–23, 234–2, 242–243, 245
   ethical 239–240
   formal 119
   professionalism of 14, 234
   yellow 66
journalists 8, 15, 61, 63, 85, 162–63, 166, 214, 218, 235–36
   investigative 173
   seized experiential 168
   service 20
   top-notch 240

King, Martin Luther 57

Lifespan of a Fact, The (D'Agata and Fingal)
   hybridity 81–82
   pedagogical lessons 92–94
   reading difficulties 89–92
   reflective reading 83–85
   rhetorical education 85–88
literacies 10, 12–13, 52, 96, 109, 141, 146, 197, 247–49
   21st-century 152
   academic 13, 133–35
   civic online 194
   critical 132, 143, 153, 155–56, 164, 206, 250
   defining 100
   emerging 10
   lifelong 131
   new media 132
   preexisting 133
lynching 26–27

mansplaining debate 20, 22–24, 30–31
master of resourcefulness
   pedagogical approach 105–106
   student experience 12, 96–97
media bias 98, 101–102, 108
media outlets 66, 68, 75, 101–2
   national 63

popular 223
social 65
memes 96, 103, 187, 218, 232, 249
   contemporary 218
   original 218
   partisan 232
   popular 218
Mills, Dakota 64, 106–107, 109
misinformation 8, 12, 20, 41, 43–45, 67, 107, 118, 196, 218
   combat 45
   constant 215
   expose 106
   exposing 215
   sheer amount of 214, 224
moment of reading
   digital lynching 25–28
   exactly the same thing 24–25
   expert readers are meta-readers 21–22
   it has made me look inward 28–30
   mansplaining 22–24

National Assessment of Educational Progress (NAEP) 2–3
National Oceanographic and Atmospheric Association (NOAA) 118
news-as-text
   four models 167–168
news literacy
   accountability and transparency 236
   acting independently 236
   fact *vs.* opinion 218, 230–231, 239
   legitimate *versus* overtly biased sources 232–233
   media bias, evaluation 170–172
   media ethics 233–234
   meme components 218
   minimizing harm 235
   multiple ethical criteria example 241–242
   as narrative 163–166
   neutrality principles 230–231
   photography 169–170
   professional ethics 234–235
   source recommendation 172–173
   21st century model 173–174
   truth seeking 235, 239–240
News Literacy Project 10, 157, 233, 237
news sources 3, 72, 75, 101–2, 108, 136, 145, 149–51, 153–57, 163, 165–66
Niha, Shifat 64, 107–109

online 2–3, 30–31, 41, 49, 68, 108, 140, 194, 196, 206
   forums 19, 88, 138, 242
Online Writing Lab (OWL)
   ecological model 39–41
   "man ban" controversy 36–38
   Purdue policy 36–39

Pacific Northwest Tree Octopus 129–142
peers 13, 59, 63, 133, 153–54, 165, 205
procedural rhetoric 13, 179, 181–83, 187, 190
PIL (Project Information Literacy) 165–166
postmodernism 214–215, 252
presentation 85, 106–7, 136–37, 153, 164
presidential election 10, 33, 47, 66–67, 90, 132, 134, 145, 186
professional journalists 172–73, 234, 242

quantitative reasoning (QR) 197
qualitative approach 138

reading
   compliance issue 6–7
   critical empathy 49–60
   deep 20
   five key moments 20–21
   mindful framework 9–10
   psycholinguistic features 5–6
   rhetorical 9, 20
   student's habits 1–5
   type 9–10
   See also moment of reading; reflective reading
reflective reading 82–83, 85, 89

Index

rhetorical analyses
  composition 34, 51, 58, 187, 247
  science literacy 124–125
rhetorical criticism 12, 81–82, 85
rhetorical strategies 115, 119, 129, 140, 142, 155, 187, 204–5

science literacy
  denial practices 115–117
  first-year writing (FYW) course 121–122
  network tracing 122–124
  rhetorical analyses 124–125
  source evaluation 119
  uncertainty levels 120–121
  vocabulary building 118–119
SHEG (Stanford History Education Group) 3–4, 8, 16, 33, 47, 180, 191, 193–94, 206
social media 4, 7, 41–43, 46, 99, 101–2, 108, 134, 138–40, 185–86, 188, 190, 224
SPJ (Society of Professional Journalists) 235–36, 238, 241, 243

teachers online debate
  moment of reading 21–28
  Writing Program Administrators Listserv (WPA-L). 11, 19–22, 28, 30–31
teaching
  critical empathy 56–59
  fact checking 81–89
  fake news caution 7–11
  rhetorical virtues 49–50
TED Conferences 226–227
Trump, Donald 19, 49–50, 67, 76, 90, 232
truth claims
  competing 125

  evaluating 126
  simplifying 120
  truth and fiction 82–84, 90, 200

uncertainty 12, 89–92, 114, 117, 127–28, 223
  science literacy 117, 120–123, 125
untruths
  examples, social media sites 211–213
  sources 214–216
  wolfpack and snow cases 211–213
URI (University of Rhode Island) 229–30, 236, 239, 244–45, 249–51

videos 96, 98–102, 111, 136, 182–83, 187, 189, 219, 236–37
viral videos 98–99, 109–10, 219
visual content 103
visual materials 96, 103
  unadulterated 235
visualizations 195, 201–2
visuals 102, 105, 166, 198
  edited 102
  quantitative 14, 195
vocabulary 2, 6, 9, 12, 115, 117–19, 121–22, 124–25, 201

writing
  critical empathy 49–60
  data stories 208
  older model 51
  scientific truth 117–118
  See also Writing 101
Writing 101, 49–51, 53–54, 56–57, 59

yellow journalism 69
  See also fake news
YouTube 103, 106, 186, 223, 245

Studies in Composition and Rhetoric

Edited by ALICE S. HORNING

This series welcomes both individually-authored and collaboratively-authored books and monographs as well as edited collections of essays. We are especially interested in books that might be used in either advanced undergraduate or graduate courses in one or more of the following subjects: cultural or multicultural studies and the teaching of writing; feminist perspectives on composition and rhetoric; postmodernism and the theory and practice of composition; "post-process" pedagogies; values, ethics, and ideologies in the teaching of writing; information technology and composition pedagogy; the assessment of writing; authorship and intellectual property issues; and studies of oppositional discourse in the academy, particularly challenges to exclusionary or hegemonic conventions. We also seek proposals in the following areas: the role of autobiography and of identity issues in both writing and writing pedagogy; the influence of social context on composing; the relationship of composition and rhetoric to various disciplines and schools of thought; collaborative learning and peer tutoring; facilitating and responding to student writing; approaches to empowering marginalized learners; the role or status of composition studies within English studies and the academy at large; and the role or status of student writers within the fields of composition and English studies.

For additional information about this series or for the submission of manuscripts, please contact:
        Peter Lang Publishing, Inc.
        Acquisitions Department
        80 Broad Street, 5th floor
        New York, NY 10004

To order other books in this series, please contact our Customer Service Department at:
        peterlang@presswarehouse.com (within the U.S.)
        order@peterlang.com (outside the U.S.)

or browse online by series at:
        WWW.PETERLANG.COM

www.ingramcontent.com/pod-product-compliance
Lightning Source LLC
Chambersburg PA
CBHW070838160426
43192CB00012B/2238

9781433188190